LYNN BEDFORD HALL
THE BEST OF
VEGETARIAN
COOKING

Photography by Malcolm Dare

STRUIK
TIMMINS

Struik Timmins Publishers (Pty) Ltd
(a member of the Struik Group (Pty) Ltd)
80 Mackenzie Street
Cape Town 8001

Reg. No.: 54/00965/07

First published in 1991

Text © 1991 Lynn Bedford Hall
Photographs © 1991 Struik Timmins Publishers (Pty) Ltd

All rights reserved. No part of this publication may be reproduced, stored in a retrieval system, or transmitted, in any form or by any means, electronic, mechanical, photocopying, recording or otherwise, without the prior written permission of the copyright owner(s).

Editor: Sandie Vahl
Designers: Janice Evans and Joan Sutton
Cover designer: Abdul Amien
Photographer: Malcolm Dare
Food Stylist: Georgia Schubitz

Typesetting by: CAPS of Cape Town
Reproduction by: Unifoto (Pty) Ltd, Cape Town
Printed and bound by: Leefung-Asco Printers Ltd, Hong Kong

ISBN 0 86978 551 6

CONTENTS

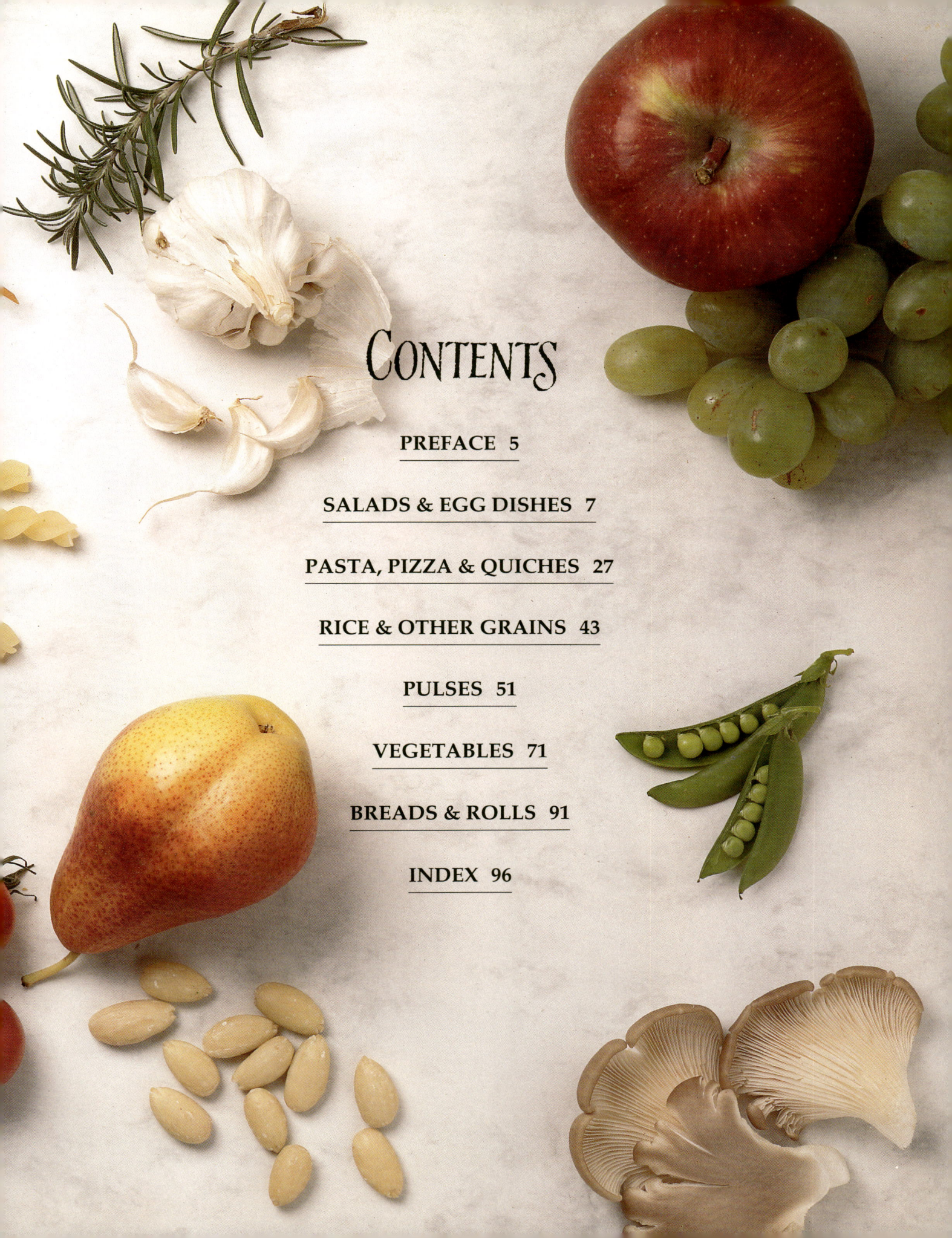

PREFACE 5

SALADS & EGG DISHES 7

PASTA, PIZZA & QUICHES 27

RICE & OTHER GRAINS 43

PULSES 51

VEGETABLES 71

BREADS & ROLLS 91

INDEX 96

Author's acknowledgements

A book of this kind involves creative input from several people. In particular, I wish to thank Sandie Vahl for her amazing dedication, meticulous editing, and the endless hours of overtime she cheerfully contributed in order to get the book published on schedule; Malcolm Dare, who is responsible for the superb photographs, both on the cover and inside; and his talented and hard-working team — especially cook Mampula Swanepoel, and stylist Georgia Schubitz who's bubbling energy and enthusiasm produced such eye-catching compositions; Janice Evans and Joan Sutton for the exceptionally hard work they put into designing a bulky manuscript; Abdul Amien for the striking cover design; Linda de Villiers and George Vine for their encouragement and support in helping this book see the light of day.

I would also like to acknowledge *The Sunday Times*, in which paper some of these recipes were first published in my weekly column.

Last, but definitely not least, thank you to my family who patiently have to help me test my efforts and have never once, during the course of eating this vegetarian book, put in a plea for frikkadels.

Photographer's acknowledgements

The publishers and photographer would like to thank the following for their contribution to the wonderful photographs in this book:
- Georgia Schubitz for styling the photographs
- Mampula Swanepoel for preparing and cooking the food
- Lucienne Vermeulen for finding props
- Lee-Ann Edwards for her assistance in the studio
- Block & Chisel Interiors, Bric-A-Brac-Lane, Collectors Corner Antiques, Garlicks and Stuttafords for the loan of crockery
- Trend Textiles for the loan of fabric

By the same author:

Best of Cooking in South Africa (Struik Publishers)
Lynn Bedford Hall's Biscuits and Breads (Struik Publishers)

METRIC VOLUME EQUIVALENTS

Using metric spoons and cups is far easier, and often more accurate, than using a kitchen scale. Spoons are available in 1 ml, 2 ml, 5 ml and 12,5 ml sizes, and cups in 25 ml, 50 ml, 62 ml, 83 ml, 100 ml, 125 ml and 250 ml sizes. To simplify measuring, I have tried to keep to the following:

1 ml = ¼ teaspoon
2 ml = ½ teaspoon
5 ml = 1 teaspoon
7 ml = 1½ teaspoons
12,5 ml = 1 tablespoon
15 ml = 3 teaspoons
25 ml = 2 tablespoons
30 ml = 2 tablespoons + 1 teaspoon
50 ml = ⅕ cup
60 ml = ¼ cup
80 ml = ⅓ cup
100 ml = ⅖ cup
125 ml = ½ cup
190 ml = ¾ cup
250 ml = 1 cup
500 ml = 2 cups
750 ml = 3 cups

Preface

I have written this book for a number of reasons, but mainly out of desperation. I am not a vegetarian, but I love vegetarian meals, I have a keen interest in wholefoods because their merits make such good sense, and I really enjoy dishes featuring grains and pulses in particular. But so many books on the subject — despite the excellence of their content — give a lot of space to simple things like wholewheat breads and fresh-fruit puddings. I wanted recipes with substance; meatless dishes which would fill people up and not leave hungry diners longing for chops or chicken. A tossed green salad served with bread is not a meal, and besides, people don't need a cookbook to tell them how to prepare a green salad. And so I have written this book, plump with hearty dishes, as a reference book for myself, and, I hope, for lots of others who are interested in cutting down on their intake of animal protein and stepping up on other, natural products.

My aim has been to create satisfying meals without meat or fish, with the emphasis on unprocessed foods, to serve on a couple of nights of the week. This is going to involve you, not only in checking the label on everything you buy, but also in a lot of washing, chopping and cooking of veggies; soaking of beans; straining and steaming and simmering. You could end up wishing you were simply frying a steak and had never bought this book. Your family might even leave home. So why persevere? For two reasons: firstly, for most people it is becoming an economic impossibility to eat red meat, chicken or fish every day; and secondly, there's the healthy spin-off that comes with eating less fat and sugar, while stepping up on fibre, and using carbohydrates for fuel. This is not a crankish approach. Obesity, high cholesterol levels, diabetes, and all sorts of other ailments are often caused by eating too much of the wrong foods, too often. Changing one's eating habits can change one's whole life.

But fanaticism is a mistake. Becoming a committed vegetarian means knowing your oats; it's an involved and scientific way of eating which has many pitfalls for the uninitiated, such as a possible lack of protein. One has to be on the ball when it comes to combining foods to achieve a nutritional balance — like always serving pulses with whole grains, for example — and I don't claim to be an expert in this sphere. With pasta dishes, particularly, a proper balance can be a problem. But it cannot be denied that more and more people are looking to a style of wholesome eating in which processed foods, with all their colourants, flavourings and other additives, play no part.

There is no need to go overboard; food is interesting and exciting, and eating should be a pleasure. To deny yourself the enjoyment of sampling all kinds of foods can simply stamp you as an eccentric and leave you undernourished. Be sensible, and be moderate. If you suddenly have the urge (as I sometimes do) to eat chicken in cream, or herby, garlicky roast lamb, then have it and love it. But at the end of the day (as they say) the bottom line (as they say) is how you *feel*: and if eating vegetarian dishes makes you feel lighter, healthier and happier with yourself, then go for it. Once you've got the hang of substituting items like pasta and vegetables, rice and lentils, on a couple of nights a week, you'll find that the whole concept really is no more trouble than fathoming the workings of a new washing machine. And the rewards are all on line: you should both feel and look a jolly sight better — and if you're looking and feeling good anyway, be prepared for a quantum leap.

I have made a point of using ingredients that are readily available. There's nothing exotic or wildly expensive in any of the dishes. The vegetables are all familiar; the pulses and grains are available at either supermarkets or wholefood shops; the spices can be found at supermarkets or speciality shops. And although some of the dishes do need advance planning and time in the kitchen, there are many which are really quick and easy.

Starting to include wholefoods in your diet could be a turning point. Do try. There's a whole new world of healthy ingredients and flavours just waiting to be enjoyed.

Lynn Bedford Hall

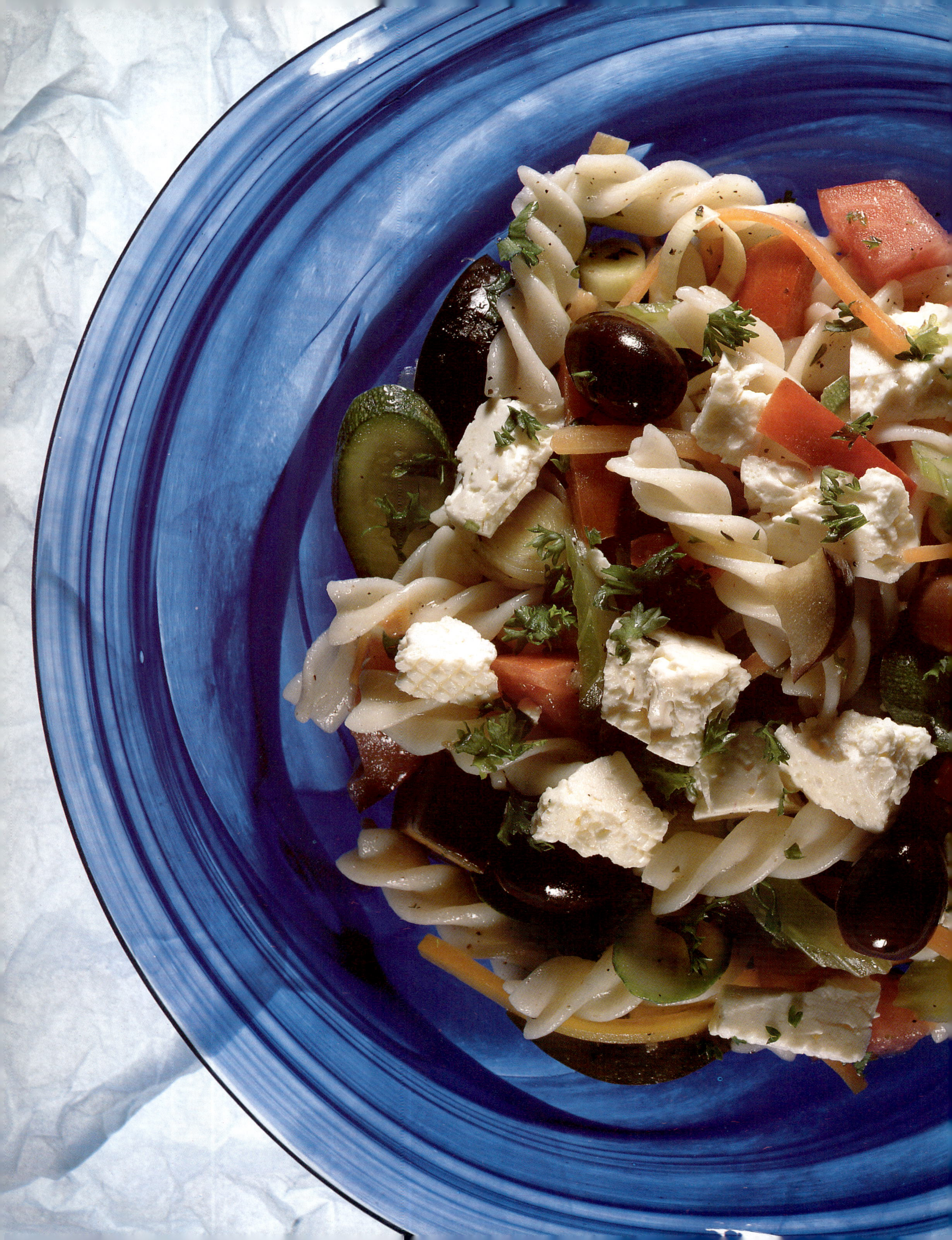

Salads & Egg Dishes

BEAN SLAW

A simple salad, and an excellent way of subtly enhancing salad greens with beans for a wholesome, unpretentious summer lunch. Add a loaf of wholewheat bread and you have a nourishing and low-cost meal. I usually mix haricot and soya beans in equal quantities, but feel free to adjust according to personal preference.

**4 x 250 ml cooked beans of choice
4 carrots, coarsely grated (500 ml)
8 slim spring onions, chopped
2 sweet apples, peeled, diced and tossed in lemon juice
4–5 x 250 ml coarsely shredded cabbage
250 ml raisins or sultanas, briefly plumped in hot water and drained
herbed sea salt to taste
walnuts or toasted sunflower seeds**

**DRESSING
250 ml mayonnaise
250 ml cultured sour cream or Bulgarian yoghurt or half-and-half
15–20 ml prepared mustard**

Mix all salad ingredients, except walnuts or sunflower seeds, in large bowl. Stir ingredients for dressing until well mixed. Fold dressing into salad ingredients, cover and chill. Just before serving, mix in walnuts or sunflower seeds.
Serves 8.

Mediterranean Pasta and Vegetable Salad (p. 18).

HARICOT BEAN SALAD (1)

Also known as Flageolet Vinaigrette, this happy combination of French and Greek flavours is an economical, substantial salad to serve with wholewheat bread as a complete meal. Serve with Tzatziki (page 76).

500 g haricot beans
2 bouquets garnis
2 bay leaves
5 ml sea salt
3–4 leeks, thinly sliced
1 green or red pepper, seeded
and chopped
1 large stick table celery, sliced
100 ml chopped parsley
a large pinch of sugar
tomato, black olives and feta cheese
for garnish

DRESSING
100 ml sunflower oil
50 ml olive oil
1 clove garlic, crushed
25 ml fresh lemon juice
2 ml sea salt
5 ml dried origanum

Soak beans in cold water overnight. The next day, drain and rinse the beans, cover them with fresh water, add bouquets garnis and bay leaves, and boil until soft, adding 5 ml salt towards the end of cooking period.

Mix all ingredients for dressing, then leave to stand while the beans are cooking.

Drain cooked beans, and spoon into a large bowl. Toss, while hot, with dressing, using a fork and taking care not to mash the beans. Add leeks, pepper, celery, parsley and sugar. Cover and stand for at least 2 hours, or chill overnight.

To serve, adjust seasoning, then spoon onto a large serving platter. Surround with chunks of tomato and top with olives. Sprinkle generously with crumbled feta.
Serves 8.

BOUQUETS GARNIS

It is possible to buy these, but if you wish to make your own from the herbs in your garden, tie together a few stalks of parsley, a bay leaf and a sprig or two of thyme. They may also be parcelled up in a small square of muslin.

PEPPERS

Red and yellow peppers are nice and mild but green peppers have a strong flavour, when served raw, that will dominate any salad.

A real cop-out salad served by some restaurants consists of raw green peppers and onions (another pungent vegetable when served raw), tossed with lettuce and tomatoes, and doused with a vinegary dressing.

To tone down the strong flavour of raw green peppers and raw onions in a salad, blanch them. They still look attractive and should retain their crunch, but the boiling water removes the bite. Place the rings in a bowl, add a pinch of sugar, pour boiling water over them to cover, leave them in the water for a few minutes, then drain them thoroughly.

AÏGROISSADE WITH AÏOLI-YOGHURT DRESSING

A fancy name for a very simple, chunky salad of Provençal origin, combining steamed vegetables, chickpeas and a garlic dressing. This is my version, using vegetables which are available throughout the year. Serve with hot wholewheat rolls and, if liked, a bowl of grated cheese for sprinkling. It is important either to steam the vegetables, or to cook them in the very minimum amount of water, adding them in relays, as described. For this method, you'll need a wide, deep saucepan or a frying pan with a lid.

2 leeks, sliced
2 medium potatoes (± 300 g), scrubbed
and cut into eighths
250 g slim green beans, trimmed
and sliced
3–4 carrots, julienned
250 g broccoli, most of stalks discarded
and coarsely chopped
500 ml cooked chickpeas
250 ml sprouts of choice
100 ml finely chopped parsley
5 ml sea salt and milled black
pepper to taste

DRESSING
250 ml mayonnaise
250 ml Bulgarian yoghurt
2 cloves garlic, crushed

Heat a small quantity of water in a pan and add leeks and potatoes. Cover and steam on low heat for about 7 minutes. Top with the beans, carrots and broccoli. Cover and steam for another 12–15 minutes. Test potatoes with tip of a knife and, if tender, the dish is done.

Tip the cooked vegetables into a bowl (if correctly cooked, no draining should be necessary). Add the chickpeas, sprouts, parsley and seasoning. Set aside to cool while making dressing.

Stir together the mayonnaise, yoghurt and crushed garlic. Gently fold half the mixture into the vegetables. If not serving immediately, cover the salad and refrigerate until needed.

To serve, mound onto a large salad platter. Serve the remaining half of the garlic dressing separately.
Serves 6.

BLENDER AÏOLI

Crudités, being fresh and raw, are the appropriate snack to serve with drinks before a vegetarian meal. Choose from a variety of fresh, very young vegetables: thinly sliced baby carrots, sliced sticks of celery, raw cauliflower florets, button mushrooms on toothpicks, fingers of English cucumber and baby marrows. Arrange them in bright little bundles with a bowl of boldly flavoured mayonnaise in the middle.

The following mayonnaise is thick and garlicky, and will not drip all over the carpet. For a milder variation, use only 2 cloves garlic and add 5 ml Dijon mustard and a generous 2 ml of dried dill before adding the oil.

4 cloves garlic
2 ml sea salt
1 whole egg and 1 egg yolk
25 ml fresh lemon juice
125 ml each sunflower
and olive oil

Place garlic, salt, egg and yolk and lemon juice in a blender and blend until well combined. With blender running, add the oils in a slow, thin stream through the hole in the top. Stop when mixture has formed a thick emulsion. Spoon into a bowl, cover, and chill to mellow the flavour.
Makes about 275 ml.

SALADS AND EGG DISHES

> ### SPROUTS
>
> Sprouts are a very healthy 'living' food. Use them in salads, sandwiches and stir-fries. Only use seeds from wholefood stores for sprouting as seeds meant for planting are often treated with pesticide. My favourites are alfalfa and lentil. They are easy and quick to sprout and grow like a forest. I find mung beans often go musty before fully grown and have to be turfed out. Various seeds, peas, wheat and chickpeas may also be sprouted. Remember that certain beans, like butter or kidney beans, become toxic when sprouted, as are potato sprouts. The most convenient and cheapest sprouter is simply a jar with a mesh top.
>
> Rinse seeds of choice and soak overnight. Drain and place in jar. Allow heaps of room for growth; some sprouts increase up to six times in volume so you need only a handful at the bottom of the jar. Tilt the jar downward (rest it on a saucer) in a dark cupboard. Rinse twice a day, draining well each time. (They will sprout more quickly in warmer weather.) When the leaves appear, the jar may be placed in the sun for a while for chlorophyll to be formed; the sprouts should become slightly greener. When ready, they should be rinsed, dried, and kept in the fridge. They should be eaten within a few days.

CREAMY CURRIED SOYA BEAN SALAD

This salad is sheer goodness, cheap, easy to make and much tastier than it sounds. Serve it with bowls of chutney, coconut for sprinkling, lettuce and tomato, and introduce a grain in the form of tiny rice timbales, made by packing a rice salad into ramekins and turning out prettily.

4 x 250 ml cooked soya beans (or half soya and half haricot)
1 small pineapple, cut into small dice
1 bunch spring onions, chopped
100 ml seedless raisins
2 Golden Delicious apples, peeled, diced, and tossed in lemon juice
onion salt or sea salt to taste
± 200 ml coarsely chopped walnuts

DRESSING
20 ml curry powder
200 ml thick mayonnaise
200 ml Bulgarian yoghurt
a pinch of sugar

Mix all salad ingredients together except chopped walnuts.

Make the dressing by steeping the curry powder in 40 ml boiling water for a few minutes to remove the raw taste. Stir the mayonnaise with the yoghurt until smooth, then add the curry powder and a pinch of sugar. Stir to mix.

Fold dressing into salad, and chill for several hours. Toss in the walnuts just before serving.

Serve as suggested
Serves 8.

CHICKPEA, RICE AND SPROUT SALAD

Bright and crunchy, this is a cheerful luncheon salad. Top with crumbled feta cheese and/or wedges of hard-boiled eggs for added nutrition and surround with slivers of avocado and cherry tomatoes. Pass hot Pita Bread (page 93) or wholewheat rolls with herb butter.

200 ml brown rice
2 ml turmeric
50 ml sunflower oil
2 large leeks, sliced
10 ml ground coriander
5 ml each ground cinnamon and cumin
750 ml cooked chickpeas
125 ml finely chopped parsley
375 ml lentil sprouts
6 small baby marrows, pared and coarsely grated or 250 ml coarsely grated raw butternut squash
herbed vegetable salt (e.g. Garlic and Parsley) or sea salt to taste
± 125 ml lemony French dressing

Boil the rice in 450 ml salted water with turmeric. Do not undercook — it must be quite dry and fluffy. Meanwhile, heat oil and sauté leeks until softened. Stir in spices, and toss over low heat for 1–2 minutes.

Tip cooked rice into large bowl. Fork in spicy leeks and rest of ingredients, except French dressing. Finally, toss with enough dressing to moisten thoroughly. At this stage, salad may be refrigerated overnight.

To serve, pile onto a platter, and garnish as suggested.
Serves 6.

RICE, CHICKPEA AND FETA SALAD

With the addition of spinach, olive oil and fresh marjoram this salad is spot-on for lovers of Middle Eastern flavours. Serve with thick yoghurt or Tzatziki (page 76), and Greek Garlic Bread (page 94).

DRESSING
60 ml each sunflower and olive oil
50 ml fresh lemon juice
30 ml finely chopped fresh marjoram leaves
2 ml sea salt
2 ml mustard powder
a pinch of sugar

150 ml brown rice
500 ml cooked chickpeas
50 ml finely chopped parsley
4 spring onions, chopped
2–3 baby marrows, pared and coarsely grated (about 150 g)
500 ml shredded spinach
sea salt and milled black pepper to taste
1 large tomato, chopped
crumbled feta cheese and toasted sesame seeds for garnish

Whisk together ingredients for dressing, then cover and stand for about 1 hour.

Meanwhile, boil rice in 325 ml salted water. When done, tip into bowl and fork in dressing while rice is hot. Add chickpeas, parsley, onions, marrows and spinach. Season very lightly, then cover and stand at room temperature to cool and to allow flavours to blend. Just before serving, toss in tomato. Pile onto serving platter and top generously with feta and sesame seeds.
Serves 4.

> ### MUSTARD
>
> Remember that most types of prepared mustard need to be kept in the fridge once opened. Most types of vinaigrette dressing benefit from the addition of mustard powder, while Dijon mustard is the favourite for using in sauces and mayonnaise.

Overleaf: Moulded Cream Cheese and Vegetable Salad (p. 20), Piperade (p. 24) and Curried Weet-Rice Salad (p. 12).

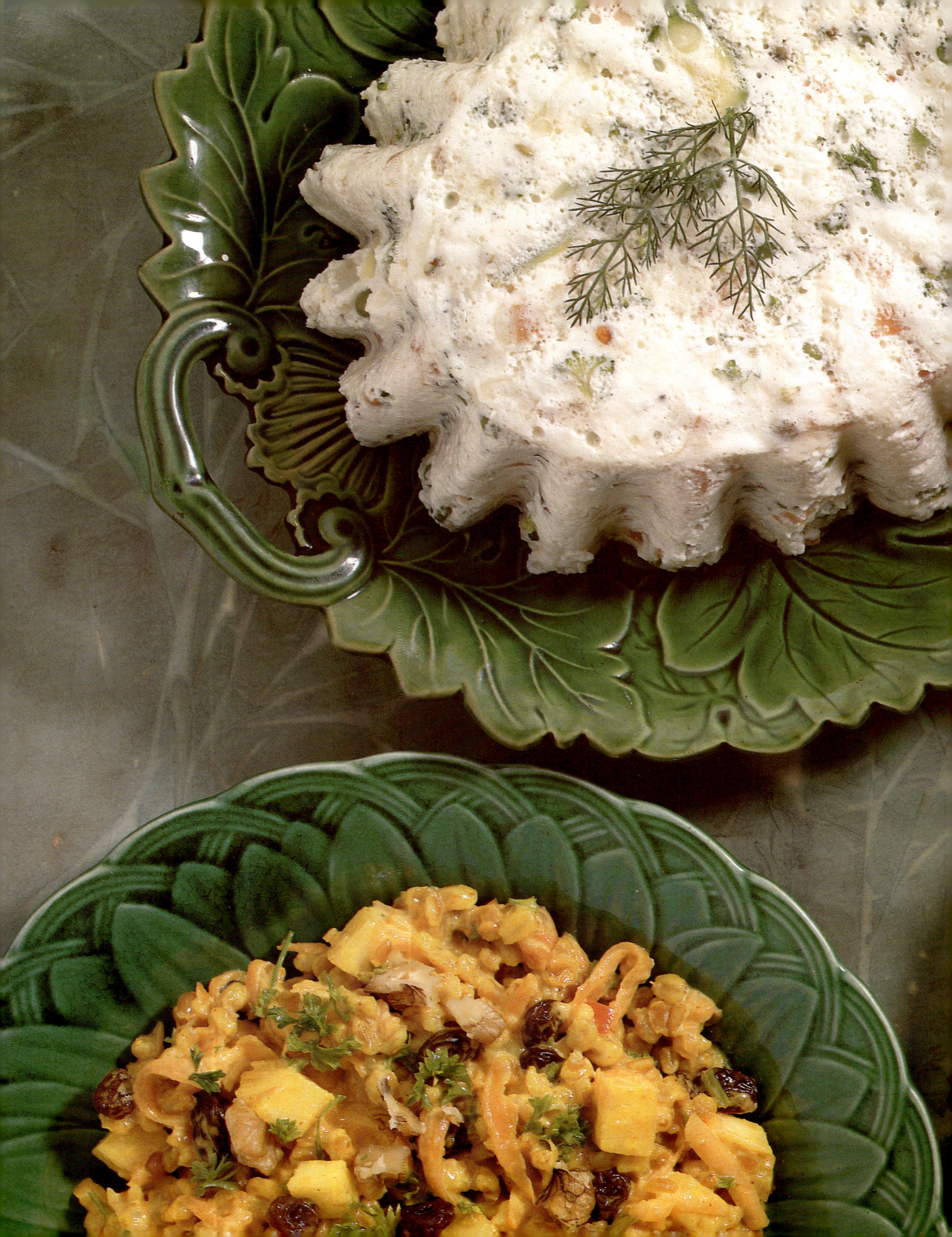

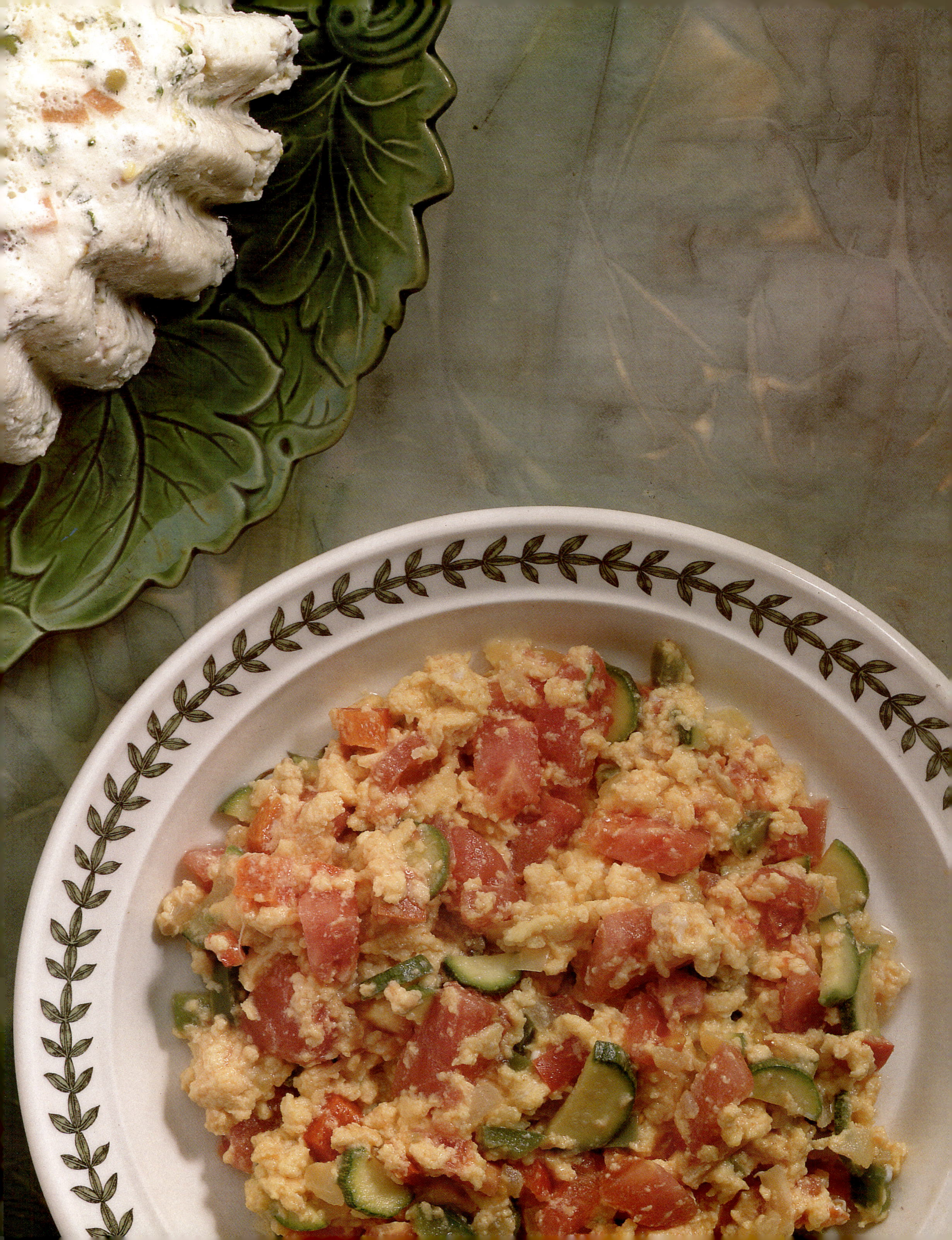

> **MAYONNAISE**
>
> With the use of a blender, making mayonnaise is a speedy and simple operation (see page 21), with the added advantage of being able to add different flavours (like garlic) or different colours (like green herbs) when making. However, a good commercial brand is Kraft Real Mayonnaise. It is tasty and thick, and may be thinned down with a little buttermilk or Bulgarian yoghurt to reduce kilojoules, or enriched with sour cream or whipped cream for a special indulgence.

CHICKPEA SALAD WITH CABBAGE AND WALNUTS

A creamy, crunchy salad which offers a good introduction to those unfamiliar with chickpeas. Serve mounded on a salad platter, sprinkle with the bright garnish and surround with shredded lettuce and segments of avocado. Pass a jug of French dressing and wholewheat rolls.

750 ml cooked chickpeas
2 Golden Delicious apples, peeled and finely diced
4 x 250 ml shredded cabbage
1 bunch spring onions, chopped
half a fresh pineapple, diced*
a shake of sea salt or herb salt
250 ml coarsely chopped walnuts
finely grated Cheddar cheese for topping
finely chopped parsley for topping

DRESSING
200 ml thick mayonnaise
200 ml Bulgarian yoghurt
5 ml prepared mustard
2 pinches of sugar

Toss all the salad ingredients together, except walnuts, cheese and parsley. Mix ingredients for dressing, stirring until smooth. Mix dressing with salad, then cover and chill for at least 2 hours, or overnight. Fork in nuts and sprinkle with the mixed cheese and parsley before serving. *Serves 6–8.*

* Cut pineapple into rings and peel. Place rings flat on chopping board, slice into thin vertical strips, then cut across into tiny dice.

BULGUR SALAD WITH RICE AND MUSHROOMS

A delectable combination of salad ingredients, tossed with a mustard-flavoured dressing. An excellent choice for a cold buffet. Then again, with the addition of nuts or sunflower seeds, and topped with feta or grated Cheddar cheese, it makes a lovely light meal. Try it with Hummus (page 84), tomatoes and Pita Bread (page 93); or simply add a creamy coleslaw. The possibilities are many and varied.

250 ml bulgur
200 ml brown rice

DRESSING
50 ml each sunflower and olive oil
40 ml fresh lemon juice
1 ml sea salt
5–10 ml prepared mustard
a pinch of sugar

30 ml sunflower oil
250 g brown mushrooms, wiped and sliced
2 cloves garlic, crushed
1 sprig fresh rosemary
25 ml sweet sherry
1 red pepper, seeded and finely chopped
6–8 slim spring onions, chopped
100 ml finely chopped parsley
⅓ English cucumber, pared and diced
a little sea salt and milled black pepper to taste
chopped nuts and toasted sunflower seeds (optional)
cheese of choice, grated, for topping

Soak bulgur in plenty of cold water for 45 minutes. Cook rice in 450 ml salted water. Whisk together ingredients for dressing and put aside.

Meanwhile, heat the 30 ml sunflower oil and add mushrooms, garlic and rosemary. Stir-fry over low heat until just softening, then add sherry and allow to evaporate. Remove pan from heat, add red pepper, cover and leave to stand.

Drain bulgur in colander and squeeze very well to release excess moisture. Spoon into large bowl and add rice, onions, parsley, cucumber and seasoning. Remove rosemary and add mushrooms to mixture, together with any juices that have formed. Fork in dressing, then cover and stand for about 2 hours for flavour to develop.

Mix in nuts or sunflower seeds, if using, and top with cheese of choice. *Serves 6.*

CURRIED WEET-RICE SALAD

A beautifully bright and tangy salad in which Weet-rice is combined with pineapple and grated raw butternut in a creamy, curry dressing. The following quantities make an enormous salad which is both economical and nourishing. Serve with hard-boiled eggs and a home-made wholewheat loaf. Chopped walnuts or toasted sunflower seeds are an optional but super addition — fold them in before serving.

375 ml Weet-rice, rinsed and drained
5 ml each sea salt and turmeric
2 sticks cinnamon
125 ml seedless raisins
3 rings fresh pineapple, diced
500 ml coarsely grated butternut squash
125 ml finely chopped parsley
a little extra sea salt and milled black pepper to taste

DRESSING
25 ml sunflower oil
3 leeks, very thinly sliced
1 red pepper, seeded and diced (optional)
15 ml curry powder
1 x 175 ml tub Bulgarian yoghurt
125 ml thick mayonnaise
25 ml mild fruit chutney
5 ml light brown sugar

Put the Weet-rice, 5 x 250 ml water, salt, turmeric and cinnamon into a saucepan. Bring to the boil, then cover and simmer for 45 minutes. Drain the cooked Weet-rice, rinse, add raisins and steam in a colander, covered with a kitchen towel, over simmering water for 15 minutes, or until fluffy. Remove the cinnamon sticks and spoon the rice mixture into large bowl. Fork in the pineapple, butternut, parsley, and season lightly. Set the mixture aside to cool while making dressing.

Heat oil in a small pan. Add leeks, red pepper (if using) and curry powder, and stir-fry for about 2 minutes, adding a dash of water so as not to scorch the curry. Mix yoghurt, mayonnaise, chutney and sugar. Add curry mixture and stir well.

Fold the dressing into the cooled salad, then cover and refrigerate for several hours or overnight before serving.

Serve with extra chutney and a bowl of coconut, and surround the salad with sliced avocado pear. *Serves 8.*

RICE, LENTIL AND PINEAPPLE SALAD

This salad is perfect summer fare: mound salad on a large platter, and surround it with halved hard-boiled eggs, rounded sides up and drizzled with a mustard-flavoured mayonnaise. Add a bowl of salad leaves and a loaf of fresh wholewheat bread.

250 ml brown rice
250 ml brown or green lentils, picked over and rinsed
125 ml sunflower oil
30 ml soy sauce
50 ml fresh lemon juice
2 ml ground ginger
5 ml honey
½ pineapple, sliced into rings and diced
2 stalks table celery, chopped
1 green or red pepper, seeded, diced and blanched
75 ml chopped parsley
125 ml seedless raisins or sultanas, plumped in hot water and drained
2 carrots, coarsely grated
250 ml mung bean or lentil sprouts
6 spring onions, chopped
125 ml toasted sunflower seeds or toasted almond slivers

Cook rice in 550 ml salted water until dry and fluffy. Boil lentils in 500 ml salted water until soft and water is absorbed. Spoon rice and lentils into large bowl.

Blanch the green or red pepper in boiling water for 1 minute, then drain. Whisk together the oil, soy sauce, lemon juice, ginger and honey and fork into hot rice and lentils. Add pineapple, celery, drained pepper, parsley, raisins or sultanas, carrots, sprouts and onions. Toss well, cover and leave to cool, or chill overnight, to allow flavours to blend. Just before serving, fork in the sunflower seeds, or sprinkle toasted almond slivers over the salad.
Serves 8–10.

BUTTERNUT SQUASH AND BEETROOT

Beetroot, especially, is a neglected vegetable because it takes time to cook. Try raw butternut squash and/or beetroot, peeled and grated in salads for extra vitamins, some bright colour and a nice crunch.

RICE, LENTIL AND MUSHROOM SALAD WITH FRESH HERBS

This is a most delicious combination and a splendid choice for a light, hot-weather lunch. It is particularly good served with butter lettuce and avocado, a bowl of Tzatziki (page 76), hot sesame rolls and cheese. It is important to use fresh herbs in the dressing, which should be made about an hour before using to allow the full flavour to develop.

DRESSING
100 ml sunflower oil
25 ml fresh lemon juice
2 cloves garlic, crushed
2 ml sea salt
25 ml fresh mixed herbs, chopped*
a pinch of sugar

250 ml brown rice
250 ml brown or green lentils, picked over and rinsed
50 ml sunflower oil
250 g brown mushrooms, wiped and sliced
3 sticks table celery, sliced, plus a few leaves
25 ml soy sauce
100 ml finely chopped parsley
1 large onion, thinly sliced into rings
1 red pepper, seeded and diced
a pinch of sugar
toasted slivered almonds for garnish

Mix ingredients for dressing, cover and set aside for flavour to develop.

Boil rice in 550 ml salted water until fluffy and dry. Boil lentils in 500 ml salted water until soft and water is absorbed.

Meanwhile, heat oil and sauté mushrooms and celery until softening. Remove from heat and add soy sauce and parsley.

Tip the hot rice and lentils into bowl and fork in the dressing. Add the celery and mushroom mixture, plus any juices that have formed.

Pour boiling water over onion rings and diced red pepper, add a pinch of sugar and leave to stand for a few minutes. Drain and fork into salad, taking care not to mash the lentils or break up the onion rings. Cover and leave to cool.

Serve at room temperature, sprinkled with the almonds.
Serves 6.

* Choose from parsley, chives, basil, tarragon or marjoram, depending on what you have in your garden.

LENTIL SALAD

This is a favourite summer lunch salad. Surround with wedges of hard-boiled eggs and serve with cheese and wholewheat bread for a nourishing, complete meal. Brighten up the lentils by drizzling a little plain yoghurt or sour cream over them and topping the salad with fresh chopped mint or a sprinkling of nuts of your choice.

375 ml brown lentils, picked over and rinsed
2 ml sea salt
2 bay leaves
2 ml turmeric
100 ml French dressing
3–4 spring onions, chopped
2 large carrots, grated
2–3 sticks table celery, chopped
50 ml chopped parsley
250 ml mung bean sprouts (or sprouts of choice)
25 ml soy sauce

Put the lentils into a saucepan with 750 ml water, salt, bay leaves and turmeric. Bring to the boil, then cover and simmer gently until soft and liquid has been absorbed.

Tip the cooked lentils into a large bowl and discard the bay leaves. Fork in the French dressing, taking care not to mash the lentils. Add the spring onions, carrots, celery, parsley, sprouts and soy sauce. Toss lightly to mix, and then set aside, covered, for about 2 hours for flavours to develop, or chill for longer.

Serve as suggested.
Serves 6.

SUGAR

I often use a little sugar in savoury dishes. It brings out the flavour, and helps to cut the acidity of ingredients such as tomatoes and buttermilk. If using white sugar, use less; if using soft, dark brown sugar, remember that it has a rather distinctive flavour.

Overleaf: Spicy Indian-Style Salad (p. 21), Green Pasta Salad with Herbed Dressing (p. 17) and Coronation Egg Salad (p. 24).

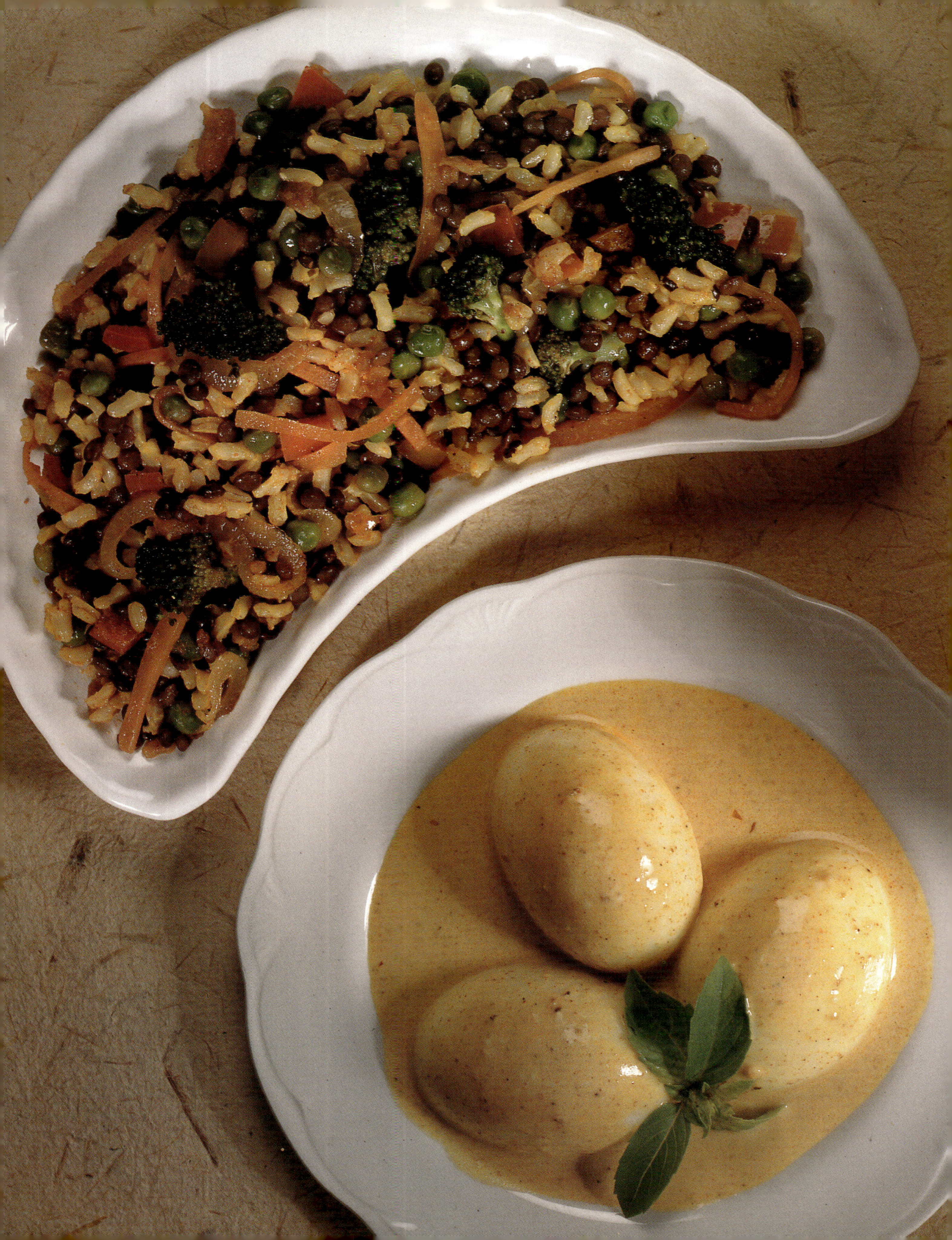

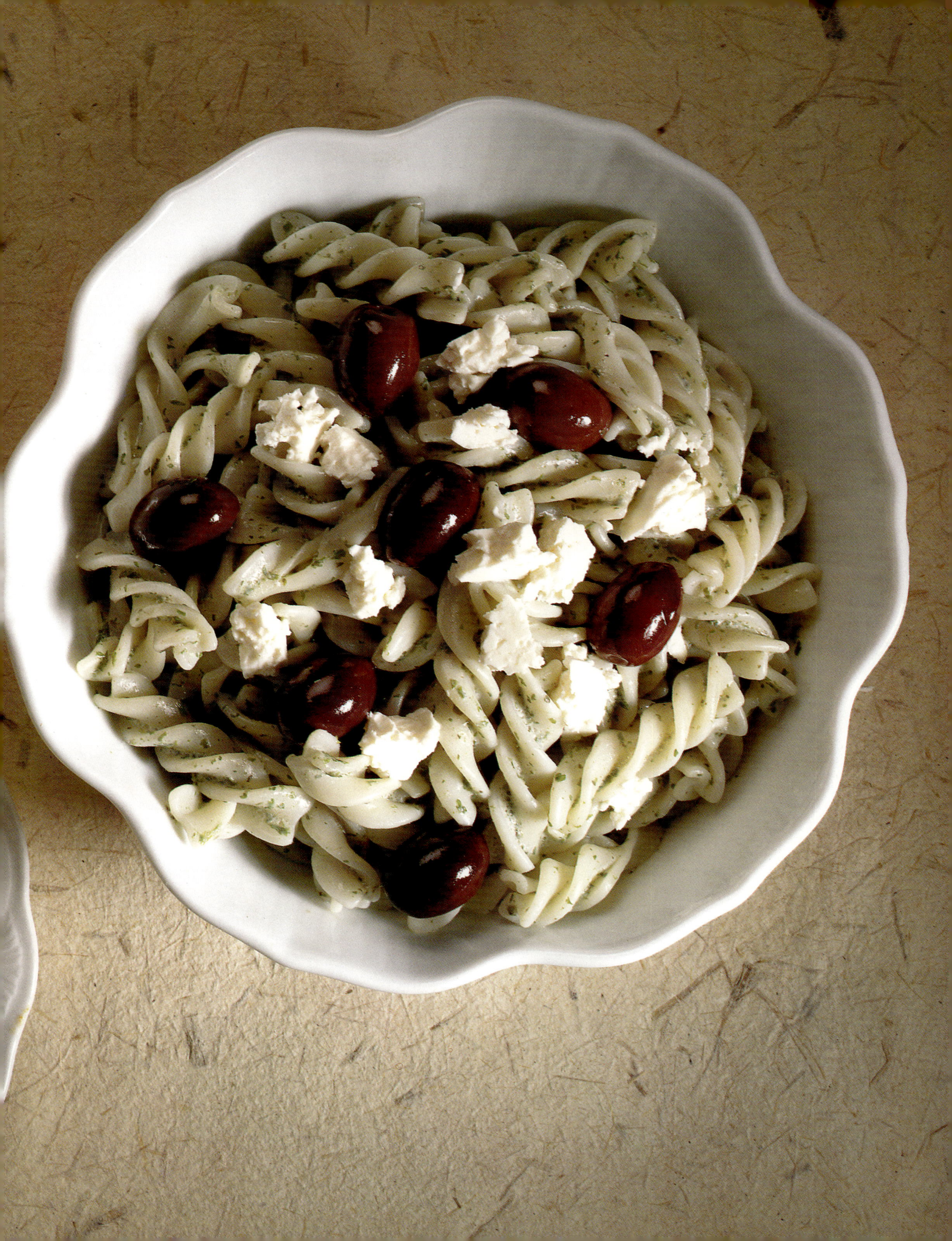

> ### GARLIC
>
> There was one thing about Italian ladies which dismayed the poet Shelley. 'Young women of rank actually eat — you will never guess what — garlick!' he wrote. Undismayed, I put it into everything. If I remember, I eat parsley afterwards. Peel a whole bulb of garlic, or buy those convenient little punnets of ready-peeled cloves and keep them in a bottle of sunflower or olive oil in the fridge. Grab a clove whenever a recipe calls for it, and use the oil in salad dressings. Garlic is reputed to be a herbal antibiotic. This is just a bonus; the important thing is its matchless aroma and flavour.

TWO-GRAIN SALAD WITH MUSHROOMS AND BABY MARROWS

Weet-rice (also known as stampkoring or pearled wheat) has a lovely nutty texture and flavour and adds a new dimension to this rice and vegetable salad, which is subtly flavoured with sesame oil. The salad may be served very simply, with greens and a bowl of thick yoghurt, or accompanied with halved hard-boiled eggs in a lemony mayonnaise for a more substantial meal.

200 ml Weet-rice, well rinsed
250 ml brown rice
25 ml each sunflower and
dark sesame oil
250 g brown mushrooms,
wiped and sliced
1 large sprig fresh rosemary
6 spring onions, chopped
6 baby marrows (about 150 g),
pared and very thinly sliced
100 ml finely chopped parsley
125 ml toasted sunflower seeds
or 100 g toasted almond strips

DRESSING
100 ml sunflower oil
25 ml soy sauce
25 ml fresh lemon juice

Cook the Weet-rice in 800 ml salted water in a covered saucepan on low heat until soft and most of liquid has been absorbed — for about 45 minutes. Rinse the cooked Weet-rice in colander, then steam over boiling water until dry and fluffy.

Cook brown rice in 550 ml salted water until tender. While rice is cooking, mix ingredients for dressing. When rice is cooked, tip the hot grains into a large bowl and fork in the dressing.

Heat sunflower and sesame oils, add mushrooms and rosemary and stir-fry over medium heat until browned and beginning to soften. Remove the rosemary and add mushrooms to grains. Add remaining ingredients, toss gently, check seasoning, then cover and stand for at least 1 hour for

Mound onto a large salad platter, and serve as suggested.
Serves 8.

> ### MARINATED MUSHROOMS WITH SPROUTS
>
> The easiest way to marinate mushrooms is simply to slice them, toss them with a well-flavoured vinaigrette dressing, and then leave them in the fridge for a couple of hours or overnight. The following recipe, not quite as simple, is more in the line of a deliciously light and crunchy salad.
>
> 40 ml olive or sunflower oil
> 10 ml butter
> 500 g white mushrooms,
>   wiped and sliced, and
>   halved (unless very small)
> 2 leeks, finely shredded
> 25 ml soy sauce
> 30 ml sweet sherry
> 25 ml toasted sesame seeds
> 25 ml extra olive or
>   sunflower oil
> 500 ml lentil sprouts
>
> Heat sunflower oil and butter in a large frying pan. Add mushrooms, and toss over medium heat until just beginning to brown and shrink. Do not overcook the mushrooms. Transfer them to a large, shallow salad bowl and carefully mix in the leeks.
> Mix together soy sauce, sherry, sesame seeds and extra oil for dressing, and add to mushrooms.
> Cover the mushrooms and refrigerate for several hours or overnight. Add the lentil sprouts just before serving, mixing in lightly.
> Serves 6.

RICE AND SPROUT SALAD WITH SESAME DRESSING

A wonderfully nutritious combination of ingredients goes into this super salad: brown rice, lentil sprouts, fresh pineapple, baby marrows or butternut, and sunflower seeds, all tossed together with a richly flavoured, unusual dressing. This is a good buffet salad, or serve it for lunch with halved hard-boiled eggs tucked into a mustard mayonnaise or simply with crusty rolls and a tub of chunky cottage cheese. Garnish with red lettuce, chopped parsley, chives and/or bright nasturtium flowers for colour. For special occasions, add a bowl of marinated mushrooms.

DRESSING*
125 ml sunflower oil
30 ml dark sesame oil**
30 ml soy sauce
50 ml toasted sesame seeds
50 ml fresh lemon juice
20 ml light brown sugar

400 ml brown rice
4 x 250 ml lentil sprouts
8 small baby marrows, pared
and coarsely grated or 500 ml coarsely
grated butternut squash
6–8 spring onions, chopped
4 thin rings fresh pineapple, diced
200 ml toasted sunflower seeds

Using a fork, whisk together all the ingredients for the dressing, cover and leave it to stand.

Cook rice in 850 ml lightly salted water. When done, drain (if necessary) and tip the hot rice into a large bowl. Fork in the dressing until rice is well moistened, then gently mix in the marrows, butternut, onions, pineapple and sunflower seeds. Cover the salad and leave it to stand at room temperature for about 2 hours to allow flavours to blend, or cover and chill until needed, but return to room temperature before serving.

Spoon onto a salad platter, and garnish as suggested.
Serves 8.

* To add a lovely flavour to a tossed green salad, combine this dressing with regular French dressing, using a ratio of 1:2.

** If using a light sesame oil, use about 50 ml and decrease the amount of sunflower oil accordingly.

BASIC BLENDER SALAD DRESSING

Why buy expensive salad dressing when you can mix your own in a trice? This is a good, simple version to have on hand in your fridge. Vary the recipe by adding fresh or dried herbs, or more garlic. I prefer using fresh lemon juice to wine vinegar, but it makes a dressing sour rather than sharp, so I add a little honey to enhance the flavour. If you use vinegar, go for a good wine vinegar — plain, herbed or sherry-flavoured.

600 ml sunflower oil
125 ml fresh lemon juice
1–2 cloves garlic
a few sprigs of parsley
5 ml mustard powder
5 ml sea salt
2 ml paprika
± 15 ml honey

Place all ingredients in a blender and blend well. Pour into a glass jar, screw on lid, and refrigerate.

SESAME RICE SALAD

A delectable combination of rice, mushrooms, cucumber and seeds, this salad has an Oriental touch. Serve as part of a cold buffet, or as a wholesome, light meal, with the addition of stuffed hard-boiled eggs and a wholewheat loaf.

200 ml brown rice
200 ml brown lentils, picked over and rinsed
60 ml sunflower oil
2 leeks, sliced or 1 large onion, finely chopped
1 red pepper, seeded and diced
250 g brown mushrooms, wiped and sliced
½ English cucumber, pared and julienned
2 sprigs fresh rosemary or 2 ml dried dill
100 ml chopped parsley
100 ml toasted sunflower seeds
25 ml toasted sesame seeds
sprouts of choice for garnish

DRESSING
50 ml soy sauce
25 ml sweet sherry
5 ml light brown sugar
15 ml dark sesame oil

Boil rice in 450 ml lightly salted water and lentils in 400 ml lightly salted water. Keep the heat low, the saucepans covered, and avoid stirring and looking. They should be done in 50 minutes.

Meanwhile, heat the sunflower oil and stir-fry leeks or onion and red pepper. When softening, add mushrooms, cucumber and rosemary or dill and toss over low heat until just tender. Remove from heat, remove rosemary, mix in parsley and seeds and set aside.

Mix ingredients for dressing. Drain cooked rice and lentils, if necessary, and tip into large bowl. Fork in mushroom mixture, adding all the juices. Toss with dressing. Cool, then cover loosely and stand for 1–2 hours. Serve with a garnish of sprouts.
Serves 6.

BULGUR SALAD WITH TOMATOES AND BLACK OLIVES

Bulgur wheat is used extensively in the Middle East. The grains are soaked then toasted, after which they need only be soaked in water. Cracked wheat cannot be substituted, but bulgur is sold at some health-food shops. It makes a delicious and unusual salad, and can be served as a light first course with cheese or Hummus (page 84) and Pita Bread (page 93).

DRESSING
50 ml each sunflower and olive oil
35 ml fresh lemon juice
1 clove garlic, crushed
sea salt and milled black pepper to taste
2 ml dried origanum

250 g bulgur (375 ml)
6 small spring onions, finely chopped
100 ml finely chopped parsley
25 ml finely chopped fresh mint
2 medium tomatoes, chopped
black olives, sliced
lettuce and sliced cucumber to garnish

Mix ingredients for dressing first, and stand for several hours to blend flavours.

Cover bulgur generously with water and soak for about 45 minutes. Drain in colander and squeeze out excess moisture with hands. Put into large bowl and add onions, parsley and mint. Pour prepared dressing over bulgur, toss, cover and stand for 30 minutes. Adjust seasoning, then fold in tomatoes and olives. Serve garnished with lettuce and sliced cucumber.
Serves 6.

GREEN PASTA SALAD WITH HERBED DRESSING

This is a stunning salad in which pasta screws, or fusilli noodles, are coated with a pale green sauce, subtly spiked with basil. Pretty to look at and deliciously flavoured, it is bound to find favour with lovers of pesto and those who enjoy Mediterranean-style foods. The sauce is quickly whipped up in a blender while the pasta is cooking and the dish is then chilled for several hours or overnight, making it a perfect choice for a do-ahead summer supper or buffet. It is not, however, a dish that can stand alone, but it does make a beautiful accompaniment to chickpea or bean salads; or for a light, bright meal simply add a well-dressed spinach salad with croûtons, mushrooms and hard-boiled eggs.

250 g pasta screws, fusilli noodles or elbow macaroni
125 ml parsley tufts
125 ml shredded fresh basil leaves, quite tightly packed
1 small clove garlic
2 spring onions, chopped
125 ml thick mayonnaise
125 ml buttermilk
50 ml olive oil
2 ml sea salt and a pinch of sugar
extra olive oil or a little French dressing
chopped walnuts (optional)
black olives and feta or Parmesan cheese for garnish

Cook pasta in plenty of rapidly boiling salted water, drain, toss with a dash of oil, and leave to cool.

Put parsley, basil, garlic, onions, mayonnaise, buttermilk, oil, salt and sugar into a blender and blend well to a medium-thick mixture, flecked with green.*

Tip pasta into a large bowl, mix in sauce, cover and chill.

Before serving, gently fork in a little olive oil or French dressing to add shine and loosen the pasta. Check seasoning (it will probably need a little salt), add walnuts if using, pile onto large serving platter, tuck in some olives and top with either crumbled feta or grated Parmesan. Pass a pepper mill at the table.
Serves 4–6, depending on the rest of the meal.

* The longer you blend the sauce, the brighter the colour will be. A very well blended sauce should be a bright peppermint green colour.

MEDITERRANEAN PASTA AND VEGETABLE SALAD

This jumbo salad is known in our house as El Cheapo, but the economy of the salad in no way detracts from its delicious appeal. Visually it's quite beautiful: screwy fusilli noodles tossed with vegetables in all the bright colours. Instead of a traditional feta cheese topping, grated Cheddar may be used, but a hot crusty loaf is an essential accompaniment. This salad is a top favourite.

250 g fusilli noodles
30 ml each sunflower and olive oil
1 onion, chopped
2 large leeks, sliced
2 cloves garlic, crushed
1 red pepper, seeded and diced
5 ml dried origanum
2 ml dried thyme
500 g brinjals, cubed and dégorged
50 ml each water and white wine
3–4 carrots, julienned
2 sticks table celery, sliced
350 g baby marrows (about 8), pared and thinly sliced
100 ml chopped parsley
sea salt and milled black pepper to taste
2–3 tomatoes, chopped
25 ml French dressing
a pinch of sugar
feta or Cheddar cheese and a few black olives for garnish

Cook noodles in plenty of salted water, drain well, toss with a dash of oil and place in a large bowl.

Heat the sunflower and olive oils in a large pan, add the onion, leeks, garlic, red pepper and herbs. Sauté for a few minutes, while you sniff the marvellous aroma released by the herbs. Add the brinjals, water and wine, then cover the pan and simmer for about 10 minutes, until the brinjals are cooked.

Mix in carrots, celery, baby marrows, parsley and seasoning, then cover and simmer for 5–6 minutes until vegetables are just wilted. Do not overcook. Pour the vegetable mixture over the noodles, carefully fork in the tomatoes and dressing, and add a pinch of sugar to bring out the flavour. Cover the salad loosely and stand for about 2 hours to mellow flavour, or refrigerate overnight.

Spoon onto large salad platter. Top with plenty of crumbled feta or grated Cheddar cheese and stud with a few olives.
Serves 8–10.

CREAMY PASTA, CHEESE AND PINEAPPLE SALAD

An interesting combination of ingredients goes into this delicious salad. The list may be long, but the ingredients are all easily obtainable and the salad itself is a breeze to put together. Although it may be chilled overnight, it should be served at room temperature. Surround with red lettuce leaves for colour and garnish with sliced avocado pear. If serving as a light meal on its own, add a hot crusty loaf and pats of herb butter.

500 ml elbow macaroni (250 g)
25 ml each sunflower and sesame oil
2 red or yellow peppers (or one of each) seeded and diced
2 sticks table celery, plus a few leaves, sliced
250 g white button mushrooms, halved or left whole
sea salt and milled black pepper to taste
1 x 425 g can pineapple rings in natural juice, drained and diced (reserve juice)
6 spring onions, chopped
750 ml shredded cabbage
2 large carrots, coarsely grated
200 g cheese (preferably low-fat Edam), cut into small cubes
± 200 ml coarsely chopped walnuts or 125 ml toasted sunflower seeds
50 ml mayonnaise

DRESSING
100 ml sunflower oil
100 ml drained pineapple juice
50 ml soy sauce
a big pinch of sugar

Cook pasta in lots of salted water with a dash of oil. Drain very well.

Heat sunflower and sesame oils and stir-fry peppers and celery until tender-crisp. Add mushrooms and toss over medium heat until softening but still chunky — do not overcook. Remove from heat, season and tip into a large bowl with the drained pasta. Add the pineapple, onions, cabbage and carrots.

Mix ingredients for dressing and pour over salad. Toss well, and then mix in cubed cheese and walnuts or sunflower seeds. Cover the salad and cool for at least an hour, or chill overnight (but return to room temperature before serving).

Just before serving, fold in mayonnaise and serve as suggested
Serves 8.

PASTA AND BUTTER BEAN SALAD

Plain and spinach fusilli noodles, creamy butter beans, a stir-fry of bright vegetables — this is such a pretty salad, and so easy to make. The cheese and sunflower seeds add nutrition, and with the addition of a hot herbed loaf it makes a super summer meal. Keep it simple, or add fresh salad leaves, baby tomatoes, small spears of corn and/or segments of avocado for a colourful garnish.

375 ml each plain and spinach fusilli noodles, loosely measured*
50 ml sunflower oil
30 ml olive oil
1 bunch spring onions, chopped
1 leek, sliced
2 cloves garlic, crushed
1 green or red pepper, seeded and diced
4 medium carrots, julienned
2 ml each dried origanum and basil
500 ml shredded spinach
125–250 g button mushrooms, wiped and halved
25 ml sweet sherry
1 x 410 g can choice grade butter beans, drained
5 ml sea salt and milled black pepper to taste
250 ml finely grated low-fat cheese (such as low-fat Edam)
125 ml toasted sunflower seeds (optional)

Boil fusilli noodles in plenty of salted water with a dash of oil.

Meanwhile, heat both oils in a large pan. Add onions, leek, garlic, diced pepper, carrots and herbs and stir-fry over medium heat. When softening, add spinach, mushrooms and sherry and toss together until spinach wilts and sherry has evaporated.

Drain pasta and tip into a large bowl. Add beans and fork in vegetable mixture. Season and set aside to cool. Fork in cheese and sunflower seeds, if using, when cold.

Serve this salad at room temperature.
Serves 6.

* Or use only one kind if preferred, but the salad won't be as cheerful.

Bulgur, Chickpea and Spinach Salad (p. 25) and Two-Bean Fruit and Nut Salad in Lemon Mayonnaise (p. 21).

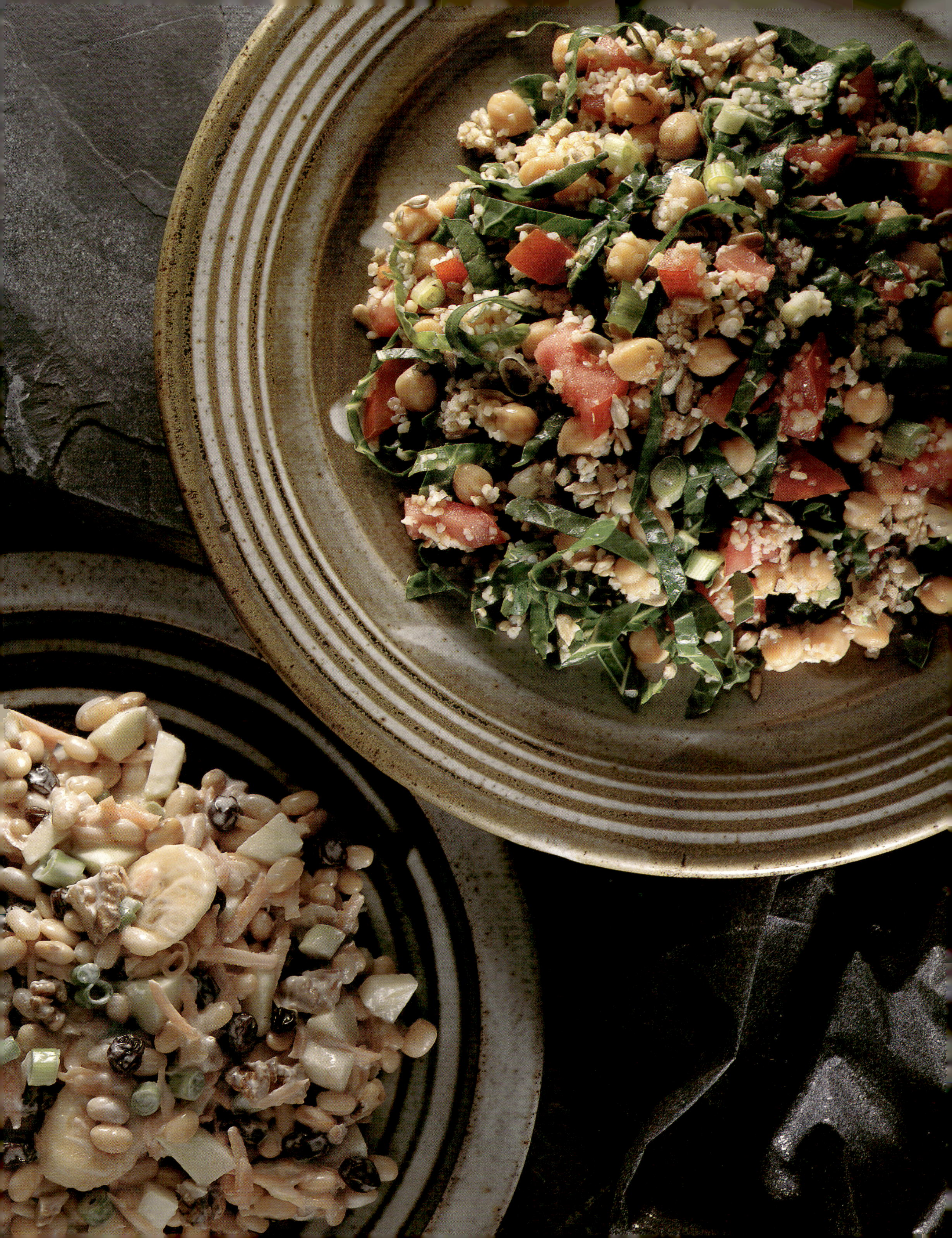

MOULDED CREAM CHEESE AND VEGETABLE SALAD

A super crunchy luncheon salad in which steamed vegetables are folded into a creamy mixture, chilled until set and then turned out. Surround with bright salad leaves and serve with a rice and mushroom salad, which makes the perfect companion. This is a flexible recipe (see notes below).

500 g mixed fresh vegetables of your choice*
5 ml each sea salt and dried tarragon
250 g cream cheese or smooth cottage cheese
125 ml cultured sour cream
125 ml mayonnaise
10 ml Dijon mustard
250 ml sprouts (about 60 g)**
50 ml finely chopped parsley
20 ml gelatine
2 egg whites, whisked
milled black pepper

Steam the prepared mixed vegetables in the minimum amount of salted water until just cooked. Towards end of cooking period, add the sea salt and crushed tarragon. Set aside to cool.

Stir together the cream cheese or smooth cottage cheese, sour cream, mayonnaise and mustard until smooth. Mix in the vegetables (drained if necessary), sprouts and chopped parsley.

Sprinkle gelatine onto 60 ml cold water in a small container and dissolve over low heat, then slowly dribble into the cheese mixture while stirring. Fold in the egg whites and pepper, and pour into a rinsed mould (capacity at least 1½ litres), then refrigerate until set.

Unmould and garnish as suggested. This recipe may be made a day in advance and the salad kept in the fridge.
Serves 8.

* I use a mixture of chopped broccoli, pared and sliced baby marrows, green peas, a small, diced carrot for colour and a large leek, thinly shredded. Use your own selection, if preferred, but do include a leek or a bunch of chopped spring onions.

** Use your favourite sprouts, or a mixture — maple peas and lentils are good. Instead of sprouts you could add a handful of chopped walnuts, for crunch. A couple of hard-boiled eggs, sliced, may also be folded into the mixture before chilling.

COTTAGE CHEESE, CUCUMBER AND PASTA MOULD

A creamy, moulded salad. Turn out and surround with a mushroom and rice salad, segments of avocado, and cherry tomatoes to spark up the colour. Lovely for a summer lunch.

⅓ to ⅔ large English cucumber
200 ml elbow macaroni
250 g smooth cottage cheese*
100 ml thick mayonnaise
125 ml cultured sour cream*
5 ml Dijon mustard
15 ml gelatine
1 bunch young spring onions, chopped
2 hard-boiled eggs, coarsely chopped
50 ml finely chopped parsley
a little sea salt, milled black pepper
2 egg whites
a pinch of sugar
walnut halves to garnish

Pare cucumber and grate coarsely into a colander. Salt lightly, weight and leave to drain. Cook the macaroni in plenty of salted water. Drain.

Use a wooden spoon to cream together cottage cheese, mayonnaise, sour cream and mustard. Dissolve gelatine in 60 ml water over low heat and trickle slowly into cheese mixture, beating well. Add onions, hard-boiled eggs and parsley. Squeeze all moisture from cucumber between palms and add to the cheese and egg mixture, together with macaroni. Mix in seasoning. Whisk egg whites stiffly with pinch of sugar and fold in. Pour into rinsed mould, preferably a loaf-shaped china dish, at least 1,25 litres capacity. Refrigerate until set. Run a knife round edges to unmould onto a large serving platter, garnish with walnut halves, and serve as suggested.
Serves 6–8.

* For a richer mould, use cream cheese instead of cottage, or use 125 ml sweet cream, whipped, instead of the sour cream, but use one or the other alternative, not both.

CHILLED MUSHROOM AND CHEESE TART

A good choice to feature on a luncheon menu or as part of a cold buffet. It may also be made without the crust, set in a mould and then turned out. Garnish with slices of avocado and a dusting of milled black pepper.

CRUST
250 ml crushed savoury biscuits
100 ml melted butter

FILLING
25 ml sunflower oil
6 spring onions, chopped
250 g white button mushrooms, wiped and sliced
1 clove garlic, crushed
2 sprigs fresh rosemary
1 red pepper, seeded and diced
1 stalk table celery, sliced
250 g smooth cottage cheese
2 eggs, separated
20 ml gelatine
100 ml vegetable stock or water
5 ml sea salt
125 ml cream, whipped
few drops Worcestershire sauce

Mix biscuits and butter and press into base of deep, greased 20-cm pie dish. Chill.

Heat oil in large frying pan and add onions, mushrooms, garlic, rosemary, red pepper and celery. Toss over medium heat for about 3 minutes until starting to shrink and soften. Remove and set aside. So that juices are not extracted, do not season until just before adding to cheese mixture.

Beat cheese and yolks together until smooth. Sprinkle gelatine onto stock or water, dissolve over low heat, then slowly whisk into the cheese mixture. Remove rosemary from vegetables, add salt and mix into cheese mixture. Chill until just starting to thicken. Whisk egg whites with pinch of salt and fold in, with cream and Worcestershire sauce. Pour onto crust, or into mould, and chill until set. Garnish as suggested.
Serves 6–8.

To totally transform old-fashioned cabbage salad into something special, toss it with pesto-flavoured mayonnaise. Mix thick Bulgarian yoghurt until smooth, and stir in pesto (p. 28) to taste.

Fold into shredded cabbage, together with grated carrots and any other salad ingredient of your choice; sprouts are a good addition, as well as sunflower seeds or shredded spinach.

QUICK HOME-MADE MAYONNAISE

Made in a blender, this is a thick, rich mayonnaise, whipped up in minutes. Flavour, if you like, with fresh herbs, chilli sauce, green peppercorns, or whatever will complement the rest of the meal. For a lighter mayonnaise, fold in buttermilk or Bulgarian yoghurt.

2 whole eggs and 2 yolks
5 ml sea salt
5 ml mustard powder
60 ml fresh lemon juice
500 ml sunflower oil
5 ml light brown sugar
1–2 cloves garlic, chopped

Put eggs and egg yolk, salt, mustard, lemon juice, 50 ml of the oil, the sugar and garlic into blender goblet and process until well mixed. With motor running, slowly drizzle in remaining oil through the hole in the lid. When all the oil has been added, you should have a smooth, thick mixture. Store in a glass jar in the fridge.
Makes about 600 ml.

RICE AND PECAN NUT SALAD

A basic recipe for one of the simplest rice salads, using the minimum of ingredients. It is very good as it stands, but may be varied in all sorts of ways: baby marrows instead of the carrots, sunflower seeds instead of the pecan nuts, while sliced sautéed mushrooms will, as always, give it a special lift. Serve as part of a cold buffet or with stuffed, baked brinjals topped with feta.

375 ml brown rice
100 ml herbed French dressing
100 ml finely chopped parsley
6 spring onions, chopped
1–2 sticks table celery, sliced
2 carrots, coarsely grated
200 ml chopped, toasted pecan nuts
15 ml soy sauce

Boil rice in 800 ml water with 2 ml salt. When cooked and all water has been absorbed, tip into a large bowl and fork in the dressing. Add remaining ingredients, tossing gently to mix, then cover and stand at room temperature for about 1 hour.
Serves 8.

TWO-BEAN FRUIT AND NUT SALAD IN LEMON MAYONNAISE

Chock-full of protein (from the beans and nuts) and vitamins (from the fruit), this salad will appeal to those who are interested in new ways of serving health foods. The beans are covertly tucked into a combination of fresh ingredients, and the result is rather like a main-dish fruit salad. A good choice for a vegetarian summer lunch, served with scoops of chunky cottage cheese nestled in fresh lettuce leaves and a crunchy wholewheat loaf. Preparation is quick and easy, if you have your supply of cooked beans in the freezer.

500 ml cooked soya beans
500 ml cooked haricot beans
2 Golden Delicious apples, peeled, diced and sprinkled with lemon juice
3–4 rings fresh pineapple, diced or
2 firm bananas, thinly sliced and sprinkled with lemon juice
200–250 ml coarsely chopped walnuts
2 large carrots, coarsely grated
6 spring onions, chopped
125 ml seedless raisins, plumped in hot water and drained
2 ml sea salt

DRESSING
1 x 175 ml tub Bulgarian yoghurt
200 ml thick mayonnaise
10 ml thin honey
5 ml finely grated lemon rind

Mix all the salad ingredients together in a large bowl. Stir the ingredients for the dressing together until smooth. Fold the prepared dressing into the salad until well combined, and then cover and chill for 2–3 hours or overnight for flavour to develop. Toss the salad again just before serving.
Serve as suggested.
Serves 6–8.

HERBS AND SPICES

These are extensively used in vegetarian cooking, which otherwise runs the risk of being rather bland. When bought in packets, they should be transferred to glass jars and kept tightly closed, as the flavours diminish quite quickly, and certain varieties, like sage and cumin, become musty.

SPICY INDIAN-STYLE SALAD

A bright and flavourful mix of rice, lentils and vegetables which will team up well with any bean or chickpea salad. Looks great on a cold buffet or may be served as a complete meal, topped with strips of cold omelette and accompanied with a bowl of mint-flavoured yoghurt. Toasted almonds are an optional but excellent addition.

125 ml brown rice
125 ml brown lentils, picked over and rinsed
10 ml sea salt
3 star anise
2 ml turmeric
6 white cardamom pods
2 bay leaves
2 ml ground cinnamon
80 ml sunflower oil
10 ml fresh lemon juice
2 medium onions, sliced into thin rings
2 cloves garlic, crushed
1 red pepper, seeded and diced
10 ml each masala for vegetables and ground coriander
4 carrots, julienned
250 g broccoli sprigs
250 ml green peas, fresh or frozen

Put rice, lentils, 550 ml water, 5 ml of the salt, anise, turmeric, cardamom, bay leaves and cinnamon in a saucepan, stir to mix, bring to the boil, then cover and simmer on very low heat for 50 minutes to 1 hour. While rice is cooking, prepare vegetables.

Remove spices from the rice and then tip rice into a large bowl. Mix 30 ml of the sunflower oil with the lemon juice and fork through the rice mixture.

Heat the remaining 50 ml oil in a large frying pan and soften onions, garlic and red pepper. Add masala and coriander and sizzle for 1–2 minutes. Add vegetables, toss to coat with spices, then add the remaining 5 ml salt and a splash of water. Cook, half-covered, until vegetables are just tender, then add to rice mixture, tossing with two forks to combine. Cover, and set aside to cool or chill overnight.

Garnish as suggested.
Serves 4–6.

Overleaf: Pasta and Butter Bean Salad (p. 18), Chickpea Salad with Cabbage and Walnuts (p. 12) and Aïgroissade with Aïoli-Yoghurt Dressing (p. 8).

SALADS AND EGG DISHES

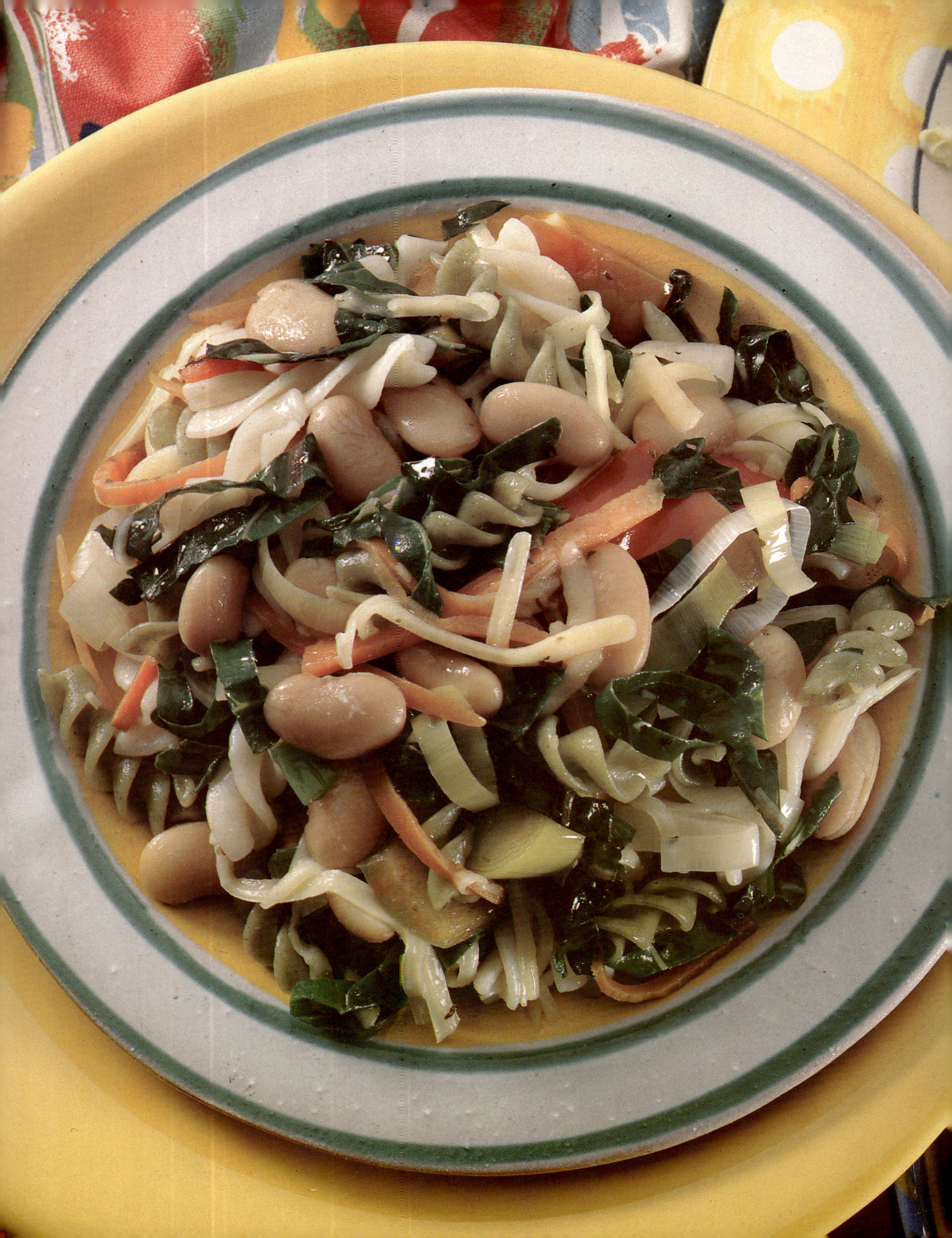

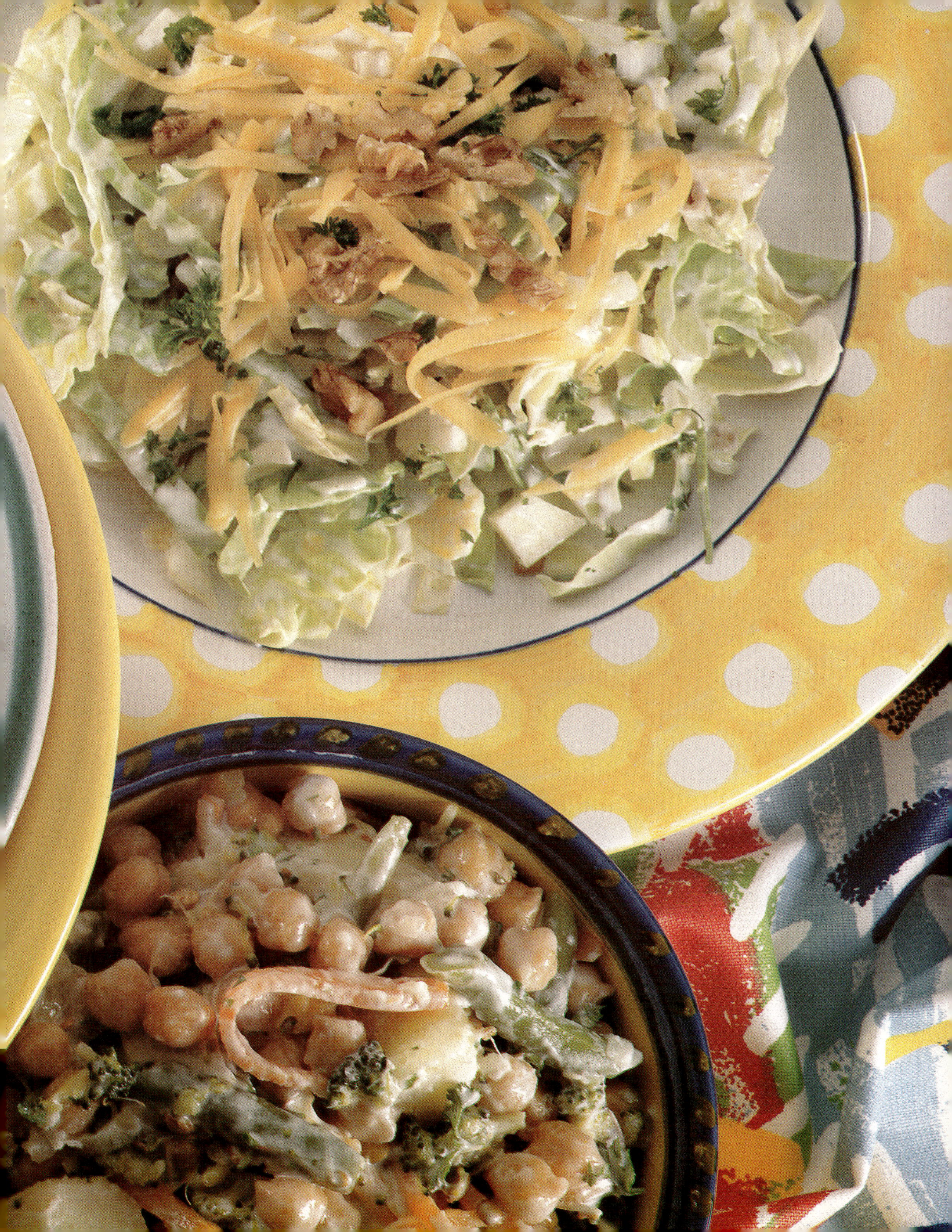

CORONATION EGG SALAD

Based on the popular recipe for Coronation Chicken, this dish features hard-boiled eggs smothered in a creamy, spicy sauce. It is a perfect choice for an elegant, light luncheon, served with a rice salad and bowls of chutney, coconut, sliced bananas, and chopped tomato with spring onions.

12 eggs (hard-boiled and sliced
in half lengthwise)
15 ml sunflower oil
1 large onion, finely chopped
5 ml each curry powder, ground
coriander, cumin and fennel
2 ml turmeric
10 ml tomato paste
100 ml each red wine and water
1 bay leaf
15 ml smooth apricot jam
200 ml thick mayonnaise
200 ml buttermilk
paprika and toasted almonds (optional)
for garnish

While eggs are boiling, heat oil in a small saucepan, add onion and cook gently until just softening — do not brown. Add all the spices and toss to mix, then add just a dash of water to prevent scorching and cook over very low heat for a minute or two. Add tomato paste, wine, water, bay leaf and jam. Stir to mix, then simmer, uncovered, for about 10 minutes until reduced and thickened. Strain mixture and discard onions. You should have just over 100 ml of richly coloured sauce. Allow to cool, then slowly stir into mayonnaise. When combined, slowly stir in buttermilk.

Arrange eggs, rounded sides up, on a large serving platter. Blanket with sauce, dust eggs with paprika and scatter with almonds, if using. Chill for at least 1 hour.
Serves 6.

CORIANDER

Fresh, chopped coriander (dhania) may be used for sprinkling on curries and breyanis, but as it has a distinctive, rather pungent flavour, it is often used simply as a garnish, like its cousin, parsley. It is obtainable from Indian markets and other outlets which sell fresh herbs.

TOMATOES

Even when cooked for a long time, as in sauces and casseroles, the flavour of fresh tomatoes is always the best. However, cans are convenient, but choice grade should always be used. Brands differ with regard to the number and size of tomatoes, and the amount of juice, so be prepared to adjust how much you use so that sauces do not end up too thick or too watery.

To skin fresh tomatoes, pour boiling water over, stand a few minutes, then run under cold water. Nick out stem ends, and then slip off the skins.

PIPERADE

A Spanish dish of eggs gently scrambled in a mixture of cooked onions, peppers and tomatoes. Although this is not a main-course dish, it does make a tasty light meal and a change from plain scrambled eggs. The Basques like to eat it with their light, white Shepherd's Bread, but it is also good atop wholewheat toast, or with croûtons; it may also be served cold, in hollowed out rolls, or as a stuffing for Pita Bread (page 93).

15 ml each sunflower and olive oil
1 small red pepper, seeded and diced
1 small green pepper, seeded and diced
4 small baby marrows, pared and diced
1 medium onion, finely chopped
2 medium tomatoes, skinned
and chopped
1–2 cloves garlic, crushed
sea salt and milled black pepper to taste
a pinch of sugar
8 eggs, lightly beaten
a little finely chopped parsley and/or
fresh basil for garnish

Heat sunflower and olive oils in a large pan and add red and green peppers, marrows and onion. Toss over low heat for about 5 minutes until softening and shrinking, then add tomatoes, garlic, seasoning and a pinch of sugar. Cover and simmer gently until the vegetables are cooked, stirring occasionally. If the tomatoes are very juicy, remove lid towards end of cooking period to drive off excess moisture. When vegetables are cooked, add eggs and stir over low heat until thick and creamy.

Turn onto warmed serving platter and sprinkle with parsley and/or basil.
Serves 4.

CURRIED EGGS

Eggs in a simple, tangy sauce; for best flavour, make in advance and leave to cool, then reheat. A little coconut and cream stirred in at the end are optional but delicious additions, and the coconut should also thicken the sauce to just the right consistency. Serve on brown rice, with condiments of your choice.

8–10 hard-boiled eggs
75 ml sunflower oil
2 onions, finely chopped
2 green or red peppers, seeded and diced
2 Golden Delicious apples, peeled
and finely diced
25–30 ml curry powder
5 ml turmeric
125 ml brown flour
1,2 litres hot vegetable stock or water
(4 × 250 ml plus 200 ml)
30 ml tomato paste
sea salt to taste
2 bay leaves
100 ml chutney
30 ml fresh lemon juice
5 ml dried mint
a big pinch of sugar
60–100 ml desiccated coconut (optional)
50 ml thick cream (optional)

While the eggs are boiling, make the sauce. Heat the sunflower oil in a large pan and lightly fry the onions, peppers and apples. Add the curry powder and turmeric and stir for 1 minute. Stir in the flour, then slowly add the stock or water, stirring until thickened. Add the tomato paste, sea salt, bay leaves, chutney, lemon juice, mint and sugar. Bring to the boil, then turn heat to very low and simmer the sauce, covered, for about 25 minutes, stirring occasionally. If working ahead, cool, transfer to a fridge container and chill until needed.

To serve, remove bay leaves and reheat (if necessary), adding the hard-boiled eggs, and coconut and cream if using.

Serve as suggested
Serves 5–6.

BULGUR

This is a fibre-rich, pre-cooked, cracked wheat which needs no further cooking if the fine-grated variety is used. For salads, simply soak it for 30–45 minutes, squeeze it dry in your hands, and it is ready for use.

SHERRIED SESAME SEED DRESSING

A rich, slightly smoky dressing made in a blender, and such a welcome change from regular salad dressings. It adds a new dimension to many salad combinations, particularly items such as steamed green beans, blanched button mushrooms, spring onions and sprouts. The dressing should be stored in a glass jar in the fridge.

250 ml sunflower oil
60 ml toasted sesame seeds*
60 ml fresh lemon juice
2 cloves garlic
10 ml thin honey
15 ml soy sauce
50 ml cooking sherry

Blend ingredients together in blender goblet or simply shake up in a glass jar. Decant and store as suggested. Shake before pouring over salads. Be judicious as only a little will be necessary. Then wait for the compliments.

* Spread dehusked sesame seeds on large biscuit tray and bake in moderate oven until lightly toasted, or use a non-stick frying pan on top of stove.

BULGUR, CHICKPEA AND SPINACH SALAD

A total departure from the regular bulgur, mint and parsley combination, this salad makes a splendid filling for Pita Bread (page 93), or serve it on a big salad platter, topped with feta and olives. Add a lettuce and sprout salad and include a hot crusty loaf and Garlic Butter (page 92), or Greek Garlic Bread (page 94).

250 ml bulgur
4 × 250 ml finely shredded, young spinach leaves, ribs removed
500 ml cooked chickpeas
1 bunch slim spring onions, chopped
a little sea salt and milled black pepper to taste
25 ml finely chopped fresh marjoram leaves
a handful of rocket leaves (if available)
100–125 ml toasted sunflower seeds
2 tomatoes, chopped
crumbled feta cheese and olives to garnish

DRESSING
50 ml each sunflower and olive oil
40 ml fresh lemon juice
1–2 cloves garlic, crushed
1 ml each sea salt and paprika
10 ml Dijon mustard
10 ml honey

Soak the bulgur in lots of cold water for 45 minutes. Mix all the ingredients for the dressing, cover and leave to stand for flavour to develop.

Drain bulgur in colander and squeeze very well with hands to release all moisture. Spoon into large bowl and add spinach, chickpeas, onions, seasoning and herbs. Add dressing, toss to mix thoroughly, then cover and stand for 1–2 hours or chill overnight.

Just before serving, fork in sunflower seeds and tomato. Garnish as suggested.
Serves 6.

TAHINI AND YOGHURT DRESSING

Made from crushed sesame seeds, tahini is not unlike peanut butter, and if you like hummus, you'll enjoy the unusual flavour of this dressing. It is full of healthy ingredients, but bear in mind that tahini has a very pronounced flavour, and the dressing is as far removed from vinaigrette or mayonnaise as you can get. Spoon it over a chickpea or grain salad, or use it to moisten a filling in Pita Bread (p. 93).

100 ml tahini
25 ml fresh lemon juice
5 ml ground cumin
2 ml sea salt
100 ml water
250 ml natural yoghurt
25 ml finely chopped parsley
1 small clove garlic, crushed
1 small spring onion, chopped with a little of the green top

Beat together the tahini, lemon juice, cumin and sea salt with a fork. The mixture will thicken to a stiff paste. Gradually beat in the water, and when pale and creamy, stir in the rest of the ingredients. Cover and chill for a few hours for the flavour to develop.
Makes about 450 ml.

SESAME NOODLE SALAD WITH TAHINI

Unusual and delicious, this looks like a rice salad but it actually consists of tiny rice noodles, mixed with vegetables and a creamy tahini dressing. Top with strips of rolled, thinly sliced omelette, and serve with a bean or chickpea salad for a different and delicious cold meal.

25 ml sunflower oil
10 ml dark sesame oil
2 cloves garlic, crushed
6–8 spring onions, chopped
1 red or green pepper, seeded, diced and thinly shredded
1 stick table celery, sliced
250 g baby marrows, pared and julienned
1 knob root ginger, peeled and grated
250 g white mushrooms, wiped and thickly sliced
375 ml rice noodles
125 ml toasted almond strips or toasted cashew bits or a handful of toasted sesame seeds
3-egg omelette and sprouts for garnish (optional)

DRESSING
50–60 ml tahini
25 ml soy sauce
± 30 ml water

Heat sunflower and sesame oils and stir-fry garlic, onions, pepper, celery, baby marrows and ginger. Add mushrooms and toss over medium heat until just changing colour — they should still be firm. Do not season. Remove from heat, cover and stand while cooking noodles.

Boil the rice noodles in plenty of salted water until just *al dente* — do not overcook. Drain, rinse under cold water, and tip into a large bowl.

Using a fork, carefully mix vegetable mixture into noodles.

Using the back of a spoon, cream together tahini, soy sauce and just enough water to make a mayonnaise-like mixture. This takes a few minutes, as tahini is thick.

Using a fork, toss the tahini dressing with noodle mixture, adding nuts or seeds. Check seasoning and add a little salt if necessary. Do not be tempted to add more soy sauce as you don't want too dark a colour. Cover loosely and leave to stand for about 1 hour.

Serve at room temperature, and garnish as suggested.
Serves 6.

SALADS AND EGG DISHES

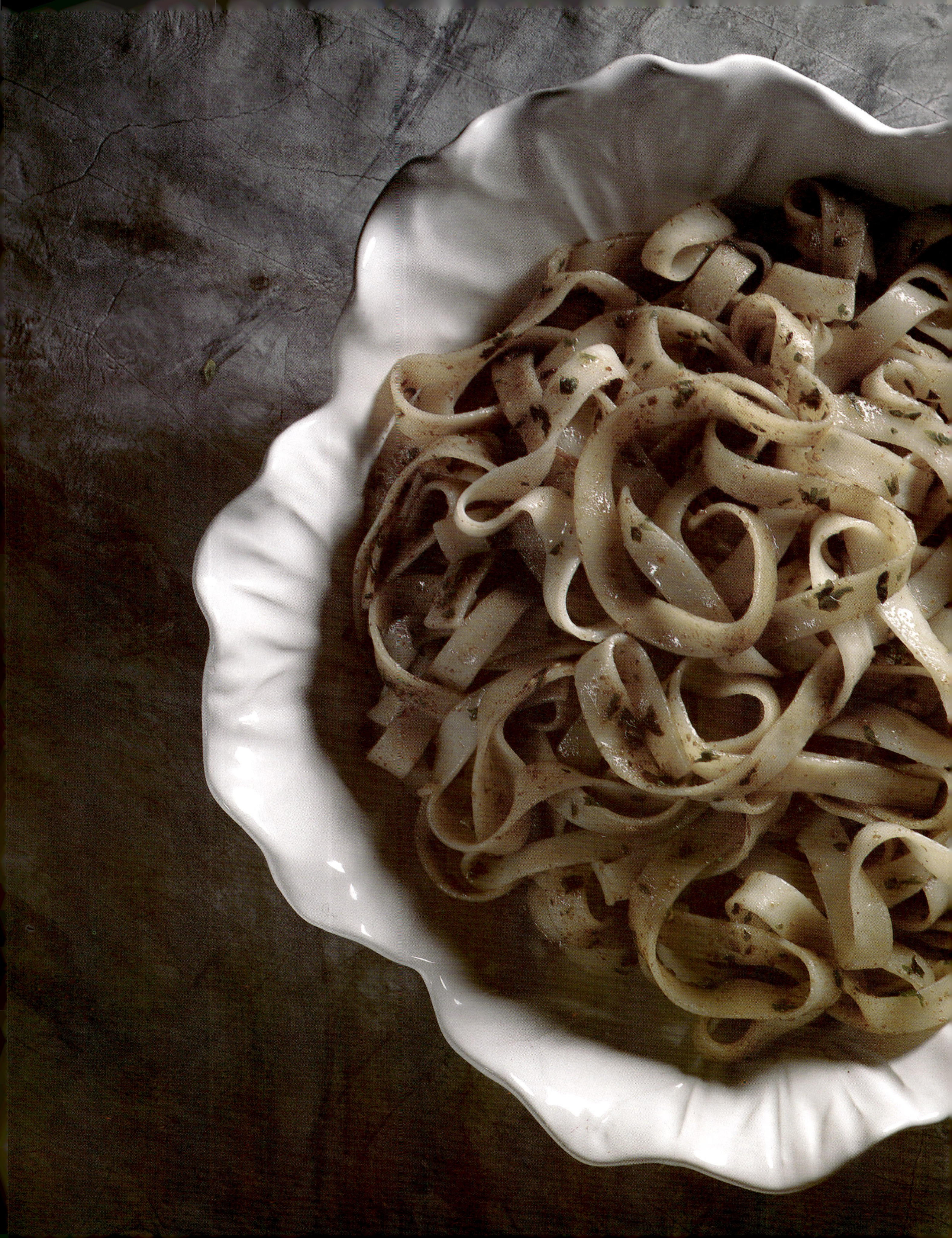

Pasta, Pizza & Quiches

PASTA WITH HERBS AND EGGS

No heavy sauces here: in this dish pasta is lightly coated with a delicately perfumed mixture of herbs and just-cooked eggs. A dish for the gourmet rather than the gourmand and a good standby when you have four people with finely attuned palates to please — in a hurry. It should be served with lots of freshly grated Parmesan and milled black pepper, a round of fluffy, crusty bread and a green salad. Home-made pasta is called for— my preference being mixed green and white fusilli noodles.

250 g pasta
60 ml olive oil
10 ml butter
1–2 cloves garlic, crushed
1 bunch slim spring onions, chopped
75 ml sunflower seeds
1 ml dried origanum
4–5 eggs, beaten
2 ml sea salt
60 ml chopped fresh basil leaves
60 ml chopped parsley

Cook pasta in plenty of salted water, toss with a dash of oil and set aside.

Heat oil and butter in a large frying pan, add garlic, onions, sunflower seeds and origanum and toss over low heat until seeds are golden brown. Mix in cooked, drained pasta, and when thoroughly heated, add lightly beaten eggs with salt and herbs. Stir over lowest heat until eggs are just cooked and serve immediately.
Makes 4 modest servings.

Tagliatelli with Pesto (p. 28).

PESTO

Although pesto is a traditional Genoese sauce which is used to top all types of pasta and gnocchi, there are many subtle variations in the recipe. Some cooks use lashings of oil and cheese and the minimum amount of basil, others load it with garlic and some even add butter. Fortunately it's a most adaptable mixture — ripe with flavour, bright in colour and very rich. (Some people like to dilute it, before serving, with water in which the pasta was cooked.) The first recipe contains the standard ingredients, except for pine nuts, which are by far the best to use but exorbitant in price; the second, which takes liberties with the nuts and the cheese, is my favourite — it is 'lighter', cheaper and tastes superb. However, both may be adjusted with regard to both ingredients and quantities, according to personal taste. Remember that pesto need not be limited to pasta. Try a teaspoonful stirred into minestrone, for instance, or serve with vegetables, tomato salad or baked potatoes instead of sour cream. However you use it, bear in mind that a little goes a long way. In the case of both sauces, remove from fridge about 30 minutes before serving, stir to mix, and make sure that the pasta and the plates are very hot, as pesto is not heated.

RECIPE 1

750 ml fresh basil leaves, washed and dried
250 ml parsley sprigs
2–3 cloves garlic
12 large walnut halves (± 50 g)
± 75 ml finely grated Parmesan cheese
± 175 ml good quality olive oil
a little sea salt and milled black pepper to taste

Place all ingredients, except oil and seasoning, in a processor fitted with the grinding blade and process until very finely chopped. With motor running, slowly dribble in the oil in a steady stream to make a thick, green purée. Add seasoning, then spoon into a jar. Run a thin film of olive oil over the top, cover and refrigerate. Pesto will keep for a couple of days and may also be frozen. Some cooks prefer to omit the Parmesan if pesto is to be frozen, adding it when the pesto is thawed and just prior to serving.

> Always rinse feta cheese before use to remove saltiness.

RECIPE 2

2 bunches of spinach
125 ml toasted sunflower seeds
3 cloves garlic
500 ml fresh basil leaves, washed and dried
250 ml finely grated Cheddar cheese
a little sea salt and milled black pepper to taste
± 125 ml each sunflower and olive oil

Trim and wash spinach — you should have 500 g leaves, weighed after treatment. Cook until soft (the water adhering to the leaves is sufficient moisture to cook it in). Drain well, pressing out moisture with a wooden spoon.

Using a processor fitted with the grinding blade, process the sunflower seeds, garlic and basil until finely chopped. Add the cooked spinach, cheese and seasoning. Process again, and then add the oils in a thin, steady stream. The final mixture should be thick and creamy. Spoon into a jar, run a thin film of olive oil over the top, close and store in fridge.

MEDITERRANEAN VEGETABLE SAUCE

Regard this as a basic recipe as other vegetables, like mushrooms or baby marrows, may be added or substituted. The following is a simple version which cooks into a delicious, thick stew. Ladle it over pasta of choice, or brown rice, and top each serving with a dollop of sour cream mixed with chopped chives, then sprinkle with grated Cheddar or Parmesan cheese or crumbled feta.

25 ml each sunflower and olive oil
4 large leeks, thinly sliced
3 cloves garlic, crushed
1 green pepper, seeded and diced
2 sticks table celery, sliced
2 medium brinjals, rinsed, dégorged and diced
400 g tomatoes, skinned and chopped
25 ml tomato paste
5 ml dried basil
100 ml chopped parsley
sea salt and milled black pepper to taste
5 ml sugar
125 ml vegetable stock or water
sliced black olives (optional)

Heat oils in a very large, heavy frying pan. Add leeks and garlic. Reduce heat to low and simmer, covered, until soft.

Add the green pepper, celery, brinjals, tomatoes, tomato paste, basil, parsley, seasoning, sugar and stock. Cover the pan and simmer for about 45 minutes, stirring occasionally and adding a little more more liquid as required for the sauce. (Bear in mind that the sauce should be thick enough to coat the pasta.)

Adjust seasoning and, if desired, add a few sliced black olives just before serving. Serve as suggested.
Serves 4.

PARSLEY PESTO

This is certainly not a regular pesto, but I have used the title for want of a better label. Strictly for pesto lovers who miss this delicious pasta sauce when fresh basil is out of season; also for those who are willing to try a version toned down with the somewhat astonishing addition of cottage cheese. Nevertheless, it is still a highly flavoured mixture best served atop very hot pasta (as the pesto is not heated). Try it once, and you could become hooked. Serve it with a tossed green salad which includes plenty of tomato.

500 ml parsley sprigs, firmly packed for measuring
1 large clove garlic
5 ml dried basil
250 ml coarsely broken walnuts
125 ml each olive and sunflower oil
100 ml grated Parmesan cheese
2 ml sea salt and milled black pepper to taste
500 g chunky cottage cheese (2 tubs)
500 g pasta, preferably wholewheat spaghetti

Put parsley sprigs, clove of garlic, basil and walnuts into processor fitted with grinding blade and chop. With motor running, add olive and sunflower oils in a slow stream. When thoroughly combined, switch off motor and add Parmesan cheese and seasoning. Process briefly to mix the mixture and then scrape the mixture into a bowl. Mix in the chunky cottage cheese, then cover and refrigerate for at least a few hours, or preferably overnight, to mellow the flavour, but return to room temperature and give it a good stir before serving.

Spoon dollops of the sauce onto each serving of freshly cooked, hot pasta on warmed plates. Additional Parmesan cheese is not necessary, but pass the pepper mill at the table.
Makes about 10 servings.

TWO-SAUCE PASTA

This dish takes a bit of care. The pasta should be home-made and preferably a mixture of green and white fusilli noodles. The tomato sauce requires fresh, not canned tomatoes. And the creamy spinach and mushroom sauce must be cooked at the last moment. However, if you can claim about 30 minutes of solitude in your kitchen, and have six pasta-loving friends with gourmet tastes to feed, try it. It's different, delicate and delicious. Serve with plenty of Parmesan cheese and ground pepper. Add a tossed salad with origanum-flavoured dressing.

TOMATO SAUCE
30 ml sunflower oil
1 large onion, finely chopped
2 cloves garlic, crushed
500 g ripe and juicy tomatoes,
skinned and chopped
25 ml tomato paste
50 ml each white wine and water
5 ml each sea salt and light brown sugar
2 ml mixed dried herbs
1 bay leaf
100 ml chopped parsley

SPINACH AND MUSHROOM SAUCE
1 x 250 g packet frozen spinach, thawed
and very well drained
125 ml thick, sweet cream
125 ml buttermilk
2 ml sea salt
25 ml sweet sherry
a pinch of grated nutmeg
250 g white mushrooms, wiped
and coarsely chopped

350 g fusilli noodles

For tomato sauce, heat oil and sauté onion and garlic. Add rest of ingredients, bring to boil, then cover and simmer very gently for about 25 minutes, stirring occasionally to mash tomatoes. When done, sauce should be slightly thickened, but still juicy.

To make the spinach and mushroom sauce, put all ingredients into a medium saucepan first rinsed out with water to prevent mixture from catching on the bottom. Bring to the boil, stirring, then simmer slowly, uncovered. Stir now and then, and cook for about 10 minutes until thickened.

Meanwhile, boil noodles until *al dente* in plenty of salted water with a dash of oil. Drain, then tip into saucepan with tomato sauce. Toss until thoroughly mixed, then pile into large, warmed serving dish. Pour spinach and mushroom sauce over the top or serve separately. Serve at once.
Serves 6.

NOODLE, CHEESE AND VEGETABLE CASSEROLE

This dish is especially good with a green salad tossed with nuts.

2 x 250 g packets frozen spinach, thawed
250 g medium ribbon noodles
25 ml sunflower oil
250 g brown mushrooms,
wiped and sliced
1 onion, chopped
5 ml chopped fresh rosemary needles
25 ml soy sauce
250 g smooth cottage cheese
4 large spring onions, chopped
2 eggs
250 ml buttermilk
sea salt and milled black pepper to taste
2 tomatoes, thinly sliced
2 cloves garlic, crushed
dried origanum for sprinkling
mozzarella cheese for topping
50 ml grated Parmesan cheese

Drain spinach in a colander, pressing out all moisture with a wooden spoon. Boil noodles, drain and toss with a dash of oil.

Heat the 25 ml oil and sauté mushrooms, onion and rosemary. When browned, remove from stove and add soy sauce.

In a large bowl, mix the spinach, cottage cheese and spring onions (add some of the green tops). Beat eggs with buttermilk, salt and pepper and add to spinach mixture. Stir in the mushroom mixture and noodles.

Spoon into greased, 28 cm x 23 cm baking dish. Cover top of casserole with tomatoes and sprinkle with garlic and origanum. Finally, top with a thick layer of thinly sliced mozzarella and, sprinkle with the Parmesan cheese.

Bake at 160 °C for 45 minutes, then switch off the oven and leave for about 10 minutes to settle before serving. This dish does not reheat successfully.
Serves 6.

ROSEMARY

This is the 'herb of remembrance'. Make a habit of adding a sprig or two of fresh rosemary when frying mushrooms. It imparts a lovely flavour. Remove the sprigs once mushrooms have browned.

ITALIAN TOMATO SAUCE WITH FRESH HERBS

Based on the classic pizzaiola sauce, this is a colourful and aromatic sauce which every cook should have at her/his fingertips. Ignore those recipes which suggest that you add six leaves of basil and a few sprigs of marjoram or a pinch of dried herbs; the tomatoes will simply obliterate their flavour. Herbs should be added with bold generosity, tomatoes should be fresh, not canned, and the sauce simmered very gently to develop the flavours while it thickens. A departure from tradition is the addition of butter beans (I do this for hungry vegetarians) which marry perfectly with the other ingredients. Serve this basic but tasty sauce with home-made pasta, a green salad and grated Parmesan, Romano or Pecorino cheese for a simple, inexpensive meal.

50 ml olive oil
2 large onions, chopped
2–4 cloves garlic, crushed
1 green pepper, seeded and diced
500 g ripe, juicy tomatoes,
skinned and chopped
25 ml tomato paste
2 bay leaves
125 ml chopped fresh basil leaves
15 ml fresh, chopped origanum leaves
15 ml fresh thyme leaves — simply strip
them off the stalks
5 ml light brown sugar
2 ml sea salt and milled black
pepper to taste
1 ml paprika
100 ml chopped parsley
50 ml white wine
1 x 410 g can choice grade butter
beans, drained
a couple of black olives, slivered

Heat oil and lightly sauté onions, garlic and green pepper. Add remaining ingredients, except beans and olives, bring to the boil, then cover and simmer on low heat for about 30 minutes. Stir occasionally to mash tomatoes. (This sauce is usually cooked uncovered, but this makes it rather too thick if using beans.) Stir in beans and olives, and a dash of water if necessary, and heat through. Serve as suggested.
Serves 4.

Overleaf: Pasta Primavera (p. 33), Creamy Mushroom, Walnut and Pepper Pasta (p. 36) and Italian Tomato Sauce with Fresh Herbs (above).

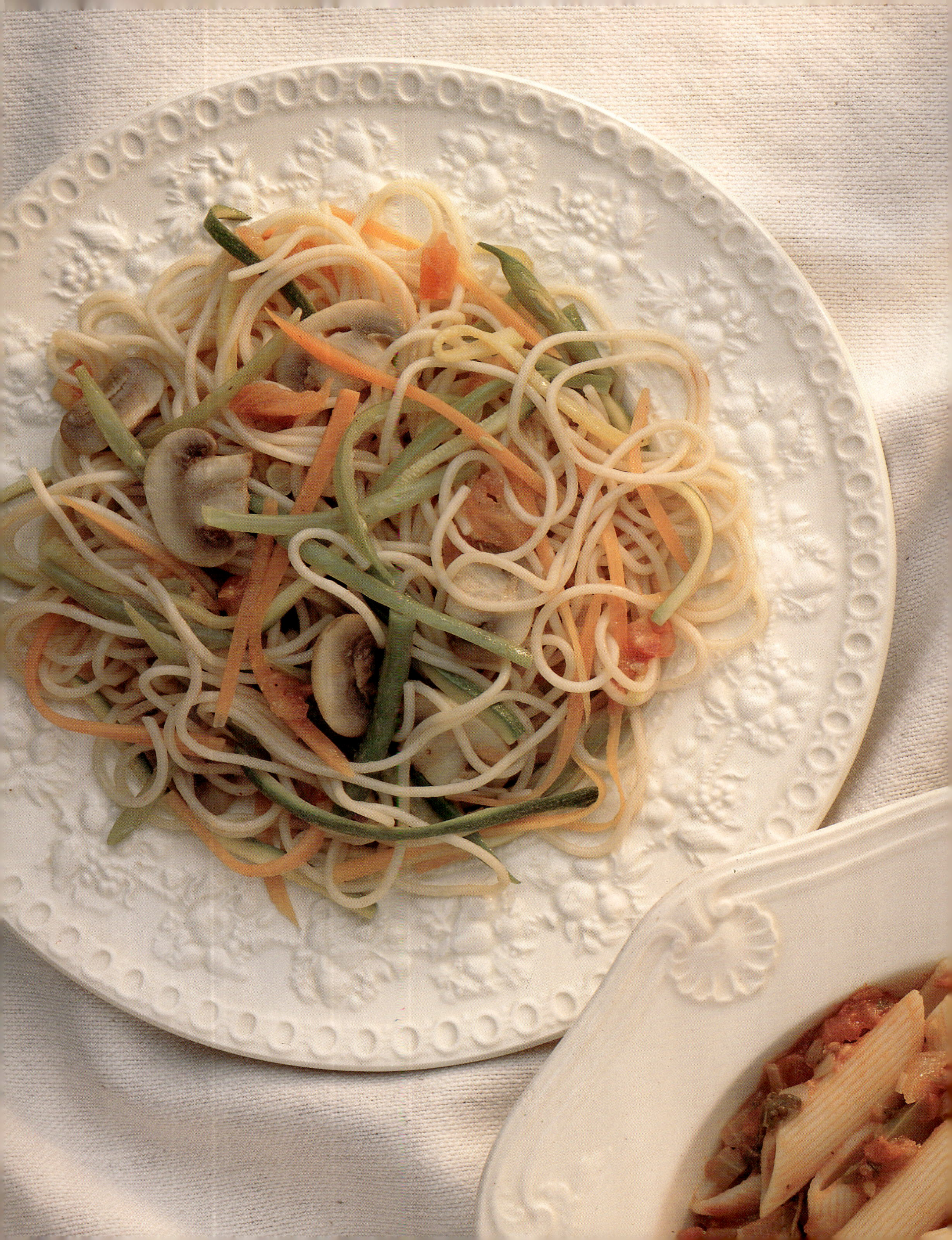

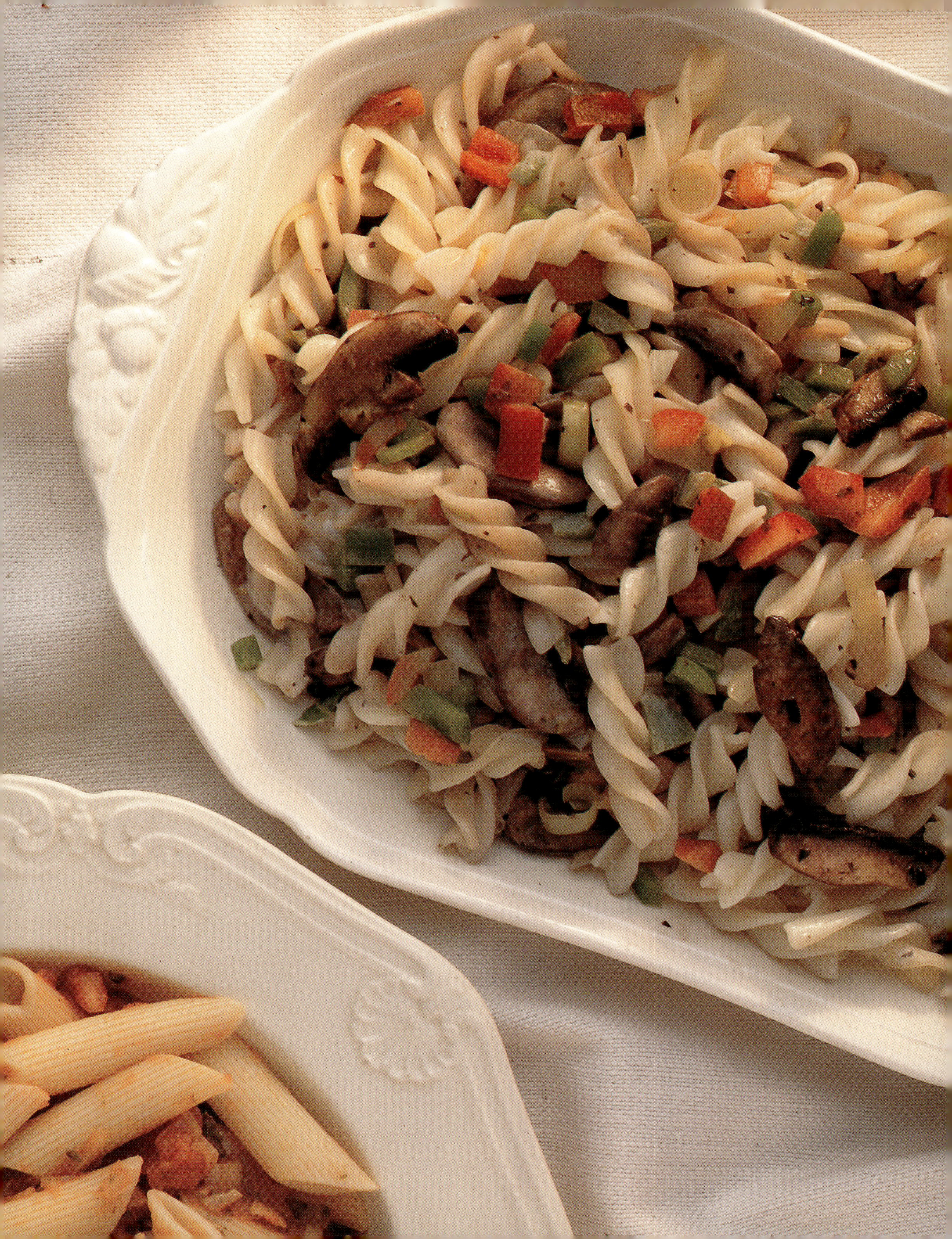

PASTA, VEGETABLE AND LENTIL BAKE

In this hearty, Italian-type dish, ribbon noodles are layered with vegetables and lentils and topped with a cheese sauce. As is usually the case with layered pasta dishes, there are three steps in the preparation, so it does take a little time. However, it may be completely assembled in advance and baked when wanted, and makes a most economical and filling meal if served with a hot garlic loaf and green salad.

**250 ml brown lentils, picked
over and rinsed
30 ml sunflower oil
2 onions, chopped
2 cloves garlic, crushed
1 green pepper, seeded and diced
1 x 400 g can tomatoes, chopped
250 g baby marrows, pared and sliced
500 ml shredded spinach leaves or
6 large leaves Swiss chard
5 ml sea salt and milled black
pepper to taste
10 ml light brown sugar
5 ml dried origanum
2 ml dried basil
50 ml each white wine and water
250 g medium ribbon noodles
grated Parmesan cheese**

SAUCE
**50 ml sunflower oil or butter or
25 ml of each
60 ml brown flour
5 ml mustard powder
500 ml milk, preferably heated
2 ml sea salt
250 ml finely grated Cheddar cheese**

Cook lentils in 500 ml salted water until soft and liquid is absorbed.

Meanwhile, heat oil and sauté onions, garlic and green pepper. Add tomatoes plus the juice, baby marrows, spinach, seasoning, sugar, herbs, wine and water. Bring to the boil, then cover and simmer on lowest heat, stirring occasionally, for 25–30 minutes. Stir in cooked lentils. There should be quite a bit of excess liquid to the mixture; this is necessary as the finished dish is baked uncovered, and the juices will then be absorbed.

For sauce, heat oil/butter, stir in flour and mustard, and, when bubbling, add milk slowly, stirring until thickened. Use a balloon whisk. As brown flour takes longer to cook than white flour, allow sauce to simmer gently for a few minutes. Remove from heat and stir in salt and cheese.

Boil noodles in plenty of salted water and drain well.

To assemble, oil a 30 cm x 20 cm baking dish and cover the base with half the vegetable/lentil mixture. Spread half the noodles over the mixture. Repeat layers. Pour cheese sauce evenly over the top and dust with Parmesan. (Set aside at this stage if working ahead.)

Bake the dish, uncovered, at 180 °C for 30 minutes, then switch off oven and leave for a further 15 minutes.
Makes 6 large servings.

SPINACH, ONION AND ROSEMARY CREAM SAUCE

This is a versatile, rather surprising sauce, distantly related to an aromatic, very thick soup. It is quick and easy to prepare, and makes a nice change from sour cream on baked potatoes. Top the potatoes with a knob of butter first and serve chunky cottage cheese on the side.

It also makes an unusual topping for pasta, finished off with a sprinkling of Parmesan cheese.

**25 ml each sunflower oil
and butter
2 medium onions, chopped
2 leeks, sliced
2 cloves garlic, crushed
2 fairly large sprigs rosemary
1 x 500 g packet frozen spinach,
thawed
5 ml sea salt
100 ml chopped parsley
±125 ml thick cultured
sour cream or
sweet cream**

Heat the sunflower oil and butter in a heavy-based saucepan. Add the onions, leeks, garlic and rosemary and sweat over low heat for about 10 minutes until softened. Add the thawed spinach, sea salt and chopped parsley, and cook, stirring, for about 5 minutes. Put aside to cool slightly before tipping the sauce into a blender. Blend until smooth, then return to the saucepan. Add enough of the cream to make a medium-thick sauce, and heat through gently, stirring.

Serve at once, as suggested.
Makes about 4 large servings.

VEGETABLE SAUCE

A chunky, robust sauce, with lots of vegetables and a touch of red wine and herbs. Serve on pasta of choice — spinach noodles are ideal — and top with plenty of feta cheese. This sauce should be made in advance, cooled and then reheated before serving.

**25 ml each sunflower and olive oil
3 leeks, sliced
1 onion, chopped
2 cloves garlic, crushed
2 large stalks table celery, sliced
2 ml each dried basil, thyme
and origanum
500 g brinjals, cubed and dégorged
500 g baby marrows, pared and sliced
125 ml tomato purée
125 ml red wine
500 ml vegetable stock or water
100 ml chopped parsley
5 ml sea salt and milled black
pepper to taste
5 ml light brown sugar
2 bay leaves
a few leaves of spinach,
shredded (optional)
250 g whole button mushrooms**

**500 g spinach noodles, cooked
and drained
feta cheese, rinsed and crumbled
for topping**

Heat sunflower and olive oils in a very large pan. Add leeks, onion, garlic, celery and herbs. Stir to mix, then cover and sweat over low heat for a few minutes, being careful not to scorch the vegetables and herbs. Add brinjals and marrows, toss until hot, and then add remaining ingredients, except the mushrooms, noodles and feta. Stir to mix, then cover and simmer on lowest heat for about 30 minutes, stirring occasionally — the vegetables will slowly soften and release their juices. Add the mushrooms and simmer the sauce for a further 10 minutes. Transfer to a suitable container and cool.

When reheating, you will probably have to bind the mixture and add a little more liquid — use about 15 ml brown flour (you can even use toasted wheatgerm for extra oomph) and enough stock or water to make a good sauce. Bring to the boil, stirring, until sauce thickens.

Remove bay leaves and check seasoning before serving. Ladle the sauce over the spinach noodles, and top with crumbled feta cheese.
Serves 6–8

> ### SOUFFLÉS
>
> I have not included any recipes for soufflés. I think they are always a bit of a let-down if served as a main course as they are not filling enough to constitute a hearty meal. They are also high in dairy products (butter, milk, eggs, often cheese as well). Of course, quiches are too, but they are far more substantial and can often be made in advance, with a wholewheat crust adding something extra.

PASTA WITH MUSHROOM SAUCE

I find this one a real life-saver. All you need are a few basic ingredients and 20 minutes in hand and you can produce a delicious meal for four to six people. Protein is added by tossing the spaghetti with some chopped nuts and topping each serving with Parmesan, Cheddar or, for a super change, feta cheese.

**300 g spaghetti, fettucini, tagliatelle or noodles
25 ml each butter and sunflower or olive oil
4 leeks, thinly sliced
2 sticks table celery, chopped
1 green pepper, seeded and diced
500 g brown mushrooms, wiped and sliced
1 sprig fresh rosemary, chopped
2 cloves garlic, crushed
40 ml brown flour
375 ml hot vegetable or Marmite stock
40 ml soy sauce
50 ml sweet sherry
50 ml sour cream**

Cook pasta or noodles in plenty of salted boiling water.

Meanwhile, heat butter and oil in a large saucepan and add leeks, celery and green pepper. When beginning to soften, add mushrooms, rosemary and garlic. Toss over medium heat until smelling really good, then sprinkle in the flour and stir to mix. Slowly add stock, soy sauce and sherry. Stir well and then allow to thicken slowly, half covered.

Just before serving, swirl in the sour cream, then spoon the sauce onto hot, drained pasta or noodles.
Serves 4–6.

PASTA PRIMAVERA

Primavera, in Italian, means spring and this is the name given to dishes combining spring vegetables and pasta. Both the pasta and choice of vegetables can be varied, so you could have Tortellini Primavera, or, as in this case, Vermicelli Primavera, with vegetables of your choice, as long as they are fresh and young. This version is a personal favourite. I make it in summer, rather than in spring, because I like to include lots of fresh basil — it adds a really special fragrance. This dish is fashionably light, quite delicious and please don't be put off by the number of vegetables to clean and steam because you can do without a salad with this meal. Just add a chunk of garlic bread, plenty of grated Parmesan or Pecorino cheese and ground pepper.

**500 ml sliced, young green beans
4–6 young carrots, julienned
250 g baby marrows, pared and julienned
30 ml olive oil
1 bunch spring onions (about 6), chopped
2–3 cloves garlic, crushed
250 g brown or white mushrooms, wiped and sliced
2 large ripe tomatoes (about 250 g), skinned and chopped
10 ml sea salt and a pinch of sugar
2 ml dried origanum
50 ml semi-sweet white wine
350 g vermicelli (just less than ¾ of a packet)
25 ml butter
125 ml chopped fresh basil leaves**

Steam the beans, carrots and marrows until just tender, starting with the beans and adding the carrots and marrows after a few minutes. Do not season. They may also be poached in a wide saucepan with just a dash of water.

In another pan, heat the olive oil and sauté the onions, garlic and mushrooms. Add the tomatoes, the steamed vegetables, salt, sugar, origanum and wine. Cover and simmer very gently for about 10 minutes.

Meanwhile, boil the vermicelli until it is *al dente*. Remember that it is thin and cooks very quickly. Drain and tip into a large baking dish. Add butter and basil and toss, using two forks, until well mixed and smelling fabulous — just like pesto. Cover and keep warm in a low oven.

When vegetable mixture is ready, pour it over the vermicelli (or pasta of choice), add an extra knob of butter, toss again with two forks, and serve at once.
Serves 6.

> ### PASTA
>
> Use heaps of fast-boiling, salted water and add the pasta slowly so as to keep the water on the boil. Adding a dash of oil to the water to prevent sticking is optional (the Italians say that this should not be necessary with quality pasta) but stirring off and on, with either a two-pronged fork or special tongs, is a good idea. Home-made pasta cooks very quickly and overcooking is regarded as a culinary disaster. It should be slightly resilient to the bite — the overworked phrase in use these days is *al dente*, or 'to the tooth'. Drain cooked pasta thoroughly and, to be on the safe side, add a dash of oil to keep strands separate.

QUICK TOMATO MACARONI CHEESE

Especially for busy people, this is an old favourite with a different flavour. It makes a simple, satisfying supper and the quantities can be doubled or trebled without adding to the preparation time.

**375 ml elbow macaroni
250 ml finely grated Cheddar cheese
1 x 410 g can Tomato-And-Onion Mix
50 ml finely chopped parsley
250 ml milk
1 egg
5 ml mustard powder
5 ml sea salt and a pinch of cayenne pepper**

TOPPING
**100 ml fine, fresh wholewheat breadcrumbs
60 ml finely grated Cheddar cheese
a few slivers of butter**

Cook macaroni in boiling salted water. Drain well and tip into a bowl. Mix in the Cheddar, Tomato-And-Onion Mix and chopped parsley.

Whisk together milk, egg, mustard and seasoning. Stir into macaroni mixture and turn into oiled baking dish — a deep, 20-cm pie dish is just right. Mix crumbs and cheese and sprinkle over, then dot with butter. Bake at 160 °C for about 30 minutes or until just set.
Makes 4 large servings.

SPINACH AND MUSHROOM SAUCE

This recipe is for spinach lovers. Fresh is better here, and cheaper, but frozen is fine and quicker. Whichever you use, be sure to drain it very well after cooking. Serve this flavoursome sauce over fettucini, ribbon noodles or spaghetti and top with grated Parmesan, strong Cheddar or crumbled feta cheese.

2–3 bunches of young, bright green
spinach or 500 g frozen spinach, thawed
25 ml sunflower oil
5 ml butter
1 large onion, chopped
2 cloves garlic, crushed
1 red pepper, seeded and diced
250 g brown mushrooms,
wiped and sliced
5 ml finely chopped fresh
rosemary needles
sea salt and milled black pepper to taste
200 ml vegetable or Marmite stock
125 ml thick cultured sour cream
5 ml Worcestershire sauce
10 ml cornflour or 25 ml toasted
wheatgerm

If using fresh spinach, wash and trim off stalks and thick ribs. You should have 500–600 g. Put, wet, into a very big saucepan and cook until soft. Drain and press out all moisture, using a colander. Chop finely. You should have 500–700 ml. If using frozen, thaw quickly by placing the unopened bags in a bowl of cold water. Weight with a saucepan. Drain well.

Heat the sunflower oil and butter in a large frying pan, add onion, garlic and red pepper and allow to soften. Add mushrooms and rosemary and stir until aromatic and lightly browned. Add spinach, seasoning and stock, and simmer until just cooked, stirring occasionally. To bind mixture, mix sour cream, Worcestershire sauce and cornflour or wheatgerm, and add to spinach mixture. Stir until hot and thickened. Serve at once, spooned over pasta.
Serves 4.

CHEDDAR CHEESE

Very well chilled Cheddar grates finely and easily in a processor fitted with the grinding blade. Do a batch and store it in the freezer for instant use.

QUICK VEGETABLE AND BEAN LASAGNE

No lasagne is really quick. This recipe does, however, offer a few shortcuts. You'll never find this dish in Italy and the ingredients will seem quite improbable, but the result is a very satisfying meal, especially designed for time-strapped cooks. The beans add protein and the dish can be assembled in advance. Toss a crisp green salad at the last moment.

50 ml olive oil
1 x 750 g packet frozen stir-fry
vegetables, just thawed*
5 ml sea salt
2 x 425 g cans choice grade baked beans
in tomato sauce
1 onion, finely chopped
2 ml dried origanum
225–250 g lasagne or 18 sheets
measuring 7,5 cm x 16 cm
375 ml finely grated strong
Cheddar cheese
grated Parmesan cheese and toasted
sesame seeds for topping

SAUCE
50 ml sunflower oil
10 ml butter
60 ml brown flour
500 ml milk
10 ml prepared mustard
2 ml sea salt

Heat olive oil. Stir-fry vegetables until just done. Remove from stove and add salt, beans, onion and origanum. Set aside.

For sauce, heat oil and butter in heavy-based saucepan. Sprinkle in flour and cook, stirring, until mixture forms a paste. Slowly add heated milk while stirring, or whisking. When smooth, simmer gently for a few minutes to thicken, then add mustard and salt. Whisk before using.

Cook lasagne in boiling, salted water, adding sheets one by one. When just tender, drain and rinse under cold water.

Lightly oil a baking dish. Arrange one third of lasagne on base. Cover with half the vegetable mixture and sprinkle with half the Cheddar cheese. Top with another third of lasagne, then the remaining vegetables and cheese. Top with final layer of lasagne and pour the sauce over. Sprinkle with Parmesan and sesame seeds and bake on middle shelf of oven at 160 °C for 45 minutes.
Serves 8.

*Use a mix including beans, baby marrows, mushrooms, red pepper and celery.

MACARONI, CHEESE AND SPINACH BAKE

A lovely casserole, with cooked spinach and raw baby marrows layered between pasta, cheese and white sauce. Serve with a crusty loaf, or Greek Garlic Bread (page 94), and a tomato and basil salad for a perfect mix of flavours and textures.

25 ml olive oil
1 large onion, chopped
2 cloves garlic, crushed
500 g frozen spinach, thawed
sea salt and freshly grated
nutmeg to taste
250 g baby marrows, pared
and coarsely grated
500 ml elbow macaroni (250 g)
375 ml finely grated low-fat cheese
(such as mozzarella)
plenty of grated Parmesan or Romano
cheese for the topping

SAUCE
40 ml sunflower oil
10 ml butter
60 ml brown flour
2 ml dried origanum
500 ml milk
2 ml sea salt

Heat olive oil, and sauté onion and garlic until soft but not browned. Add spinach and stir until just cooked. Remove pan from heat and add salt, nutmeg and marrows (the latter will absorb any excess liquid).

Make sauce by heating oil and butter (you can, of course, use more butter and less oil if you like). Sprinkle in flour and origanum, and when bubbling, add milk slowly. Bring to the boil, stirring, and then allow to simmer for a few minutes. It should be a fairly thin consistency. Season.

Cook macaroni in boiling salted water, and drain thoroughly.

Oil a medium-sized rectangular baking dish or a deep 24-cm pie dish. Cover base with half spinach mixture, then add half the cheese, half the macaroni and half the sauce. Repeat layers. (If you'd like a richer, custardy topping, beat an egg into the sauce for the top layer.) Sprinkle generously with Parmesan and bake on middle shelf of oven at 160 °C for 45 minutes. Switch off oven and leave for 15 minutes.
Makes 6 large servings.

Pasta and Brinjal Casserole (p. 36) and Italian Quiche (p. 41).

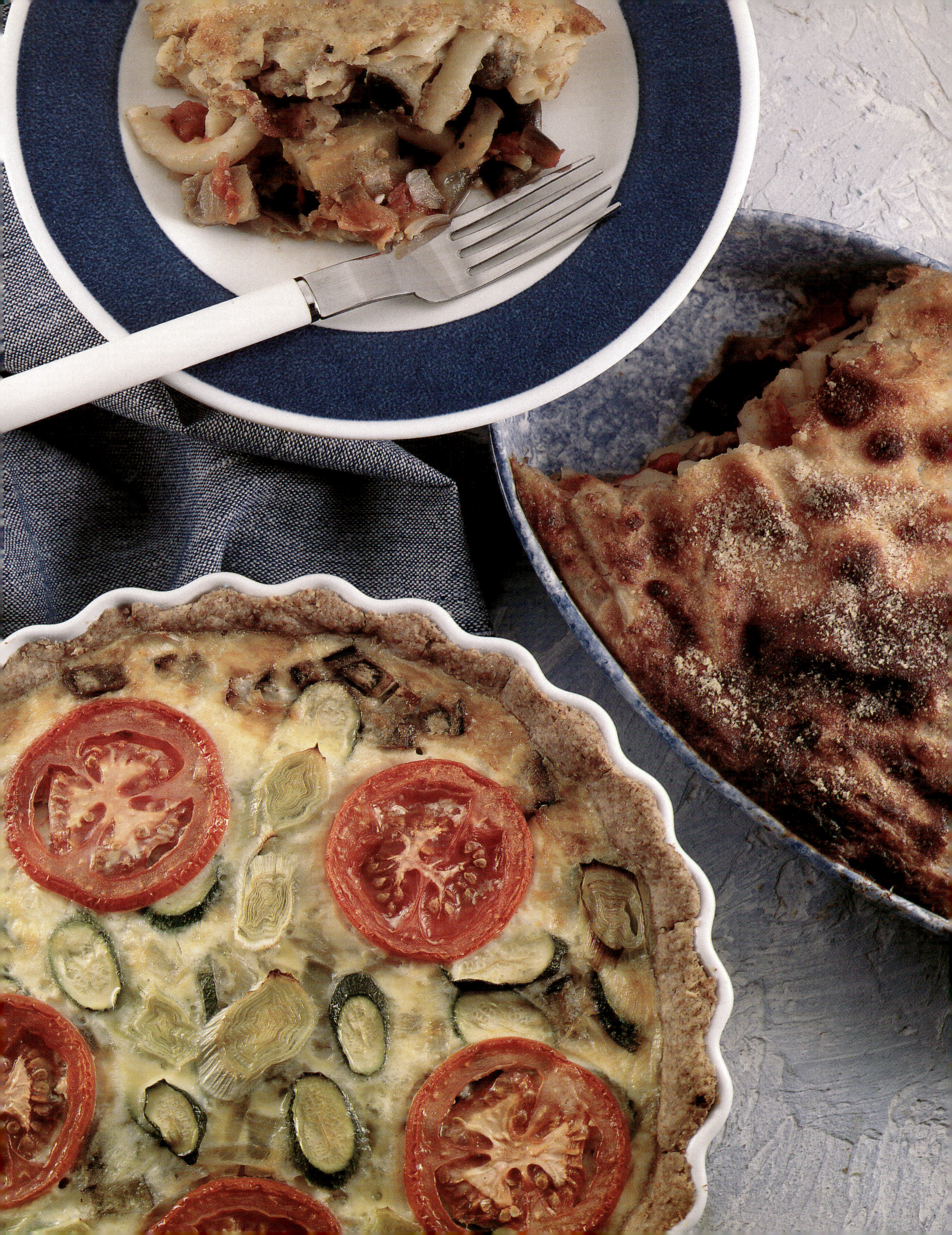

PASTA AND BRINJAL CASSEROLE

The flavour of Greece predominates in this substantial, economical dish. To cut down on preparation time, boil the pasta and make the sauce while the vegetables are simmering. Serve with a tossed lettuce and spinach salad and Greek Garlic Bread (page 94).

50 ml oil, preferably half olive
2 onions, chopped
3 cloves garlic, crushed
600 g brinjals, cubed and dégorged
7–10 ml dried origanum
500 g juicy tomatoes, skinned and chopped
125 ml white wine
2 bay leaves
5 ml sea salt and milled black pepper to taste
10 ml light brown sugar
500 ml elbow macaroni (250 g)

SAUCE
50 ml sunflower oil and a nut of butter
75 ml brown flour
750 ml milk
sea salt and milled black pepper to taste
1 ml each ground cinnamon and grated nutmeg
2 eggs, beaten
50 ml grated Parmesan cheese

Heat oil in a very large pan and lightly fry onions and garlic. Add brinjals and origanum and toss for 1–2 minutes, until hot and shiny. Add tomatoes, wine, bay leaves, seasoning and sugar. Cover and simmer on low heat for about 20 minutes, stirring occasionally to mash tomatoes. Add a dash of water if mixture seems dry. It should be thick and juicy, but not watery.

Meanwhile, cook pasta in salted water with a dash of oil. Drain well.

Make sauce by melting oil and butter, stirring in flour and slowly adding milk. Stir until smooth and then simmer for a few minutes until medium-thick. Add seasoning and spices. Spoon a little sauce onto beaten eggs, then add to sauce with half the cheese and whisk to mix.

Remove bay leaves from brinjals. Lightly oil a deep, 30 cm x 20 cm baking dish. Cover base with half brinjal mixture, top with half pasta, then repeat layers. Pour white sauce over, and then sprinkle with remaining Parmesan. Bake, uncovered, at 160 °C for 50 minutes, then switch off oven and leave for 15 minutes.
Makes 8 large servings.

WHITE SAUCE

In keeping with the unrefined ingredients used in this book, I have broken with tradition and, instead of using butter and cake flour for making white/béchamel sauces, I have substituted oil, or a mixture of butter and oil, and plain brown flour. This results in a sauce that is not white, but slightly speckled and somewhat thinner, and which needs extra simmering to cook the flour and obtain the right consistency. The flavour, although not delicate, is fine (especially if used in a cheesy casserole) and in view of the fact that meals without meat or fish often rely heavily on dairy products for protein, it makes sense to cut down on saturated fats when possible. Cordon bleu cooks may be dismayed by this method, but in the cuisine of certain countries, butter is never used in white sauces.

PASTA, MUSHROOM AND RICOTTA BAKE

Devised with an eye to short-term preparation, this casserole conveniently dispenses with the making of the sauces which usually accompany baked pasta dishes. All you need to add succulence to the basic mixture is a carton of sour cream, while a can of Tomato-And-Onion Mix does for the topping. When you're not in a hurry, however, use a fragrant, slow-simmered, home-made tomato sauce instead. Serve with a tossed green salad — either add croûtons to the salad or serve Italian breadsticks on the side.

25 ml sunflower oil and 5 ml butter
1 large onion, finely chopped
250 g brown mushrooms, wiped and finely chopped
2 sprigs fresh rosemary
400 g ricotta cheese
50 ml chopped parsley
25 ml soy sauce
250 ml cultured sour cream
5 ml sea salt
250 g medium ribbon noodles
1 x 410 g can Tomato-And-Onion Mix
5 ml dried basil
grated Parmesan cheese or any low-fat cheese

Heat oil and butter and add onion, mushrooms and rosemary. Keep heat low to allow mushrooms to soften without burning, as they will initially absorb a lot of oil. When tender and cooked, there should be no juices left in the pan. Tip into a large mixing bowl and mix in the ricotta, parsley, soy sauce, cream and salt.

Boil noodles in plenty of salted water with a dash of oil. Drain well and stir into mushroom mixture. Turn into oiled 20 cm x 30 cm baking dish, spreading evenly.

Mix Tomato-And-Onion Mix and basil, and spread over the top. Because ricotta is a fairly firm cheese, the topping will not sink in. Sprinkle plenty of Parmesan (or a low-fat cheese of choice) over the top and bake at 160 °C for 45 minutes.
Serves 6.

CREAMY MUSHROOM, WALNUT AND PEPPER PASTA

Unlike many pasta dishes made with vegetables and sauces, which have to be baked after assembling, this dish is quickly prepared on top of the stove. The addition of cream and walnuts makes it rich, but it's a lovely indulgence when you want a quick meal. Serve with a green salad and extra Parmesan.

250 g pasta (spinach or egg noodles, fettucini or wholewheat spaghetti)
30 ml olive oil
1 small onion, chopped
2 leeks, sliced
2 cloves garlic, crushed
1 large red pepper, seeded and diced
1 large green pepper, seeded and diced
2 ml each dried basil and origanum
250 g brown mushrooms, wiped and sliced
30 ml sweet sherry
250 ml cultured sour cream
25 ml grated Parmesan cheese
5 ml sea salt and milled black pepper to taste
100–125 ml chopped walnuts (optional)

Cook pasta in plenty of salted water with a dash of oil. Meanwhile, heat oil, add onion, leeks, garlic, peppers and herbs, turn heat to lowest, cover and allow to sweat until softened, shaking pan occasionally. Add mushrooms and sherry and toss, still over low heat, until mushrooms are just beginning to shrink. Stir in well-drained noodles, cream, cheese, seasoning and walnuts, if using. Heat through gently until pasta is coated with sauce. Do not overcook.
Serves 4–6.

TWO-SAUCE NOODLE CASSEROLE

This is a lovely dish with an Italian flavour and plenty of character. It is ideal for informal entertaining as it can be assembled in advance. Hot Pita Bread (page 93) with herb butter and a green salad tossed with sunflower seeds make particularly good accompaniments. As it is a dairy-rich dish, use low-fat milk for sauce.

250 g medium spinach noodles
a little grated Parmesan cheese

MUSHROOM SAUCE
50 ml sunflower oil (or half olive)
1 large onion, chopped
2 cloves garlic, crushed
1 green pepper, seeded and diced
250 g brown mushrooms,
wiped and sliced
2–3 ripe tomatoes (250 g), skinned
and chopped
25 ml tomato paste
10 ml vegetable salt or 5 ml sea salt, and
freshly milled black pepper to taste
5 ml brown sugar
2 bay leaves
2 ml dried Italian Herbs
(or herb of choice)
50 ml off-dry or semi-sweet white wine

CHEESE SAUCE
25 ml sunflower oil and a nut of butter
60 ml brown flour
5 ml mustard powder
500 ml low-fat milk
250 ml grated Cheddar cheese
sea salt and milled black pepper to taste

Boil noodles, drain and toss with a dash of oil. Leave in colander and set aside.

For mushroom sauce, heat oil and soften onion, garlic and green pepper. Add mushrooms and, when softening, add rest of the ingredients. Cover and simmer for 20 minutes, stirring occasionally. Remove bay leaves.

For cheese sauce, heat oil and butter, stir in flour and mustard, and when nut-brown, add milk slowly. Cook until thickened, then add cheese and seasoning.

Oil a 28 cm x 18 cm baking dish or a deep, 23-cm earthenware pie dish. Cover base with half the mushroom sauce and top with half the noodles. Repeat layers. Pour cheese sauce over top, sprinkle with Parmesan and bake, uncovered, on middle shelf of oven at 180 °C for 30 minutes. Switch off oven, and leave for 15 minutes.
Serves 6.

PASTA WITH VEGETABLES AND HERBS

This is a favourite, one-saucepan pasta dish in which fusilli or screw noodles, mushrooms and baby marrows are folded into a robustly flavoured butter and oil sauce. It is very easy and exceptionally quick to make: the herby sauce is mixed in advance in order to develop the flavour and the final cook-up takes but a few minutes, if using home-made pasta. Pass the cheese separately and a loaf of crusty white bread, and, if you like, a Greek salad with plenty of feta cheese, in which case, omit the Parmesan.

SAUCE
30 ml olive oil
25 ml butter
100 ml finely chopped parsley
2 cloves garlic, crushed
5 ml dried origanum*
2 ml dried basil*
1 ml dried thyme*

250 g fusilli or screw noodles
50 ml olive oil
50 ml white vermouth
(such as Cinzano Bianco)
250 g brown mushrooms,
wiped and sliced
250 g baby marrows, pared
and julienned
5 ml sea salt
plenty of freshly grated Parmesan or
Romano or Pecorino cheese

For the sauce, heat the olive oil and butter in a small saucepan over low heat. Add parsley, garlic and the herbs and stir for 1 minute, then remove from stove, cover and leave to steep for at least 1 hour.

Just before dinner, cook pasta, and at the same time do the vegetables by heating 50 ml olive oil with the vermouth in a very large saucepan (use one that is pretty enough to take to the table). Add vegetables and salt and toss over medium heat until just softened.

Using a two-pronged fork or spaghetti spoon, fork the well-drained pasta into the vegetable mixture, and then add the herbed sauce. Toss together gently until just heated through and smelling gorgeous, and then serve at once. Pass the cheese of your choice at the table for sprinkling.
Serves 4.

* Be sure to use absolutely level measures of the herbs or the flavour will be too pronounced. Less is better than more.

EASY PIZZA WITH WHOLEWHEAT CRUST

There are surely more varieties of pizza then there are roads in Rome — not only with regard to what you put on top, but also what you do to the base. Traditionally, it's a yeast dough which I, personally, find too chompy and often very dry. The following is a quick alternative.

CRUST
250 ml wholewheat flour
250 ml white flour
2 ml sea salt
5 ml baking powder
80 ml sunflower oil
100 ml skimmed milk
10 ml fresh lemon juice

TOPPING
100 ml tomato sauce
10 ml Worcestershire sauce
2 ml each dried origanum and thyme
2 tomatoes, sliced
1 onion, coarsely grated
2 cloves garlic, crushed
grated Cheddar and Parmesan cheese*
black olives and cooked
mushrooms (optional)
a little olive oil
2 ml garlic salt

To make the crust, mix flours, salt and baking powder. Add oil, milk and lemon juice. Quickly mix to a ball (use an electric beater if possible) and press evenly onto the base of a lightly oiled 20 cm x 33 cm swiss roll tin, or a pizza pan.

Mix tomato sauce, Worcestershire sauce and herbs and spread over dough, right to the edges. Cover with tomatoes, onion and garlic. Sprinkle thickly with Cheddar cheese and dust with Parmesan. Top pizza with olives and mushrooms, if desired. Drizzle with olive oil, sprinkle with garlic salt and bake at 200 °C for approximately 30 minutes, until bubbly and cooked. Cut into fingers and serve very hot.
Serves 6–8.

* Or use soft, white Italian mozzarella cheese for a perfect topping. It melts to form a golden-brown blanket. Use sliced rather than grated. Tusser's is another alternative.

Overleaf: Pasta, Vegetable and Lentil bake (p. 32), Pasta with Herbs and Eggs (p. 27) and Easy Pizza with Wholewheat Crust (above).

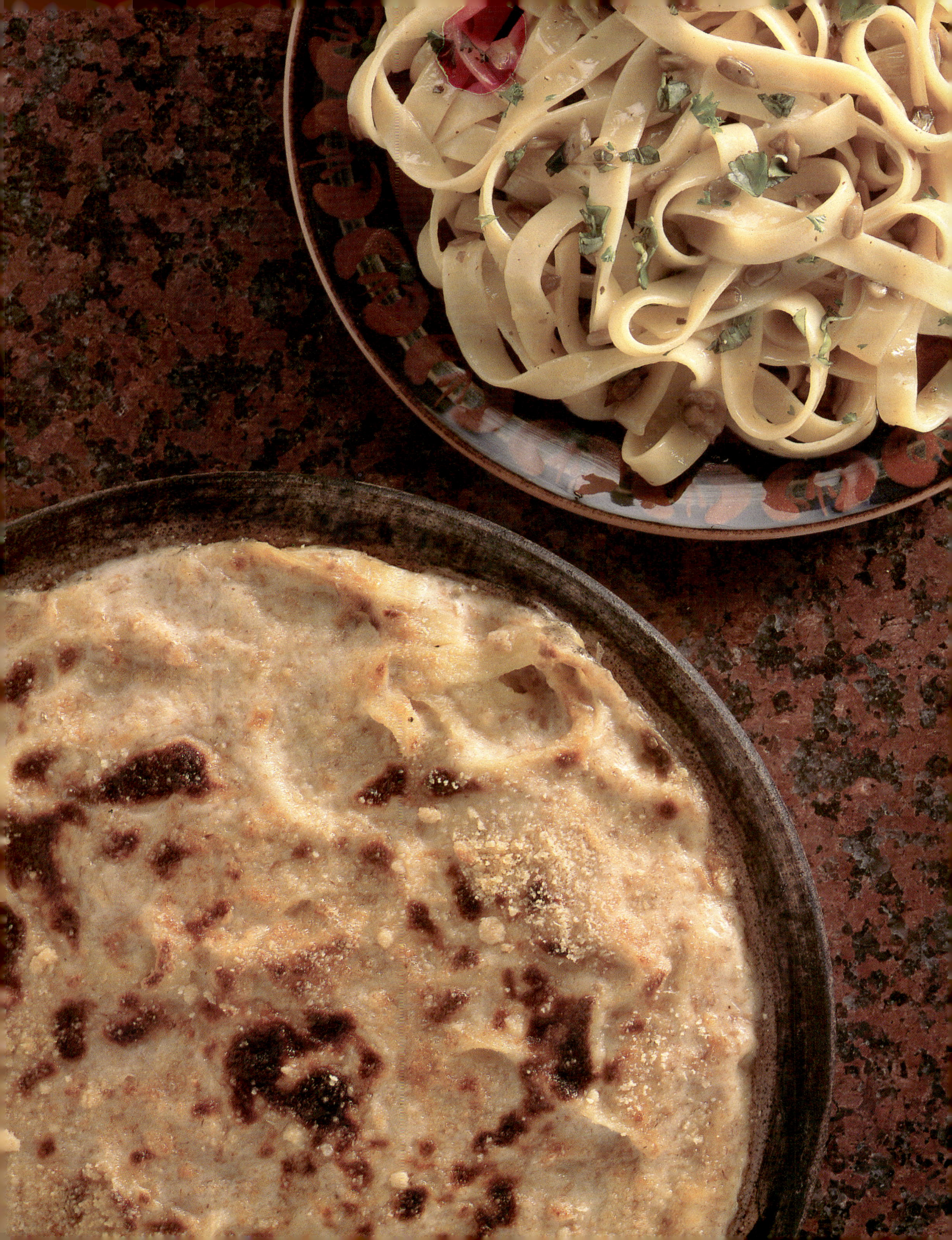

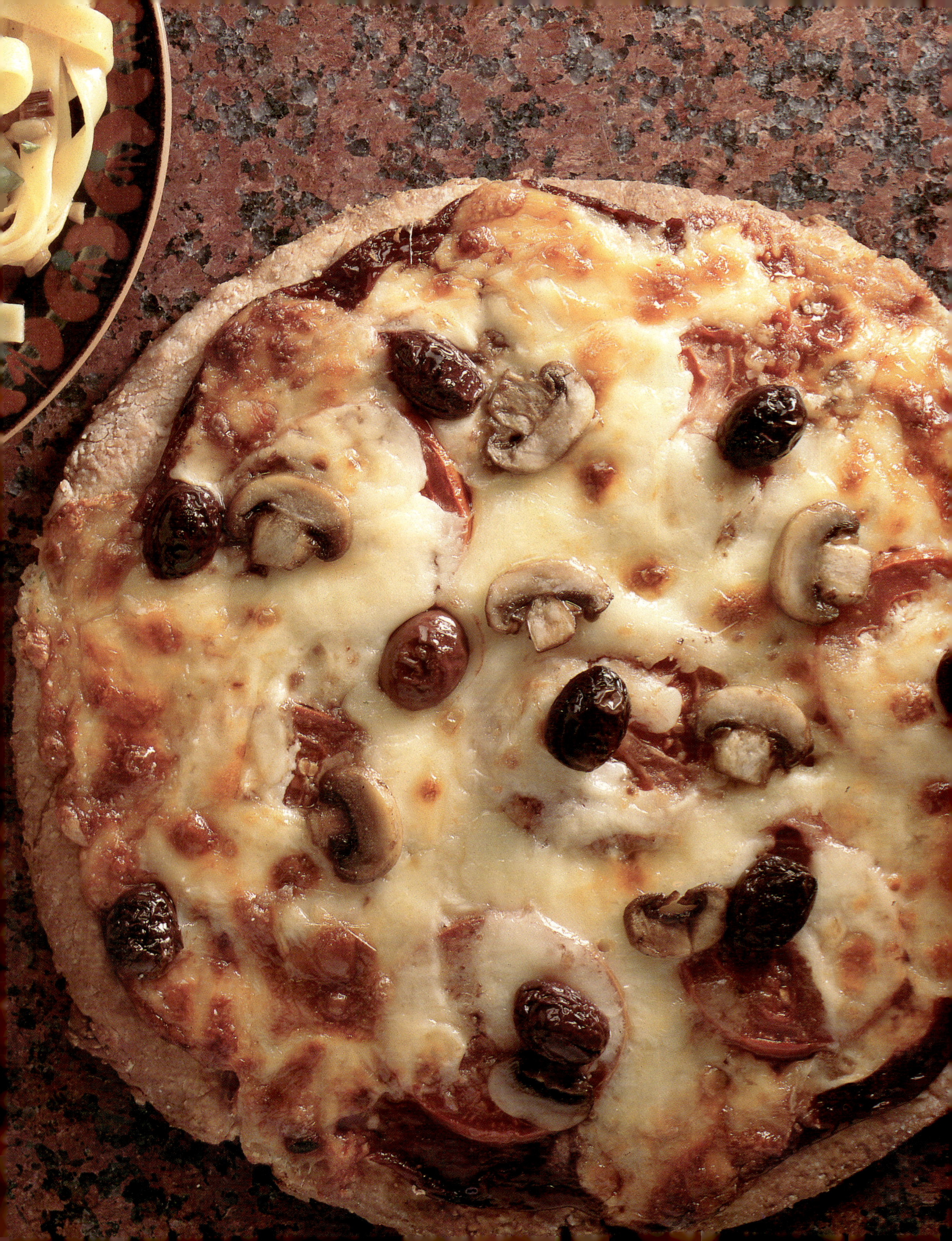

FAVOURITE MACARONI CHEESE

Quite possibly, the last time you ate macaroni cheese was at boarding school. And quite possibly this put you off it forever, which is a pity because it can be jolly tasty, especially if, when making it, you follow the one cardinal rule — never overcook the macaroni or it will never marry with the sauce and you'll end up with that dry, stick-like boarding school affair. The pasta must be al dente. A little mustard, cayenne pepper and grated onion add a super flavour to the first recipe, a touch of nutmeg to the second. The second recipe includes eggs, but is simpler and easier in that you don't have to make a sauce. Take your pick, but in neither case should you rinse the macaroni after draining as that prevents the sauce from coating it.

RECIPE 1

25 ml each sunflower oil and butter
60 ml white bread or cake flour
750 ml milk (low-fat or half-and-half)
5 ml sea salt
2 pickling-size onions, coarsely grated
10 ml prepared mustard
250 ml finely grated Cheddar cheese
a large pinch of cayenne pepper

TOPPING

125 ml fine, stale plain brown breadcrumbs
60 ml finely grated Cheddar cheese
25 ml grated Parmesan cheese
250 g elbow macaroni
a few slivers of butter

First, make a white sauce by melting the sunflower oil and the butter, stirring in the flour, and then slowly adding the milk. Stir until smooth. Simmer for a few minutes until thickened, then remove from the stove and stir in the sea salt, onions, prepared mustard, Cheddar cheese and a pinch of cayenne pepper.

Prepare topping by mixing breadcrumbs and both cheeses.

Cook pasta in boiling salted water and drain very well to avoid adding any water to the dish. Toss drained pasta with cheese sauce, and then spoon into a lightly oiled baking dish — a 20 cm x 30 cm rectangular dish or a deep, 23-cm pie dish. Sprinkle with the prepared topping and dot with slivers of butter.

Bake at 160 °C for about 30 minutes until just bubbling. Do not overbake.
Serves 6 with a salad.

RECIPE 2

250 g elbow macaroni
1 ml freshly grated nutmeg
2 eggs
500 ml milk (low-fat or half-and-half)
5 ml sea salt
250 ml finely grated Cheddar cheese

TOPPING

100 ml finely grated Cheddar cheese
paprika
slivers of butter

Cook the macaroni in boiling salted water until al dente, drain very well, and then place in a lightly oiled 23-cm pie dish. Sprinkle with the grated nutmeg.

Beat eggs with milk and salt and stir in cheese. Pour over macaroni, sprinkle with topping of Cheddar and paprika, and dot with butter. Bake at 160 °C for 30 minutes or until just set. Do not overbake.
Serves 6 with a salad.

PASTA RATATOUILLE WITH MARINATED FETA

These days there's a definite swing towards home-made pasta, cooked in just a few minutes and tossed with a non-cloying sauce. Bolognaise has certainly taken a tumble. In this recipe, a mélange of vegetables is simply stewed in its own juices. It is a particularly useful recipe for the hurried, beginner or weight-conscious cook. The latter could opt for a topping of Parmesan cheese instead of the feta. However, this recipe is a marvellous way of treating feta ('cured' in herbs and oil), which can be used in any dish or salad in which a topping of feta is required.

RATATOUILLE

1 medium onion, chopped
3–4 leeks, sliced
500 g baby marrows, pared and sliced
700 g brinjals, cubed and dégorged
500 g juicy tomatoes, skinned and chopped (not canned)
2 green or red peppers, or one of each, seeded and diced
3–4 cloves garlic, crushed
4 bay leaves
5 ml each dried origanum and thyme
10 ml each sea salt and light brown sugar
milled black pepper to taste
100 ml olive oil (preferably extra virgin)
black olives (optional)
400–500 g pasta of choice

Put all the ingredients, except the olives and the pasta, into a really big saucepan as the mixture is very bulky to start with, reducing only once it has cooked for a while. Toss all the ingredients until mixed, bring to the boil, and then cover and simmer over very low heat until the vegetables are tender — for 40–50 minutes. Stir occasionally, but be careful not to break up the vegetables. You should not need to add any liquid as the vegetables should draw their own juices. (Cool if time allows and reheat before serving.) Add the olives, if using them.

Cook pasta just before serving, and ladle sauce over each portion. Top with the marinated feta cheese.
Serves 6–8.

MARINATED FETA

To make this slightly more economical, the feta will not be completely covered with oil; so the jar should be turned upside down now and then to allow all the cheese to be submerged. It should be made about two days in advance and kept in the fridge.

400 g feta cheese, rinsed
4 whole cloves garlic
a few black olives
2 sprigs fresh rosemary
4 bay leaves
± 200 ml each olive and sunflower oil
5 ml dried origanum
1 ml dried thyme
50 ml fresh lemon juice

Pack the feta cheese into a wide-mouthed, 750-ml glass jar together with the garlic cloves, olives, sprigs of rosemary and bay leaves. Mix the olive and sunflower oils, dried herbs and lemon juice and pour over the cheese. Seal the glass jar and refrigerate until needed.

SALT

Use pure sea salt (not the table salt available from supermarkets), either fine or coarse. Grind coarse salt in a salt mill at the table — you will use far less. Apart from sodium chloride, sea salt also contains certain minerals and trace elements, so it's much healthier than ordinary table salt. It is available, reasonably priced, from health-food shops and in selected supermarkets.

ASPARAGUS AND SPRING ONION QUICHE

Serve as a light meal with a salad of lettuce, grated baby marrows and sprouts in a lemony dressing.

CRUST
375 ml white or brown flour
2 ml sea salt
2 ml baking powder
100 ml sunflower oil
a squeeze of fresh lemon juice
10 ml cornflour

FILLING
1 x 460 g can asparagus tips and cuts, well drained
6 spring onions, chopped
250 g smooth cottage cheese
2 ml dried tarragon
2 ml sea salt and milled black pepper to taste
3 eggs
125 ml milk
125 ml cream
25 ml chopped parsley
paprika and grated Gruyère cheese

To make crust, sift flour, salt and baking powder. Add oil, 50 ml iced water and lemon juice. Mix lightly with a fork, shape into a ball and roll out thinly between two sheets of grease-proof paper. Line a deep, 23-cm flan tin, prick well and bake at 200 °C for 15 minutes. Remove and dust base with cornflour. Cool. If asparagus cuts are thick, slice in half lengthwise. Arrange on base of crust, together with spring onions.

Beat cottage cheese with tarragon, salt and pepper. Beat in eggs, one at a time, followed by the milk, cream and parsley. Pour carefully onto crust, dust with paprika and sprinkle with Gruyère. Reduce oven temperature to 180 °C and heat a baking tray in it for a few minutes. Place flan tin on the hot tray and bake for 45 minutes or until set.
Serves 6–8.

SAUTÉ AND SWEAT

In the former, the vegetables are lightly browned, whereas in the latter they are cooked gently, covered with a lid, to allow them to soften in their own juices.

SPINACH AND BROWN MUSHROOM QUICHE

A substantial, large, cheesy and herby quiche which reheats well. Use a good shortcrust pastry if you like a light touch or try the bolder wholewheat version which, if preferred, may be used to line the base only — like a pizza — and then served cut into squares.

PASTRY
200 ml each cake and wholewheat flour
a pinch of sea salt
125 g butter
squeeze of fresh lemon juice
1 egg white (reserve the yolk)

FILLING
2 x 250 g packets frozen spinach, thawed
1 ml sea salt
2 ml dried dill
25 ml each sunflower oil and butter
250 g brown mushrooms, wiped and roughly chopped
2 leeks, sliced
1 small onion, chopped
1 sprig fresh rosemary
sea salt and milled black pepper to taste
250 ml milk
2 eggs plus reserved yolk
125 ml cultured sour cream
5 ml French mustard
100 g Gruyère or Cheddar cheese, grated
2 ml dried origanum

To make the pastry, mix flours and salt. Rub in butter until crumbly, then bind with 75 ml iced water and lemon juice. Form pastry into a ball, chill for about 30 minutes, then roll out and line a deep 28-cm quiche tin. Prick well and bake at 200 °C, just below centre of oven, for 20 minutes. Brush with the lightly beaten egg white, and return to oven for 5 minutes.

For the filling, drain spinach well, pressing out all moisture, then season with the sea salt and dried dill. Heat the oil and butter and sauté mushrooms, leeks, onion and rosemary. When half-soft, remove the rosemary and season the mixture lightly. Beat the milk with eggs and reserved egg yolk, sour cream, mustard and more seasoning, if needed.

Spread drained spinach over crust and spoon mushroom mixture over. Pour egg mixture over, sprinkle with cheese of your choice and the origanum, and then bake at 160 °C for 45 minutes or until set.
Serves 8.

ITALIAN QUICHE

Baked in a 29-cm pizza pan, this is a huge and hearty quiche with a wholewheat crust and a ratatouille-type filling. Serve with a salad.

PROCESSOR PASTRY
250 ml wholewheat flour
125 ml cake flour
2 ml sea salt
125 g butter, diced
10 ml fresh lemon juice
15 ml extra flour

FILLING
50 ml olive oil
2 leeks, chopped
1 small onion, chopped
1 green pepper, seeded and diced
2 cloves garlic, crushed
4 small baby marrows (250 g), pared and diced
2 small brinjals (250 g), diced
2 ml sea salt and milled black pepper to taste
50 ml chopped parsley
2 ml dried origanum
1 ml dried basil
125 g cream cheese
375 ml milk
3 eggs
1 ml sea salt
1 large tomato, thinly sliced
250 ml grated Cheddar cheese
25 ml grated Parmesan cheese

To make pastry, use grinding blade of processor to mix flours, salt and butter until finely blended. With motor running, add lemon juice and 35–50 ml cold water. Stop as soon as it forms a ball, turn out onto floured board and roll out, using floured rolling pin. Using fingers, press into pizza pan, flute edges, prick well and chill.

To make filling, heat oil in a large pan and sauté leeks, onion, green pepper and garlic. When translucent, add marrows and brinjals, then season with 2 ml salt and pepper. Cover and cook over low heat, stirring occasionally, until soft. Spoon into a bowl and add parsley and dried herbs. Cool.

Bake crust at 200 °C for 12 minutes. Distribute about 15 ml flour over base, using pastry brush. Spoon in filling.

For custard, beat cream cheese, milk, eggs and 1 ml salt.

Arrange tomato over vegetables, pour custard over, sprinkle with Cheddar and Parmesan cheese and bake at 180 °C for 30–35 minutes. Switch off oven and leave for 20 minutes to settle.
Serves 8.

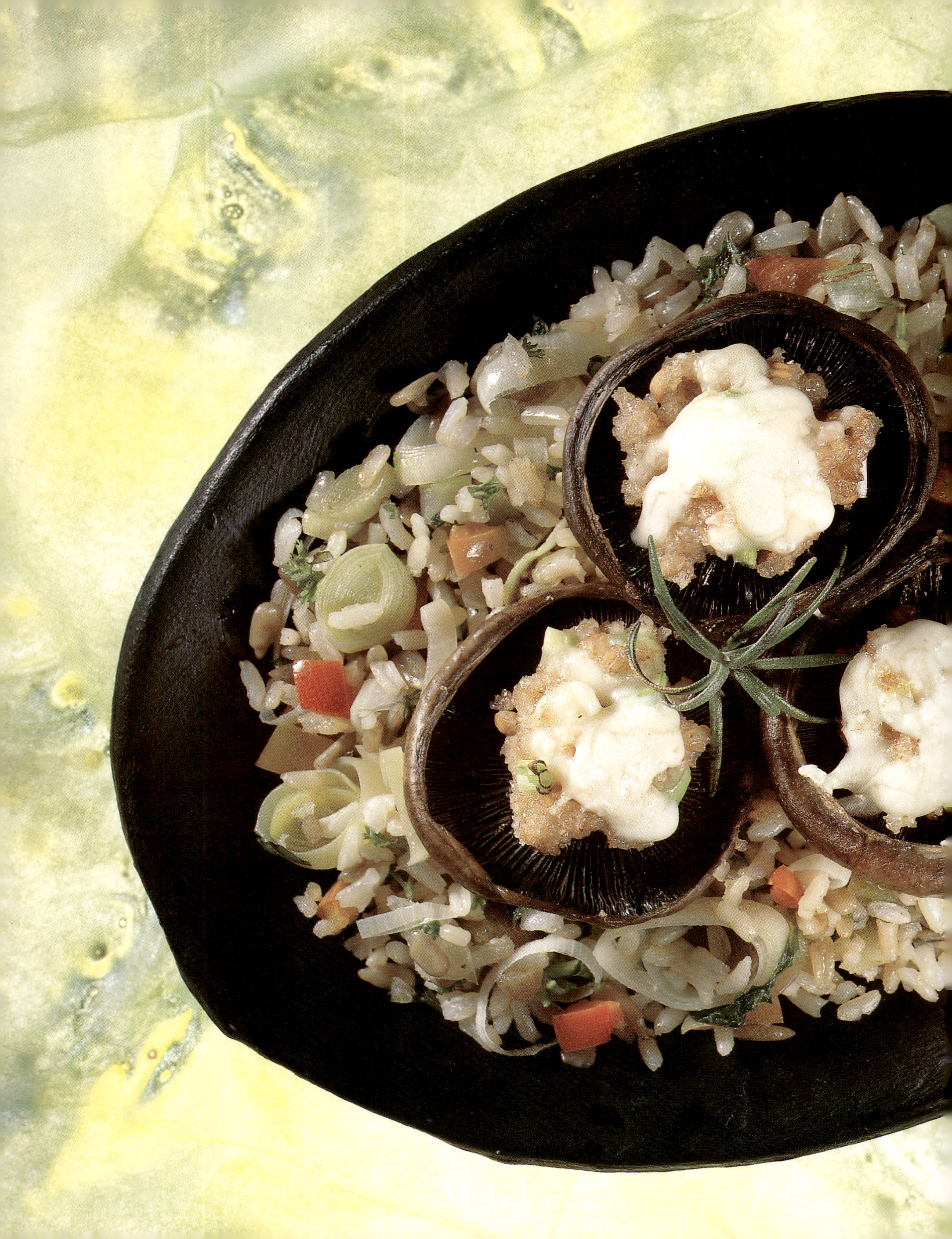

Rice & Other Grains

NUTTY BARLEY AND VEGETABLE BAKE

Barley is a sadly neglected grain which most people use only in soups. This is a pity for it has a marvellous nutty texture and is very nutritious, containing plenty of B vitamins. Try serving it instead of rice, or in a salad. Barley is also very economical and satisfying, especially when used in a vegetable casserole as follows. Cinnamon-baked pumpkin and creamed spinach are good accompaniments.

50 ml sunflower oil
2 large onions, chopped
2 sticks table celery, plus some leaves, chopped
1 green pepper, seeded and diced
250 g brown mushrooms, wiped and sliced
250 g baby marrows, pared and sliced
5 ml mixed dried herbs
5 ml sea salt
375 ml pearl barley, rinsed and drained
750 ml Marmite stock
125 ml toasted sunflower seeds (or more, if you like them)
2 tomatoes, thinly sliced into rounds for topping
plenty of sliced or grated mozzarella or Cheddar or low-fat cheese for topping

Heat oil and sauté onions, celery and green pepper. Add mushrooms, marrows and herbs and toss over low heat until just wilting and smelling good. Add salt and spoon mixture into a rectangular baking dish, about 20 cm x 30 cm. Add barley, stock and sunflower seeds and mix with a fork until well combined, spreading evenly. Cover securely and bake on middle shelf of oven at 160 °C for 1 hour. Uncover and top with tomatoes. Cover with cheese, and bake, uncovered, for 20–30 minutes more.
Serves 8.

Nutty Vegetable Rice with Stuffed Mushrooms (p. 48).

NUTTY RICE AND MUSHROOM CASSEROLE

In this dish, the vegetables are first sautéed and then baked in stock with the uncooked rice and herbs, resulting in maximum flavour with the minimum of fuss and a lovely aroma while it is in the oven. The omelette topping, sliced into strips, finishes it off beautifully. Serve with a tossed green salad — especially good is a combination of lettuce, avocado and sprouts.

60 ml sunflower oil
1 onion, chopped
2 leeks, sliced
2 cloves garlic, crushed
250 g brown mushrooms, wiped and sliced
4 young carrots, julienned
2 sticks table celery, plus some leaves, chopped
375 ml brown rice
125 ml chopped parsley
800 ml hot vegetable or Marmite stock
5 ml sea salt and a little milled black pepper to taste
30 ml (firmly packed) finely chopped fresh herbs*
30 ml soy sauce
125 ml toasted almond strips
a few pats of butter

OMELETTES
8–10 eggs
sea salt and milled black pepper to taste
a little sesame oil

Heat oil in large pan and lightly fry onion, leeks and garlic. Add mushrooms, carrots and celery and stir-fry for a few minutes until glistening, smelling good and beginning to soften. Spoon into a 20 cm x 30 cm baking dish. Add the rice, parsley, stock, seasoning and herbs. Stir with a wooden spoon until well combined, then cover and bake at 160 °C for about 1 hour 10 minutes, until rice is cooked and stock absorbed. Fork in soy sauce, almonds and butter.

During last few minutes of baking, make two omelettes by mixing eggs lightly with a little water, salt and pepper. Do not overbeat. Cook half the egg mixture in a greased pan at a time. (Do use sesame oil.) When just set, tilt pan and roll omelette over a few times. Remove to plate and slice thinly. Arrange slices on top of casserole. *Serves 6.*

* I use a mixture of rosemary, thyme, marjoram and origanum.

BROWN RICE

There are several brands of unpolished rice on the market. The one I have used in all the recipes in this book is Old Mill Stream, which is so easy to cook and comes up nice and fluffy — not quite as fluffy as white rice, but pretty good nevertheless. Use 375 ml rice to 800 ml salted water, bring to the boil, reduce heat to very low, cover and cook for about 50 minutes without looking or stirring. To prevent it from sticking, smear the base of the saucepan with a little oil before cooking. Don't rinse the rice after cooking, and if adding other ingredients, use a fork so as not to make it stodgy.

Remember that Basmati rice needs to be washed very well before cooking.

RICE WITH LENTILS, MUSHROOMS AND ALMONDS

Served with a creamy green salad, this vegetarian main dish is a real delight.

250 ml brown lentils, picked over and rinsed
1 bay leaf
a few nuts of butter
5 ml ground cumin
2 pinches of sea salt
375 ml brown rice
5 ml mixed dried herbs
25 ml each butter and sunflower oil
2 onions, thinly sliced
1 red pepper, seeded and sliced
300–400 g brown mushrooms, wiped and sliced
2 sticks table celery, chopped
100 ml chopped parsley
500 ml mung bean sprouts
50 ml soy sauce*
50 g halved, toasted almonds

Put lentils into saucepan with 500 ml water, bay leaf, a nut of butter, cumin and a pinch of salt. Bring to boil, then cover and simmer gently for about 50 minutes until water is absorbed and lentils are soft.

Meanwhile, cook the rice in another saucepan with 850 ml water, a nut of butter, a pinch of sea salt and mixed herbs, and simmer, covered, over low heat for about 45 minutes.

Toss lentils and rice together and spoon into a large, buttered baking dish, discarding bay leaf. Cover and keep warm in low oven, or set aside to reheat gently later.

To prepare vegetables, heat butter and oil in a large frying pan and add onions and red pepper. When soft and browning, increase heat and add mushrooms, celery and parsley. Stir-fry for 5 minutes, then add sprouts and soy sauce. Reduce heat and cook for a further 2 minutes, tossing with wooden spoon. Pour mixture over warm rice and lentils and scatter with almonds. *Serves 8–10.*

* Soy sauce should season the dish sufficiently, so taste before adding salt.

ONE-POT RICE, MUSHROOM AND SPROUT RISOTTO

A convenience dish which makes a lovely, light meal. The correct rice for risottos is the Italian Arborio, but I have substituted brown rice.

30 ml each sunflower oil and butter
1 large onion, finely chopped
2 cloves garlic, crushed
250 g brown mushrooms, wiped and sliced
250 ml brown rice
1 red pepper, seeded and diced
5 ml chopped, fresh rosemary needles
550 ml hot Marmite stock
50 ml finely chopped parsley
25 ml soy sauce
25 ml sweet sherry
500 ml sprouts (mung bean, lentil, maple pea or a mixture)
toasted almond strips (optional) and an extra knob of butter (plain or flavoured with herbs and garlic)
fried eggs for topping

Heat oil and butter in large frying pan with lid and sauté onion and garlic. Add mushrooms, rice, red pepper and rosemary and stir-fry over low heat until glistening and aromatic. Add hot stock, parsley, soy sauce and sherry. Stir through quickly with a fork, then cover and simmer on very low heat for about 50 minutes or until rice is tender. Do not stir, but towards the end of the cooking period, check if you need a little more stock. Fork in sprouts. If using almonds, add them now with extra butter; otherwise, spoon mixture into a serving dish, top with eggs and serve at once. *Serves 6–8.*

SPICED RICE, LENTILS AND VEGETABLES WITH YOGHURT

This dish is neither a pilaff nor a breyani, but simply an aromatic mixture of Eastern ingredients in which Basmati rice, laced with spices, is served on a dish of lentils cooked with butternut and tomatoes, drizzled with a nutty yoghurt topping and finished off with fresh mint. It is a wonderfully fragrant dish and despite the rather long list of ingredients, it really is quite simple to prepare. Furthermore, I find it does not have to be cooked and eaten immediately — often a daunting factor. Each component is prepared separately and then heated through just before dinner. Not authentic, but nicely perfumed and very tasty. Serve with a brinjal salad, or a carrot and pineapple salad, or simply a mix of tossed greens and cucumber.

TOPPING
500 ml Bulgarian yoghurt
125 ml desiccated coconut
100 ml raisins, plumped in hot water and drained
100 ml finely chopped, toasted almonds
10 ml thin honey
a pinch of sea salt
chopped fresh mint

RICE
250 ml Basmati rice, carefully picked over
25 ml each sunflower oil and butter
1 large onion, finely chopped
2 sticks cinnamon
4 whole cloves
2 ml turmeric
5 ml ground coriander
5 ml sea salt

LENTILS
25 ml sunflower oil
1 large onion, finely chopped
5 ml leaf masala (or more if you want it hot)
2 ml turmeric
5 ml each ground ginger and fennel
500 ml coarsely grated, peeled butternut squash (about 500 g unpeeled)
2 firm tomatoes (about 200 g), coarsely grated, and skin discarded
250 ml brown or green lentils, picked over and rinsed
5 ml each sea salt and sugar

Prepare the topping first by mixing all the ingredients together, except the chopped fresh mint. Cover and chill.

To prepare rice, wash well, then cover with cold water. Pour off any husks or bits that float to the top. Soak for 30 minutes. Drain. Heat oil and butter and braise (or soften) onion. Add spices and sizzle on low heat for 1–2 minutes. Add rice, 750 ml water and salt. Bring to the boil, cover and simmer gently for 20 minutes. Turn off heat and stand for 10 minutes, or longer if preparing in advance. Remove spices.

To cook lentils, heat oil in large frying pan with lid, add onion and cook until wilted. Add spices and fry for 1–2 minutes to release flavours. Add remaining ingredients, plus 500 ml water, bring to the boil, then cover and simmer on very low heat for 1 hour.

When done, both the rice and the lentil mixtures should be just moist enough to stand gentle reheating without any danger of scorching. When just heated through, pile rice into a large, warmed baking dish. Spoon the lentil mixture over the rice. If liked, keep warm, covered, in a low oven for a short while.

Just before serving, drizzle over some of yoghurt topping and sprinkle with mint. Serve rest of yoghurt topping separately.
Serves 6.

ORIENTAL RICE

A simple dish, combining rice with steamed vegetables, sprouts, soy sauce and seeds or nuts. With the addition of eggs, it makes a nourishing, light meal. It may also be served as part of a vegetarian buffet.

300 ml brown rice
500 ml sliced, young green beans (250 g)
4–6 young carrots, julienned
2 sticks table celery, plus some leaves, chopped
60 ml sunflower oil
20 ml dark sesame oil
1 large bunch spring onions, chopped
250 g brown mushrooms, wiped and sliced
25 ml sweet sherry
500 ml lentil sprouts
50 ml soy sauce
60 ml toasted sesame seeds or 125 ml toasted slivered almonds or toasted sunflower seeds
4 eggs, poached, or made into an omelette, thinly sliced

Place rice in saucepan with 625 ml water and 2 ml salt, bring to the boil, then cover and simmer very gently until cooked and water is absorbed.

Meanwhile, poach or steam (covered, in very little water) the beans, carrots and celery (cook the beans for a few minutes before adding the carrots and celery) until crisply tender and set aside. Do not season.

Heat both oils in a large frying pan and sauté onions. Add mushrooms and when softening, add sherry and cook gently for a minute or two to bring out the flavour. Fork in steamed vegetables, sprouts, soy sauce and seeds or nuts. Turn into large, warmed baking dish and fork in the rice. If mixture needs extra moisture, toss in a nut of butter, then cover and keep warm in a low oven. Prepare eggs, arrange on top of rice and serve at once, with extra soy sauce if liked.
Makes 4 large servings.

KITCHEREE WITH FRIED EGGS

From Egypt to India, the nourishing combination of rice and lentils is eaten in many forms, usually with spices and/or hot sauces. The following version is lightly spiced and makes a very satisfying and economical meal. Serve with a bowl of Bulgarian yoghurt and a layered tomato and onion salad, or a dish of baby marrows, coarsely grated and quickly stir-fried.

50 ml sunflower oil
2 large onions, sliced into thin rings
2 ml masala for medium curry
5 ml each ground cumin and fennel
2 bay leaves
2 sticks cinnamon
4 whole cloves
200 ml brown rice
200 ml brown lentils, picked over and rinsed
5 ml sea salt
2 nuts of butter
4 fried eggs

Heat oil in large frying pan with a lid. Add onions and sauté until golden. Turn heat to low, add spices and sizzle for a minute or two. Add remaining ingredients, except butter and eggs, plus 850 ml boiling water, bring to the boil, stirring to mix, then cover securely and simmer on lowest possible heat for about 1 hour, until rice and lentils are cooked and all liquid absorbed. If working ahead, turn off heat and leave for full flavour to develop.

To serve, remove spices and reheat over low heat. Fork in the butter and spoon onto large, warmed serving platter. Top with eggs and serve as suggested.
Serves 4.

BULGUR, LENTIL AND TAHINI PILAFF

This absolutely delicious dish combines 'health foods' which are sure to be unfamiliar to many. The result is so good and the flavours so subtle, that you're sure to be quizzed about the ingredients. And once you've discovered how easy it is to prepare, you're bound to make it often. This is a very light, spicy and slightly nutty pilaff which I like to top with either fried or hard-boiled eggs for extra protein. Serve it with buttered corn or a green salad with sprouts, or omit the eggs and serve it cold as a salad, tossed with an oil and lemon dressing.

200 ml green lentils, picked over and rinsed
2 ml each sea salt and turmeric
50 ml sunflower oil
1 bunch spring onions, chopped
2 cloves garlic, crushed
1 green or red pepper, seeded and diced
5–7 ml each ground cumin, coriander and fennel
250 ml bulgur
5 ml sea salt
60 ml tahini
25 ml fresh lemon juice
100–125 ml toasted sunflower seeds or chopped, toasted almonds
6 eggs

First, put lentils into small saucepan with 400 ml water, the 2 ml sea salt and turmeric and cook gently until soft and liquid is absorbed. Drain.

Heat sunflower oil in a large frying pan with a lid. Add spring onions, garlic and pepper and sauté until soft. Add the spices and toss over low heat for a minute or two. Add bulgur and toss until coated, then add another 5 ml sea salt.

Mix 500 ml boiling water with tahini and lemon juice (Don't be concerned if the tahini melts into threads.) Stir into mixture in pan, then cover tightly and cook on low heat for 5 minutes. Switch off heat and leave for another 5 minutes. Use a fork to mix in the lentils and sunflower seeds or almonds, tossing lightly until thoroughly combined, then turn onto a large heated platter and keep warm, covered, in a low oven until ready to serve.

Fry the eggs. As soon as they're done, arrange them on top of the pilaff and serve immediately. If using hard-boiled eggs, first moisten the pilaff by forking in a lump of butter, top with eggs and serve with a bowl of chutney.
Serves 6.

MILLET

An exceptional grain which matches wheat in protein content and packs in a lot of magnesia. It can be used in soups and casseroles, but the simplest way to serve it is as a nourishing alternative to rice. Use de-husked millet, and toast it lightly to bring out the flavour. Cook 250 ml millet in 625 ml salted water for 15–20 minutes on very low heat. It will expand a lot during cooking. Fork in (do not stir) a nut of butter before serving.

MILLET PILAFF WITH EGGS FLORENTINE

Although these are two completely separate dishes, they make such a good combination that I am featuring them as one meal. The eggs, baked on a bed of spinach in individual ramekins, are served to one side of the dinner plate, with a mound of the nutty pilaff alongside. This method of presentation makes a nice change, and only a fork is used to dip into the two. The result is a super combination of flavours and textures, but the pilaff can, of course, be served elsewhere as a particularly wholesome alternative to rice. Start with the baked eggs Florentine as the cooking time is slightly longer than for the millet. Cook the pilaff while the eggs are baking. For added flavour, the millet should be pre-toasted. Do this by spreading it out on a baking tray and placing in a moderate oven until a light golden brown.

BAKED EGGS FLORENTINE

500 g frozen spinach, thawed
sea salt and a little freshly grated nutmeg
8 eggs
200 ml cultured sour cream
sea salt and paprika

Cook the thawed spinach in a little water. Drain, if necessary, and then season with sea salt and nutmeg. Divide the spinach between eight small ramekins, lightly greased with butter. Break an egg into each ramekin and over each egg spoon 25 ml sour cream. Dust with a little sea salt and paprika, and then arrange ramekins, not touching, in a large tin, one third filled with water. Bake at 180 °C for about 45 minutes or until set.

NUTTY MILLET PILAFF

25 ml each sunflower oil and butter
1 bunch spring onions, chopped
1 large red pepper, seeded and finely diced
250 ml dehusked millet, toasted
5 ml sea salt
100 ml chopped parsley
500 ml lentil sprouts
125 ml toasted sunflower seeds
a nut or two of butter (optional)

Heat oil and butter in wide, heavy-based frying pan with a lid. Add spring onions and red pepper and allow to soften over medium heat. Add millet and toss until coated. Add 750 ml boiling water, the sea salt and parsley, stir to mix, then cover and simmer very gently for 25–30 minutes, until millet is tender and liquid absorbed. (Don't make it stodgy by stirring.) Fork in the sprouts and sunflower seeds and, if liked, a nut or two of butter.
Serves 6 — presuming that some diners will have 2 eggs and some will have 1.

WEET-RICE

Also known as stampkoring or pearled whole wheat, this is a natural product which really needs wider recognition. Being unrefined, it is rich in essential nutrients and fibre; it is also deliciously nutty and most economical as the grains swell up to three times in size during the cooking process. Use it with rice, or instead of rice, in main dishes, salads or even in baking, but do try it.

The cooking method is more or less the same as for brown rice, but you will need more water — at least 800 ml to 250 ml Weet-rice (rinse well before cooking). Once boiling, cover and cook on very low heat for 45–50 minutes.

To make it fluffy, I then give it a very quick rinse and then steam it in a colander over simmering water for ± 20 minutes, but this is not necessary.

Oriental Rice (p. 45) and Vegetable Breyani (p. 48) with cucumber and sour cream salad.

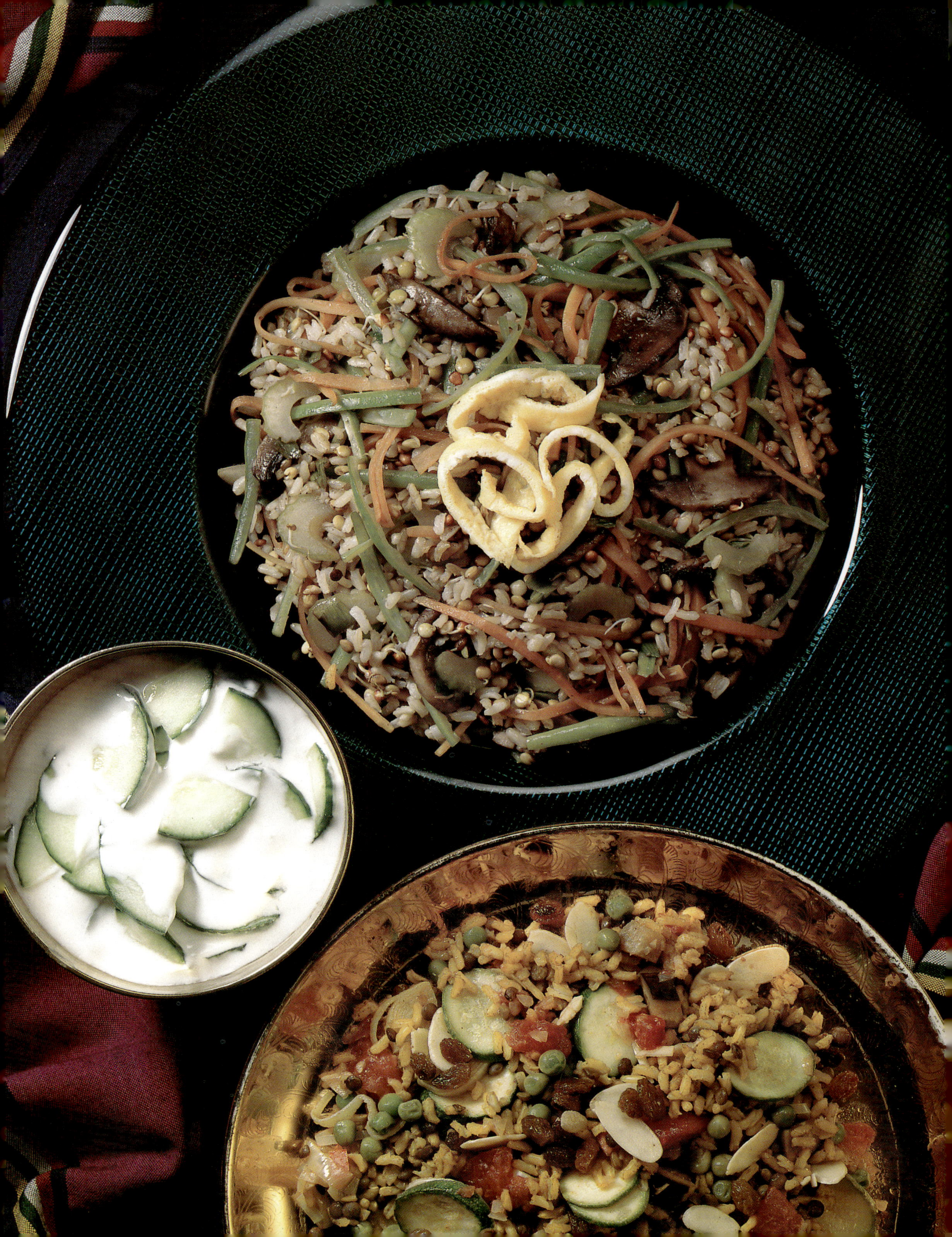

VEGETABLE BREYANI

Based on a dish from Northern India, this is an aromatic combination of rice, lentils, vegetables and spices. The dish has only a gentle bite, but the amount of masala used may be increased to taste. A cooling cucumber, mint and sour cream salad makes a fine accompaniment. See page 62 for another version of breyani, with equal quantities of lentils and rice, and layered with hard-boiled eggs instead of vegetables.

250 ml brown rice
125 ml brown lentils, picked over and rinsed
5 ml each sea salt, turmeric and ground coriander
2 ml ground cumin
1 stick cinnamon
1 brinjal, washed and cubed (200 g)
25 ml each butter and sunflower oil
2 leeks, sliced
1 large onion, chopped
2–4 cloves garlic, crushed
2 ml Pure Roasted Masala or more to taste
1 red pepper, seeded and diced
4 juicy tomatoes, skinned and chopped
6 small baby marrows (300 g), pared and sliced
250 ml green peas
a pinch each of sea salt and sugar
125 ml slivered almonds
25 ml butter
125 ml sultanas

Put rice, lentils, salt, spices and 800 ml water into a saucepan. Bring to the boil, cover, lower heat and leave to cook gently for about 50 minutes, by which time liquid should be absorbed. Fluff up with a fork and remove cinnamon stick.

Meanwhile, dégorge brinjal. Heat butter and oil in a large frying pan and sauté leeks, onion, garlic and masala. When softened, add the brinjal, red pepper, tomatoes, baby marrows and peas. Cook for approximately 10 minutes, stirring occasionally, until marrows are translucent. Remove from stove and add salt and sugar.

In a large, deep, buttered dish, layer one third of rice, half the vegetable mixture, another third of the rice, the remaining vegetable mixture, then remainder of the rice. Bake, covered, at 160 °C for 30 minutes. Just before end of baking time, fry almonds in butter. When lightly browned, add sultanas, heat through and spoon over top of breyani.
Serves about 8.

WILD RICE WITH WATER CHESTNUTS

Wild rice is the seed of a grass which grows in the shallow waters of lakes and waterways in parts of North America. Because of the locality, these slim, blackish seeds with their distinctive, nutty flavour are difficult to harvest, so they are wildly expensive and best used with other types of rice. There are different ways of cooking wild rice, but the brand I use – Pouyoukas — is simple to prepare, and may be cooked together with brown rice. The following dish is a lovely combination of flavours and textures, and delicious served with large, grilled mushrooms. Not an economical family meal, but an excellent choice for a special occasion. Quantities may easily be doubled.

125 ml wild rice, rinsed
125 ml brown rice
25 ml each butter and sunflower oil
2 medium onions, sliced into thin rings
125 ml slivered almonds
2 cloves garlic, crushed
1 red pepper, seeded and diced
1 large stick table celery, plus leaves, chopped
1 small knob root ginger, peeled and grated
3 rings fresh pineapple, diced
½ a 230-g can water chestnuts, drained and sliced
25 ml soy sauce
10 ml honey
250 ml lentil sprouts

Bring 600 ml salted water to boil in a heavy saucepan. Add wild rice, brown rice and a dash of oil, stir once to mix, and as soon as water returns to the boil, reduce heat to very low, cover and leave to simmer for 50-60 minutes, until tender and all water has been absorbed.

Meanwhile, heat half the butter and oil in a large frying pan. Add one of the onions and the almonds, and toss over medium heat until browned. Remove from pan and set aside. Add remaining butter and oil to pan and sauté the other onion, garlic, red pepper, celery and ginger. When softening, stir in pineapple, water chestnuts, soy sauce, 50 ml water and honey. Cover and simmer on a very low heat for 10 minutes. Fork in cooked rice and the sprouts. Check seasoning — a little more soy sauce may be necessary — then turn mixture, which should be moist and shiny, onto large heated platter. Top with reserved onion and almonds, and serve immediately.
Serves 4–6.

NUTTY VEGETABLE RICE WITH STUFFED MUSHROOMS

A marvellous dinner dish, smart enough for entertaining and a top favourite in our house. Cooked rice is tossed with sautéed vegetables and nuts; big brown mushrooms, stuffed and topped with cheese and garlic butter, are baked separately. Together they make a superb combination of textures and flavours. Serve with a crisp green salad.

MUSHROOMS
8 large brown mushrooms (about 500 g), wiped
4 spring onions, chopped
100 ml stale, finely crumbed brown or wholewheat breadcrumbs
12 needles fresh rosemary, finely chopped
30–40 ml thick mayonnaise
a pinch of sea salt and milled black pepper to taste
sliced mozzarella or grated low-fat Gouda or Cheddar cheese
50 ml garlic butter

RICE
50 ml sunflower oil
2 leeks, sliced
1 onion, chopped
2 sticks table celery, plus a few leaves, chopped
1 red or yellow pepper, seeded and diced
100 ml toasted sunflower seeds or
150 ml coarsely chopped pecan nuts
100 ml chopped parsley
750 ml cooked brown rice
30 ml soy sauce

Remove stalks and a little of the centre of each mushroom. Chop finely and mix with onions, breadcrumbs, rosemary, just enough mayonnaise to moisten, and salt. Lightly oil base of large baking dish and arrange mushrooms in it, hollows up. Season. Fill each mushroom with a spoon of the stuffing, then top with cheese. Put a small lump of garlic butter on each and bake at 180 °C for about 25 minutes until tender and cheese has melted.

Meanwhile, heat oil and soften leeks and onion. Add celery and diced pepper and stir-fry over low heat until just tender. Fork in remaining ingredients for rice mixture. Heat through on very low heat.

Spoon the rice into warmed serving dish. Top each serving of rice with two of the mushrooms, spooning the juices over.
Serves 4.

COUSCOUS WITH CHICKPEA AND VEGETABLE STEW

The following method is a fuss-free and quick way of preparing couscous. Do not prepare beforehand as couscous easily becomes stodgy. But as it takes only 10 minutes to prepare, it can easily be done just before dinner. The accompanying stew is thick with vegetables, chickpeas and tahini, making this a dish for those initiated into foreign flavours.

STEW
30 ml sunflower oil and 10 ml butter
1 large onion, chopped
2 cloves garlic, crushed
1 green pepper, seeded and diced
2 ml ground cumin
5 ml ground coriander
1 smallish butternut squash, cubed (500 ml)
500 ml cauliflower florets
500 ml shredded spinach leaves
12 baby potatoes, scrubbed
4 carrots, julienned
500 ml cooked chickpeas
2 sticks cinnamon
2 bay leaves
5 ml each sea salt and light brown sugar
500 ml vegetable stock or liquid from cooking chickpeas
10–15 ml tahini

COUSCOUS
250 ml refined semolina couscous
2 ml turmeric
5 ml sea salt
a nut of butter

Heat the oil and butter in a large saucepan. Add the onion, garlic and green pepper and sauté until softening. Mix in all the spices and toss for 1–2 minutes. Add all the vegetables and toss until well mixed, then add the remaining ingredients for stew, except tahini. Bring to the boil, then cover and simmer on low heat, stirring occasionally, until the vegetables are cooked and the sauce is thick. Remove cinnamon and bay leaves, and stir in the tahini.

Prepare the couscous by putting it into a saucepan with 500 ml water, turmeric and the sea salt. Bring to the boil, stir, then cover and remove from heat. Leave it to stand for 10 minutes, then lightly fork in the nut of butter.

To serve, spread couscous around the edge of a large, warmed platter and pile the stew in the middle.
Serves 4 to 6.

COUSCOUS

Couscous is not necessarily the same product in different countries. We use a pale yellow, refined type of semolina, but a dish of Armenian couscous could well use bulgur, or, in Morocco, it could be barley. Basically, couscous comprises a grain topped with a vegetable sauce. Semolina couscous is very bland, but it is easy to cook and lovingly absorbs other flavours. For this reason, it is often steamed over the saucepan in which you are cooking the vegetables. If using this method, first soak the couscous in plenty of cold water, to allow the grains to swell. If you omit this step, the fine grains will simply fall through the sieve. A quicker method is to combine the grains with twice the amount of salted water, bring to the boil, and as soon as little holes appear (looking like sea sand in which little creatures are burrowing as the tide recedes), remove the saucepan from the heat, cover and stand for 10 minutes. Now fork in some flavour, depending on the dish you are serving it with. It could do with a knob of butter, a touch of freshly grated nutmeg is interesting, and so are fresh herbs, such as parsley and basil. Use a fork, not a spoon, when making these additions, and, if possible, prepare just before serving.

MUSHROOM RICE WITH SPROUTS AND TAHINI

This dish affords a gentle introduction to the use of tahini. Mixed with lemon juice and water, it adds a creamy texture and a slightly smoky flavour to the delicious combination of rice, vegetables, sprouts and sunflower seeds. A dressed spinach and tomato salad with wedges of hard-boiled eggs makes a fine accompaniment.

SAUCE
100 ml tahini
50 ml fresh lemon juice
100 ml cold water

RICE
60 ml sunflower oil
2 leeks, sliced
1 small onion, chopped
2 cloves garlic, crushed
1 green, red or yellow pepper, seeded and diced
2 sticks table celery, sliced
250 g brown mushrooms, wiped and sliced
50 ml soy sauce
a pinch of sugar
100 ml chopped parsley
4 x 250 ml cooked brown rice
375 ml lentil sprouts
125 ml toasted sunflower seeds
feta cheese, rinsed and crumbled for topping

Stir tahini very well before using, or turn into a small bowl and whisk thoroughly. Slowly stir in lemon juice — the mixture will become thick and grainy. Add water gradually, stirring the sauce until it is smooth and creamy.

Heat oil in a large pan and soften leeks, onion and garlic. Add pepper and celery and stir-fry over low heat for a few minutes. Add mushrooms and when softening, add soy sauce, sugar and parsley. Cover and keep on very low heat for about 10 minutes until juices form, then fork in remaining ingredients. The mixture should be moist and glistening. No salt should be necessary due to the generous addition of soy sauce.

Stir in tahini sauce and heat without boiling. Turn into warmed serving dish, top with feta and place in moderate oven briefly just to heat through.
Serves 6.

BARLEY

Pearl barley is a wholesome grain, high in water-soluble fibre. It makes a lovely change from rice, and may be combined with lentils, beans or chickpeas for a protein-rich meal. It is also excellent in grain salads.

To cook, use 500 ml salted water for every 250 ml polished pearl barley (which should be rinsed well before cooking). Bring to the boil, then cover and simmer gently until the grains are tender and the moisture has evaporated — for about 1 hour. Cover saucepan with a kitchen towel, switch off the stove plate, and leave to stand for 10 minutes.

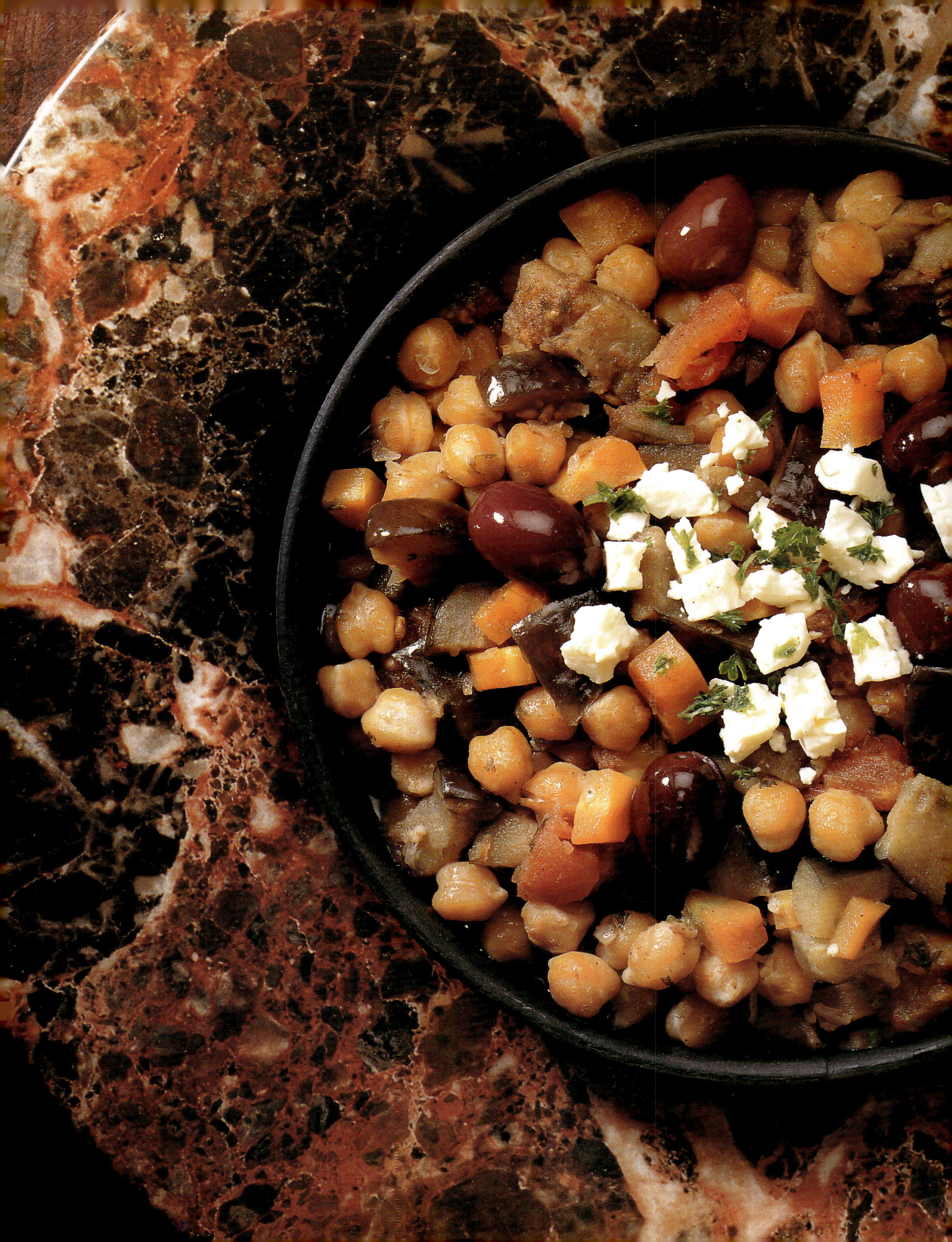

PULSES

SPICED CHICKPEAS

A fragrant stew to serve on brown rice with bowls of coconut and chopped nuts and a green salad.

50 ml sunflower oil
2 onions, chopped
2–3 cloves garlic, crushed
2 ml each ground cumin, turmeric, cinnamon and ginger
5 ml ground coriander
2 sticks table celery, chopped
1 green pepper, seeded and diced
750 ml cooked chickpeas, drained
125 ml chopped parsley
1 x 400 g can tomatoes, chopped, plus juice
2 bay leaves
250 ml water or vegetable stock
5 ml sea salt or 10 ml vegetable salt
5 ml sugar

Heat oil in a large saucepan. Add onions, garlic, spices, celery and green pepper. Cover and cook over very low heat until the onions are soft. Add remaining ingredients, bring to the boil, then cover and simmer on low heat for about 30 minutes, stirring occasionally. Add a little water if necessary, for a good sauce. Check seasoning, and serve as suggested.
Serves 4–6.

Mediterranean Chickpea Casserole (p. 53).

PULSES

I have used this term to include dried beans, peas and lentils, all of which are staple foods all over the world, although it is only the soya bean which contains all the essential amino acids. The others all need to be eaten with a whole grain, bread, wholewheat pasta or baked potatoes to provide the required amount of protein.

There is no real shortcut to cooking beans, although some varieties can be covered with cold water, brought to the boil, boiled for 10 minutes, then soaked for an hour or two before boiling again. To my mind, that's far more trouble than simply remembering to soak them overnight; and if you soak at least 500 g to 1 kg at a time, you can cook them in one batch and freeze what you don't use immediately. To do this, use small containers (those shallow plastic ones containing vegetables, which you buy in supermarkets, are ideal). Ladle the pulses in, add just enough water to cover (to prevent freezer burn), and then you simply reach for a container when you want to prepare a meal. They can easily be thawed under running water, tipped into a colander, and then rinsed under cold or hot water.

Once you've learnt to enjoy pulses, their preparation becomes a habit. Come the evening and have you put out the cat? Locked the doors? Soaked the beans? But back to the basics of how to cook pulses: pick over and rinse, place in a bowl, cover generously with cold water, then leave for 8 hours or overnight. In warm weather, you should keep soya beans in the fridge while soaking to prevent them from fermenting.

To cook pulses, drain them (you'll be throwing away some of the vitamins, but this step makes them more digestible), put them into a large saucepan, cover with water, bring to the boil, and boil rapidly for the first 10 minutes (this facilitates the availability of the protein). Reduce heat and simmer until soft (the time varies with the type of bean or pea, but slow, thorough cooking is very important for the release of essential nutrients). Add salt only halfway through the cooking process. If salt is added at the start, it prevents the pulse from softening adequately.

CHICKPEAS

Soak overnight in plenty of cold water. Drain, rinse and simmer, covered with water, for 2½ to 3 hours, until soft, adding salt after 1 hour. Pour off cooking liquid and reserve if required. Tip chickpeas into a large bowl, add cold water, and rub them between the palms of your hands to remove the skins. As skins float to the top, pour off the water. Repeat this several times.

An amount of 500 g uncooked chickpeas makes 6 x 250 ml when cooked.

CHICKPEA STEW WITH TAHINI SAUCE

If you like tahini, you'll love this chickpea dish, subtly flavoured with ginger and cumin. Spooned over brown rice, it could be classed as a major protein meal. Although the stew does contain vegetables, a crisp green salad just ties it all together. Remember to save the cooking liquid when draining chickpeas, as it gets added to the dish.

50 ml sunflower oil
2 onions, chopped
3 leeks, thinly sliced
4 sticks table celery, thinly sliced
3 cloves garlic, crushed
6 medium baby marrows, pared and julienned
5 ml each ground cumin and ginger
30 ml brown flour
6 x 250 ml cooked chickpeas (500 g uncooked)
750 ml liquid from cooking chickpeas
75–100 ml tahini
50 ml soy sauce (a little less if liquid is salty)

Heat oil in a large pan. Add onions, leeks, celery, garlic and baby marrows. Mix well, then allow them to sweat over a low heat, half-covered, until nearly soft. Mix in the spices (for a fairly 'hot' flavour, increase quantities of both spices to 10 ml) and cook a further 2 minutes. Mix in the flour, then add chickpeas. Stir the 750 ml liquid with the tahini and soy sauce. Add to stew, bring to the boil slowly, cover and simmer gently for about 15 minutes before serving. It may also be cooled and reheated.
Serves 8.

BUTTER BEAN, MUSHROOM AND WALNUT CURRY

This easy, stove-top dish, with its rather surprising combination of ingredients, is high on my list of favourites. Nourishing and quick to make, it turns out a rich caramel colour with a lovely tang. Ladle servings over brown rice and pass bowls of coconut, chutney and a crisp, green salad.

50 ml sunflower oil
1 large onion, finely chopped
1 large Golden Delicious apple, peeled and diced
10 ml curry powder
5 ml ground coriander
2 ml each turmeric and ground cumin and cinnamon
50 ml brown flour
250 ml vegetable stock or water
250 ml milk
5 ml sea salt
25 ml tomato paste
a pinch of sugar
30 ml butter
250 g brown mushrooms, wiped and sliced
1 red pepper, seeded and diced
125 ml coarsely chopped walnuts
1 x 410 g can choice grade butter beans, drained

Heat oil and lightly fry onion and apple. Add spices and allow to sizzle gently for about 2 minutes. Sprinkle in flour, then slowly stir in stock or water and milk. When thickening, add salt, tomato paste and sugar. Cover and simmer very gently for 20 minutes, stirring occasionally to prevent sticking. Meanwhile, heat butter in separate pan. Add mushrooms, red pepper and walnuts and fry until mushrooms are just softening. Stir into curry sauce, add beans, then simmer on low heat until very hot. Check seasoning (if water has been used, you may need to add a little salt).
Serves 4–5.

BROCCOLI AND CAULIFLOWER

These vegetables should be soaked ever so briefly in salted water to remove grit. Rinse and then prepare and cook as explained in the recipe.

CHICKPEAS AND BROCCOLI IN MUSTARD SAUCE

A simple but tasty combination of chickpeas and vegetables in a creamy sauce. Serve on brown rice or pasta and top with grated Cheddar or crumbled feta cheese, or with baked potatoes and chunky cottage cheese. A simple tomato and basil salad makes a good accompaniment.

500 g broccoli
60 ml sunflower oil
3 leeks, thinly sliced
1 small onion, chopped
2 cloves garlic, crushed
400 ml liquid from cooking chickpeas or vegetable stock
5 ml sea salt and milled black pepper to taste
75 ml brown flour
375 ml milk
4 x 250 ml cooked chickpeas
15 ml Dijon mustard
15 ml fresh lemon juice
75 ml cream or cultured sour cream

Prepare broccoli: remove only the tips of the stalks, chop remainder of stalks thinly and the florets fairly coarsely.

Heat sunflower oil in a large pan. Add leeks, onion and garlic and sweat over low heat, shaking pan occasionally. Add the prepared broccoli, 200 ml of the liquid and seasoning. Cover and cook gently until soft. Sprinkle in the flour and toss to mix, then slowly stir in the remaining 200 ml liquid and the milk. Stir over low heat until the sauce has thickened, then add the remaining ingredients. Heat through, stirring, and allow the mixture to bubble gently for a few minutes to blend flavours.

Check seasoning and serve at once, as suggested above.
Serves 6–8.

BEURRE MANIÉ
•

This is a paste made of butter and flour, which is kneaded together until smooth, and used for enriching and thickening sauces and stews. It should be whisked, a little at a time, into the hot liquid, which is then slowly brought back to the boil. The classic ratio of butter to flour is 3:2, but less butter may be used with good results.

CHICKPEA STEW

Serve on brown rice and top with grated cheese.

25 ml each butter and sunflower oil
1 large onion, chopped
2 cloves garlic, crushed
2 carrots, diced
1 red pepper, seeded and diced
250 g brown mushrooms, wiped and sliced
250 g tomatoes, skinned and chopped
25 ml tomato paste
125 ml chopped parsley
2 ml each dried basil and thyme
4 x 250 ml cooked chickpeas
125 ml vegetable stock
sea salt and milled black pepper to taste

Heat butter and oil in large saucepan. Stir-fry onion, garlic, carrots, red pepper and mushrooms. Add remaining ingredients. Season, cover and simmer for 30 minutes. Thicken sauce with beurre manié.
    Serve as suggested.
Serves 5–6.

MEDITERRANEAN CHICKPEA CASSEROLE

An aromatic, spicy combination of vegetables and chickpeas, slowly simmered together to make a marvellous topping for brown rice or pasta. The addition of black olives and feta cheese make it cheerfully bright and very tempting. This dish may be made in advance and reheated, and is even good cold.

50 ml olive oil
25 ml sunflower oil
2 large onions, chopped
2 cloves garlic, crushed
10 ml ground coriander
5 ml each ground cinnamon and cumin
500 g brinjals, cubed and dégorged
2 carrots, diced
400 g ripe tomatoes, skinned and chopped
4 x 250 ml cooked chickpeas
5 ml sea salt and milled black pepper to taste
5 ml sugar
2 bay leaves
125 ml chopped parsley
500 ml vegetable stock or water or liquid from drained chickpeas
black olives (optional)
feta cheese, rinsed and crumbled for topping

Heat both oils in large saucepan. Add onions and garlic, and when translucent add spices and cook for 1 minute. Add brinjals and carrots and toss, over low heat, until coated. Add remaining ingredients, except olives and feta, bring to the boil, then cover and simmer over very low heat for 45–60 minutes, stirring occasionally. When ready, mixture should be thick, like a stew, but if it needs binding, stir in a little flour slaked with water. Remove bay leaves and check seasoning. If cooking in advance, transfer to suitable container and cool. Reheat gently before serving, adding a little water or stock if necessary. Stir in a few olives, if using, and spoon into large, warmed serving dish. Top with feta.
Serves 6.

SPICED MIXED RICE AND LENTILS
•

This useful recipe, in which everything is simply simmered together until done, could easily become a favourite. As it combines a pulse and grain, it is more nutritious than serving just one or the other, and its delightful flavour marries perfectly with curries, or bean or chickpea casseroles. Or toss it with French dressing and serve cold, as a salad.

- 250 ml each brown rice and brown lentils, picked over and rinsed
- 1 litre plus 100 ml water
- 5 ml sea salt
- 4 star anise
- 2 sticks cinnamon
- 2 bay leaves
- 6 white cardamom pods
- 5 ml each ground cumin, ground coriander and turmeric
- 50 ml dried onion flakes
- a nut of butter

Put all ingredients, except butter, in a saucepan. Bring to the boil, cover and simmer on lowest heat for about 1 hour until liquid is absorbed. Remove spices and bay leaves, and fork in butter.
Serves 8.

Overleaf: Mushroom and Lentil Moussaka (p. 57), Quick Butter Bean and Mushroom Goulash (p. 56) and Pot Beans (p. 65).

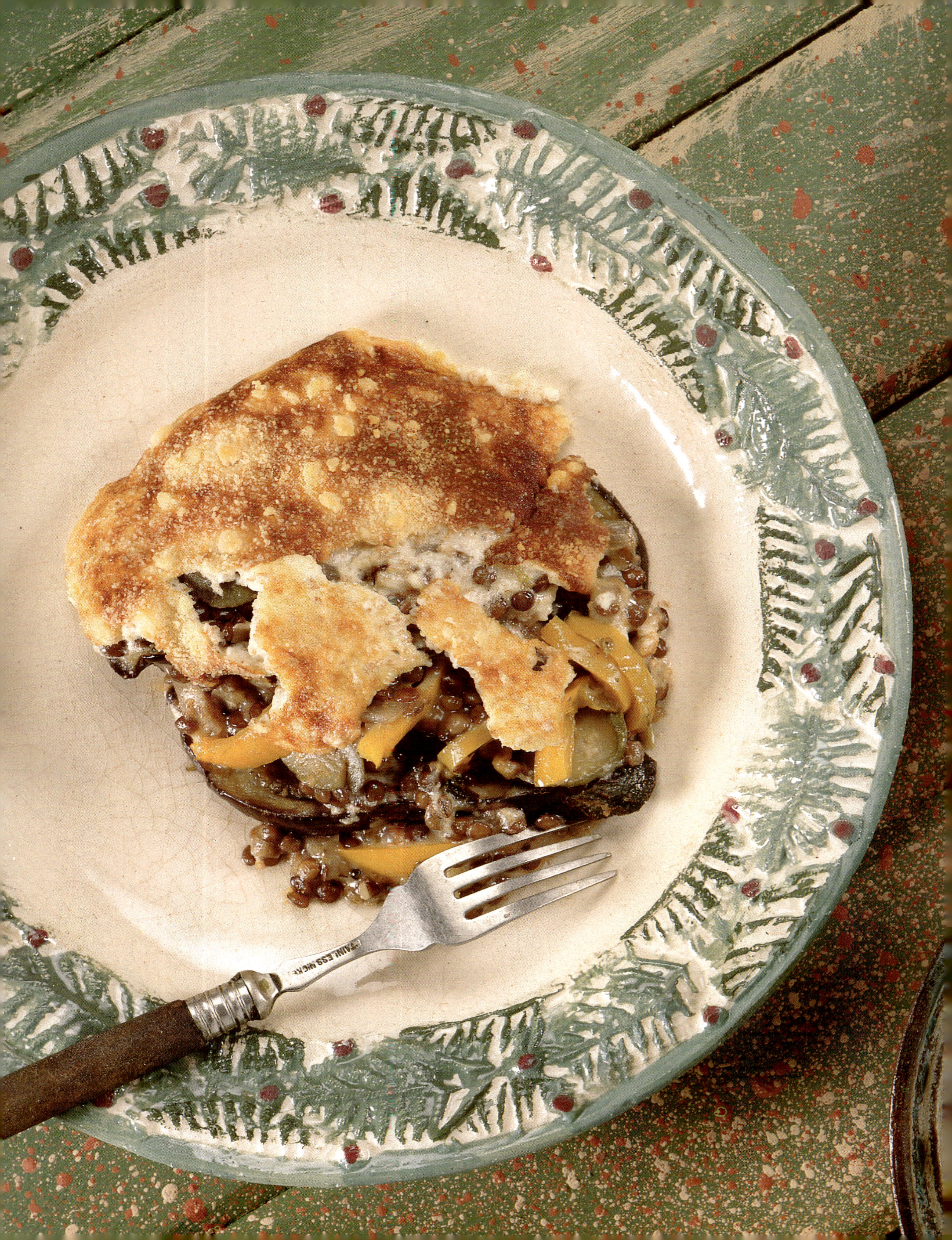

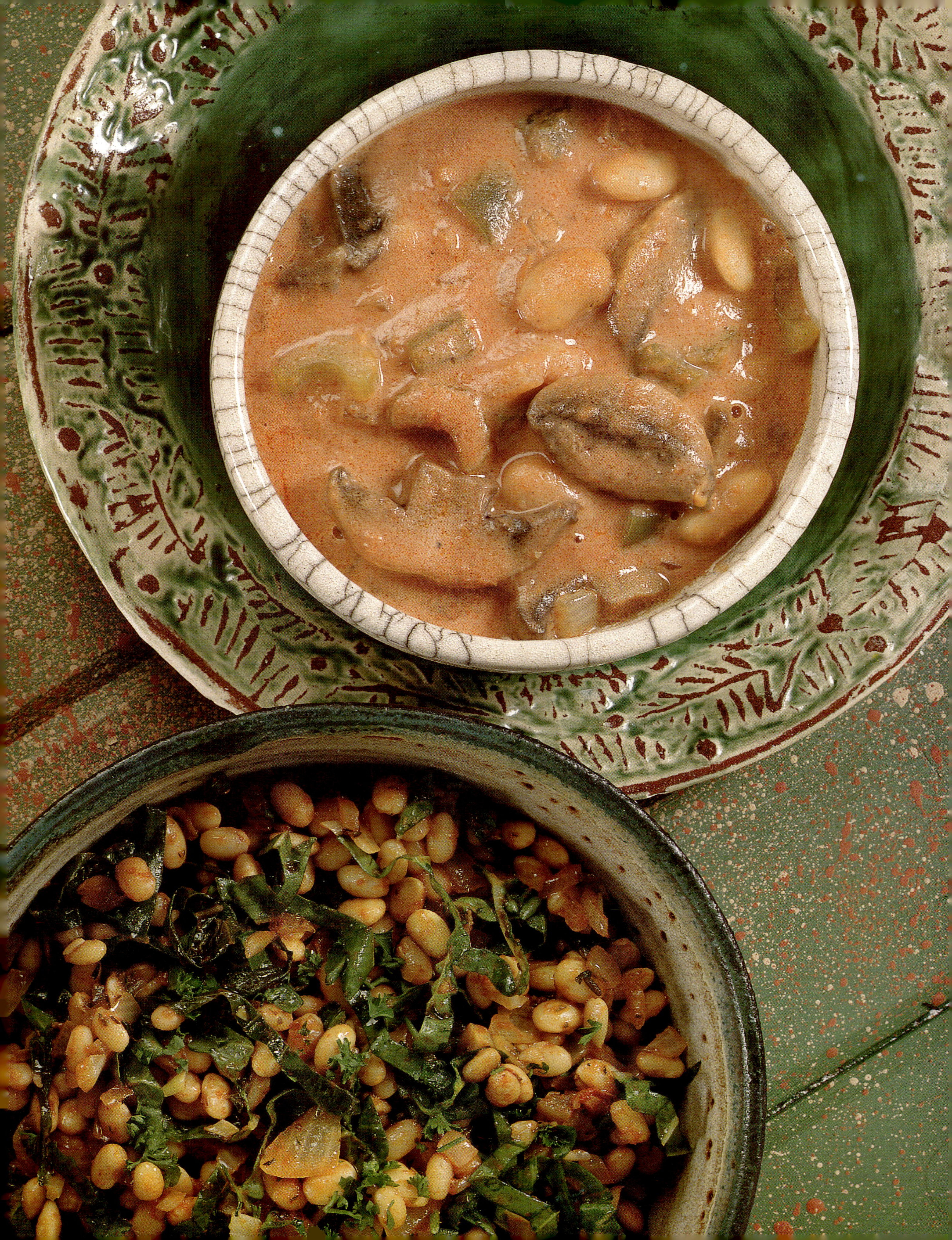

VEGETABLE AND BUTTER BEAN HURRY CURRY

There's no denying that many meatless meals are quite tough on the cook. Pulses take time to soak and cook; vegetables take a lot of cleaning and chopping. There's also no denying that these freshly prepared ingredients taste the best. But there are times when a cook simply has to cheat. This recipe is for just such an occasion. It's not gourmet fare, but it is both tasty and filling.

50 ml sunflower oil
2 large onions, chopped
2–4 cloves garlic, crushed
30 ml curry powder, or more to taste
5 ml turmeric
1-kg packet frozen vegetables (e.g. marrows, carrots, cauliflower and peas)
500 g ripe tomatoes, skinned and chopped into small pieces
500 ml vegetable stock or water
5 ml sea salt
50 ml chutney
25 ml tomato paste
2 bay leaves
2 x 410 g cans choice grade butter beans, drained
a little fresh lemon juice
125 ml desiccated coconut

Heat oil and soften onions and garlic. Add curry powder and turmeric and sizzle for a minute or two. Add just-thawed vegetables and toss to coat. Add tomatoes, stock or water, salt, chutney, tomato paste and bay leaves. Cover and simmer gently for 15 minutes. Add beans, lemon juice and coconut and heat through. Add a little extra liquid if needed. If time allows, transfer to suitable container and cool for flavour to develop. Remove bay leaves and reheat gently. Check seasoning and serve on brown rice with sambals.
Serves 8.

To me, one of the very nicest meals is one that is so simple that no recipe is required. We love it — particularly on those evenings when I just do not wish to be in the kitchen. Young potatoes, scrubbed and steamed (not baked) are served with fried mushrooms (sometimes I add spinach), chunky cottage cheese and sour cream. It's a surprisingly addictive combination.

BOSTON BAKED BUTTER BEANS

This is a tasty but totally unpretentious meal. Based on an old-fashioned American dish, my recipe includes the traditional mustard, molasses and spices, but without the fat salt belly pork which is normally added. I have also shortened the cooking time considerably — traditionally (with the pork) it is cooked for about 8 hours! The following quantities make enough to feed an army, but can easily be halved. It is astonishingly economical. The dish is perfectly rounded off with the addition of brown rice or baked potatoes, grated Cheddar or cottage cheese and a cabbage, carrot and pineapple slaw. It also reheats well. (See box on page 64.)

500 g butter (large kidney) beans
100 ml sunflower oil
4 large onions, chopped
4 sticks table celery, plus some leaves, chopped
6 medium carrots, diced into small cubes
4 bay leaves
200 ml chopped parsley
20 ml mustard powder
20 ml light brown sugar
50 ml desulphured molasses
500 ml tomato purée
10 ml ground mixed spice
500 ml vegetable stock or water
5 ml sea salt
20 ml Worcestershire sauce

Soak beans overnight, drain and rinse and put into a large saucepan. Cover with cold water, bring to the boil, boil rapidly for 10 minutes, then simmer gently until nearly tender — about 45 minutes — adding salt towards the end. Drain.

Heat oil in a large saucepan, add onions, celery and carrots and sweat over low heat until onion is glossy and carrots are tender. Mix in remaining ingredients, except beans, then turn into a large baking dish. Stir in the beans, then cover and bake at 140 °C for 1 hour. Stir to mix, adding extra liquid if necessary, then return to oven and bake for another 1 hour 15 minutes.

Remove bay leaves before serving. If making ahead, you will probably need to add a little extra stock or water before reheating, to ensure a juicy mixture.*
Serves 10–12.

* If preferred, this dish may be cooked on top of the stove. Cover and simmer very gently until beans are tender and flavour has developed, checking occasionally to see if extra liquid is needed.

QUICK BUTTER BEAN AND MUSHROOM GOULASH

Good quality canned butter beans are a useful time-saver and can be used to pad out many a dish. The following is a tasty, simple and quickly prepared example. Serve on rice or pasta, or with baked potatoes and a salad.

30 ml sunflower oil
1 large onion, chopped
250 g white or brown mushrooms, wiped and sliced
2 stalks table celery, sliced
1 green or red pepper, seeded and diced
7 ml paprika
30 ml brown flour
125 ml tomato purée
2 ml sea salt and milled black pepper to taste
2 x 410 g cans butter beans, drained
125 ml cultured sour cream
grated Cheddar cheese for topping

Heat oil and fry onion lightly. Add mushrooms, celery and pepper and toss over medium heat until softening. Sprinkle in paprika and flour and toss to mix. Add tomato purée, 250 ml water, seasoning and beans. Cover and simmer very gently for 15 minutes, stirring once or twice to prevent mixture from sticking to the bottom of the pan as it thickens, but taking care not to mash the beans.

If possible, set aside to cool for a while (see box on page 64), then reheat gently, swirling in the sour cream. Check seasoning and serve topped with Cheddar cheese.
Serves 5–6

BUTTER BEANS

Also called lima or large kidney beans, these are big, flat, white and relatively quick to cook (about 50 minutes of simmering), although they do need overnight soaking. An amount of 500 g uncooked beans will give you 7–8 cups of cooked beans.

Canned butter beans are convenient and inexpensive, and unlike our local haricot beans, are not flavoured with tomato sauce. This is a real bonus and increases their versatility in both salads and cooked dishes.

> **CLEANING PULSES**
>
> There are usually stones and other bits and pieces lurking in beans, lentils and chickpeas. They are awful to bite on when you are eating. Little rocks in chickpeas are usually easy to see and remove (pick over) before cooking, but put on your spectacles in the case of lentils and beans. When a pulse needs to be soaked, always discard anything that rises to the top.

MUSHROOM AND LENTIL MOUSSAKA

As with all moussakas, this dish takes time to prepare, but makes a delicious and nourishing meal served with a crisp salad and hot garlic bread. The dish reheats very well. If doing ahead, bake for 30 minutes at 180 °C and remove. Reheat at 160 °C for 30 minutes.

**600 g brinjals
sunflower oil for frying
250 ml brown lentils, picked over and rinsed
25 ml olive oil
1 large onion, chopped
1 green pepper, seeded and diced
2 cloves garlic, crushed
250 g brown mushrooms, wiped and sliced
400 g tomatoes, skinned and chopped
10 ml brown sugar
2 ml ground cinnamon
1 bay leaf
2 ml sea salt
100 ml chopped parsley**

**TOPPING
50 ml butter
50 ml brown flour
500 ml milk (full-cream or half skimmed and half full-cream)
2 eggs, separated
sea salt and milled black pepper to taste
2 ml freshly grated nutmeg
375 ml grated Cheddar cheese**

Cut stem ends off brinjals, slice into 5-mm thick rings, then dégorge. Fry on both sides until lightly browned and soft. If fried on a fairly low heat in a heavy-based pan and half-covered every now and then, much less oil will be absorbed.

Meanwhile, boil lentils in 500 ml salted water for 50 minutes or until soft and the water is absorbed.

In a large frying pan, heat the olive oil and soften the onion, green pepper and garlic. Add the mushrooms and when softened, add the tomatoes, sugar, cinnamon, bay leaf, salt and parsley. Cover and simmer for 20 minutes, stirring occasionally. Remove the bay leaf and stir in the cooked lentils. The mixture should be moist and fairly thick.

Make topping by melting the butter, then stirring in the flour. Cook for 1 minute, remove from heat and slowly stir in the milk. Return to stove and cook, stirring, until thickened. Beat the egg yolks with a little hot sauce and then mix in with the sauce, using a balloon whisk. Season with salt, pepper and nutmeg. Stiffly whisk the egg whites and fold in.

To assemble, cover the base of a 20 cm x 30 cm baking dish with half the brinjal slices, then spoon the lentil mixture over. Cover with the remaining brinjal slices, then pour the topping over. Sprinkle with grated Cheddar cheese and bake at 180 °C for 30 minutes, then switch off the oven and leave for 15 minutes to settle.
Serves 6.

> **LENTILS**
>
> Lentils are great to use in cooking. High in B vitamins, iron and protein, and low in fat, they are also incredibly versatile. Green lentils are the large ones obtainable at wholefood shops, and have several advantages over the brown or black varieties: they are bigger and keep their shape well; they can be used for sprouting; and they contain fewer gritty little particles which are so nasty to bite on. Brown and black are interchangeable, and good for casseroles, while red lentils quickly cook to a mush and are nice in soup. I seldom soak lentils as they'll soften within an hour, at most, at a slow simmer.
>
> To cook lentils, pick over carefully and rinse, and place in a saucepan with twice the amount of water, and a little salt. Bring to the boil, then cover and simmer until liquid is absorbed.
>
> Use in salads, loaves, patties, casseroles, curries, or mixed with rice as a complementary protein (see box on page 53).

SPICY LENTIL AND MUSHROOM STEW

A dish with an intriguing flavour; no one ever seems able to guess what all the ingredients are. Economical, easily prepared and excellent served on brown rice or pasta. Serve with additional coconut, chutney and a bowl of yoghurt with cucumber and chopped fresh coriander.

**60 ml sunflower oil
1 large onion, chopped
2 leeks, sliced
2 cloves garlic, crushed
1 green pepper, seeded and diced
15 ml curry powder
5 ml ground coriander
2 sticks cinnamon
4 whole cloves
250 g brown mushrooms, wiped and chopped
2–3 carrots, julienned
375 ml brown lentils, picked over and rinsed
1 litre vegetable stock or water
25 ml tomato paste
10 ml sea salt
5 ml honey
60 ml each desiccated coconut and cultured sour cream (optional)
6 hard-boiled eggs, quartered**

Heat oil in a large pan. Add onion, leeks, garlic and green pepper and stir-fry over medium heat until softening. Add all the spices and toss for a minute or two. Add mushrooms and carrots and toss until combined with vegetables and spices. Add lentils, stock or water, tomato paste, salt and honey. Bring to the boil, then cover and simmer on lowest heat for about 1 hour, stirring occasionally. At end of cooking period lentils should be soft and most of liquid absorbed. If possible, leave to cool in suitable container. To reheat, remove cinnamon and cloves, if you can find them, and add a little more water, as the mixture absorbs excess liquid on standing and although the stew should not be watery it should not be too thick or dry either. Stir in coconut and swirl in cream, if using, and reheat gently. Pile onto warmed serving platter and surround with eggs.
Serves 6–8.

Overleaf: Lentil Dahl with Eggs and Masala Sauce (p. 60) and Vegetarian Bobotie (p. 69), served with atjar, chopped tomato, onion and green pepper, and poppadans.

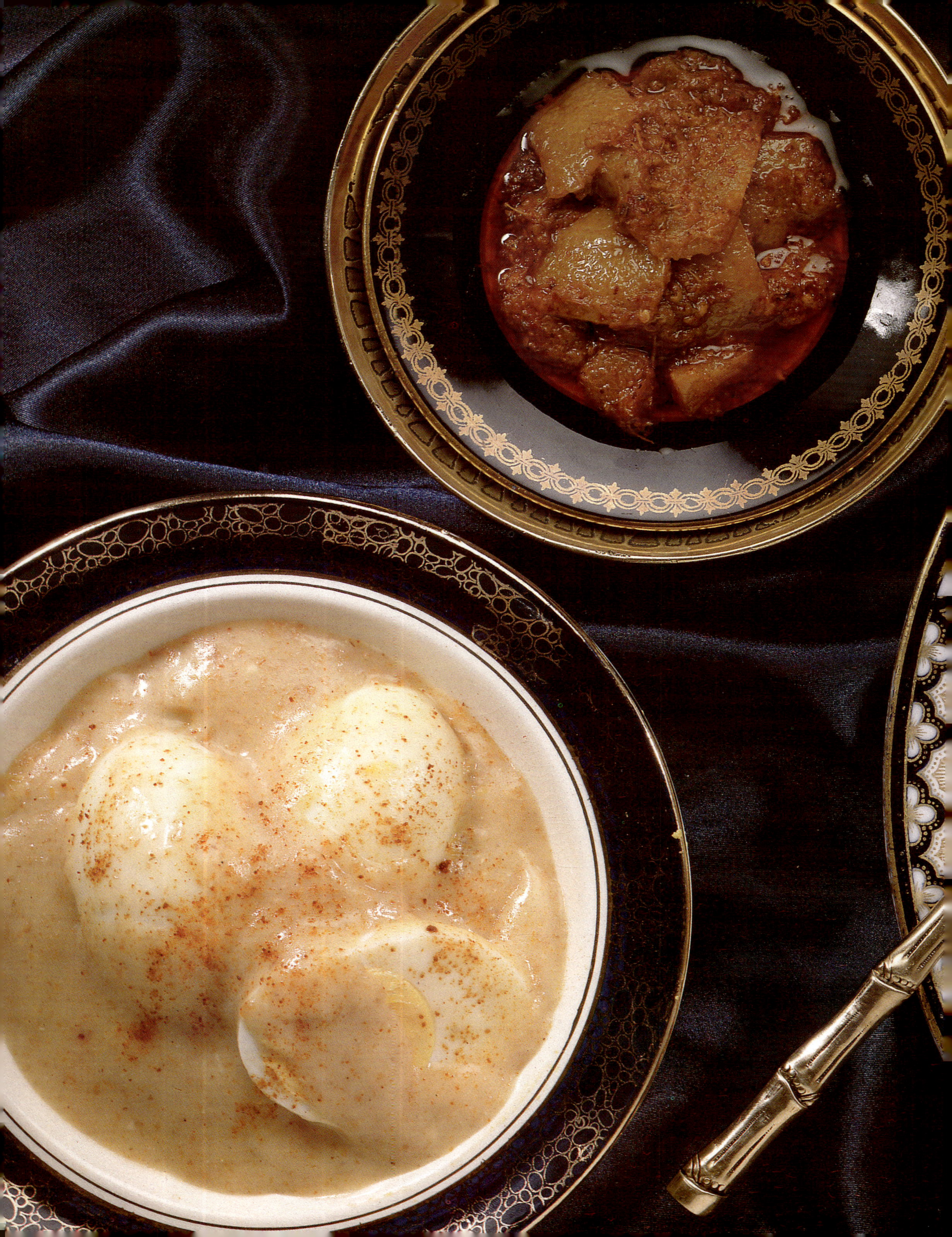

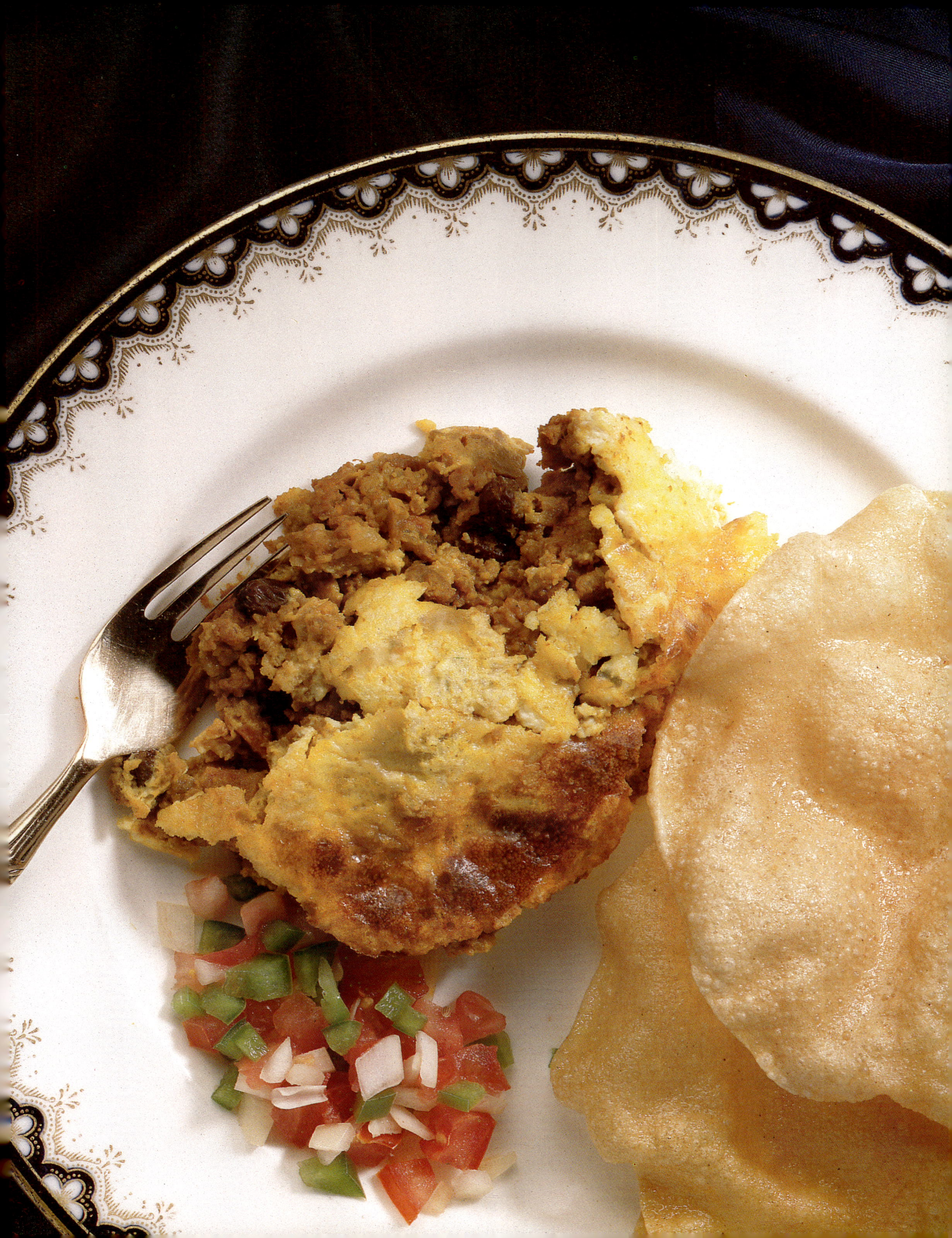

LENTIL DAHL WITH EGGS AND MASALA SAUCE

This is a bright and beautiful dish, consisting of a spicy purée of red lentils, topped with hard-boiled eggs and a sauce lightly spiked with masala. When baked, it looks rather like a humpy, golden brown soufflé. Serve with Basmati or brown rice, bowls of coconut and chutney and a crisp green salad. If you have rocket in your herb patch, chop in a few leaves for an interesting flavour. The dish may be assembled in advance and quantities can easily be doubled.

375 ml red lentils, picked over and rinsed
1 onion, finely chopped
2 cloves garlic, crushed
5 ml each turmeric and ground cumin
10 ml ground coriander
1 stick cinnamon
2 bay leaves
3 whole cloves
5 ml sea salt
6 eggs, hard-boiled and halved
paprika

SAUCE
15 ml sunflower oil
10 ml butter
1 onion, finely chopped
50 ml brown flour
5 ml leaf masala (or more to taste)
250 ml vegetable stock or water
250 ml milk
25 ml chutney
5 ml fresh lemon juice
2 ml sea salt

Put lentils, onion, garlic, spices, salt and 750 ml water into a saucepan. Stir to mix, bring to the boil, then cover and simmer on lowest heat for 20 minutes, stirring once. Red lentils soften quickly, and when done, the mixture will be mushy and moist. Remove cinnamon, bay leaves and cloves, if you can find them, and spread evenly into a lightly oiled baking dish — a deep, 23-cm pie dish is just right.

Make the sauce: heat sunflower oil and butter in a heavy-based saucepan and braise onion. Stir in flour and masala and cook gently for about 2 minutes. Slowly add the stock or water and milk, stirring until thickened. Add the chutney, lemon juice and sea salt. Half-cover the pan and simmer the sauce on low heat for about 20 minutes, stirring occasionally.

Arrange eggs, rounded sides up, on top of lentil mixture. Strain sauce through a fine sieve and pour over — it will coat the eggs and it should cover the lentil mixture completely. Dust with paprika. If working ahead, set aside at this stage. Bake at 160 °C for about 40 minutes or until just bubbling. Serves 4.

SHERRY

Cheap and sweet is fine to use in cooking. A touch of sweetness brings out the flavour in savoury foods, and it is especially useful in reducing the saltiness of soy sauce.

SPICY STOVE-TOP BEANS

An economical and easily prepared meal, using basic ingredients and canned beans. The result is a thick, bright and flavoursome stew to serve on rice. Serve with bowls of chutney, coconut and sliced bananas or a cucumber raita.

30 ml sunflower oil
1 large onion, chopped
1–2 cloves garlic, crushed
1 large green pepper, seeded and diced
5–10 ml curry powder
5 ml ground coriander
2 ml each ground fennel and cumin
2 sticks cinnamon
2 bay leaves
2 x 425 g cans choice grade baked beans in tomato, undrained
1 Golden Delicious apple, peeled and finely diced
60 ml seedless raisins or sultanas
25 ml chutney
20 ml fresh lemon juice
at least 125 ml water

Heat the sunflower oil and sauté the onion, garlic and green pepper. Add the spices and toss over low heat for 2 minutes, then add the remaining ingredients. Mix well, then bring to the boil, cover, and simmer very gently for 30 minutes, stirring occasionally to prevent sticking, and adding more water if mixture becomes too thick. When stirring, take care not to mash beans. Check seasoning, remove bay leaves and cinnamon sticks, and serve as suggested.
Serves 6

SPICED LENTILS AND MUSHROOMS WITH CORIANDER

Fresh coriander puts the finishing touch to this simple but super dish. Serve on brown rice with chutney, a green salad and a loaf of hot garlic bread. On special occasions, fork a nut of butter and some toasted almond strips into the rice.

250 ml lentils (green or brown), picked over and rinsed
60 ml sunflower oil
1 large onion, chopped
2 cloves garlic, crushed
5 ml each ground cumin, coriander, fennel and turmeric
250 g brown mushrooms, wiped and sliced
250 g baby marrows, pared and sliced
2 sticks table celery, sliced
100 ml chopped parsley
500 ml vegetable or Marmite stock
5 ml sea salt and milled black pepper to taste
desiccated coconut and fresh coriander leaves, chopped, for topping

Cook lentils in 500 ml salted water until soft and dry — for about 50 minutes.

Heat oil and soften onion and garlic. Add spices and toss for 1–2 minutes on low heat. Add mushrooms, marrows, celery and parsley and toss until coated, then add stock and seasonings. Cover and simmer gently until vegetables are cooked — for about 20 minutes. Add cooked lentils — you should have 750 ml. Mix in carefully then simmer until mixture is hot and thick — it should be juicy and moist, not watery, but if it needs reduction, simply leave the lid off for a few minutes. Spoon into a heated serving dish and sprinkle with coconut and coriander.
Serves 6.

VEGETABLE OR MARMITE STOCK

Cubes are expensive and not readily available, and home-made is excellent, but time-consuming to make. Marmite stock can often be substituted very successfully, and it is suitable for vegetarian cooking as it does not contain any animal ingredients. Use about 5 ml Marmite to 250 ml boiling water.

LENTIL AND VEGETABLE MOUSSAKA

Similar to Mushroom and Lentil Moussaka on page 57, but somewhat more Greek in character, this recipe uses baby marrows and herbs instead of mushrooms and introduces a different way of preparing the brinjals. Grilled, instead of fried, they absorb far less oil and this method may be used for most other brinjal dishes. Serve this moussaka with a garlic loaf and spinach salad.

50 ml sunflower oil (preferably half olive)
1 large onion, chopped
2 cloves garlic, crushed
8 small baby marrows (about 200 g), pared and sliced
1 red or yellow pepper, seeded and sliced
4 large, juicy tomatoes, skinned and chopped or 1 x 400 g can, chopped
375 ml brown or green lentils, picked over and rinsed
100 ml chopped parsley
5 ml sea salt and milled black pepper to taste
10 ml brown sugar
2 ml each dried basil, thyme and origanum
750 g brinjals, sliced and dégorged
half olive, half sunflower oil for grilling brinjals

SAUCE
40 ml sunflower oil and a nut of butter
50 ml brown flour
500 ml milk (full-cream or low-fat)
sea salt and milled black pepper to taste
1 ml grated nutmeg
375 ml finely grated Cheddar or low-fat cheese
2 egg yolks, beaten
4 egg whites, stiffly whisked

25 ml grated Parmesan cheese for topping

Heat the 50 ml sunflower oil and lightly fry the onion. Add garlic, marrows and pepper and allow to soften over medium heat. Add the tomatoes (plus juice if using a can), lentils, parsley, 750 ml water, seasoning, sugar and dried herbs. Bring to the boil, and cover and simmer very gently for about 1 hour, stirring occasionally. The lentils should be soft, and the vegetable mixture thick and juicy.

Grill brinjals while vegetables are cooking. First rinse them, then pat very dry. I find this is most easily done by spinning the slices in a salad spinner and then patting dry with paper towels. Cover one very large or two medium biscuit trays with a fairly thin layer of oil — preferably half olive and half sunflower. Arrange brinjal slices in single layer, turning once to coat, and then grill about 15 cm below griller until brown, turning once. Contrary to expectations, they will not scorch as the juices are soon extracted and they will soften at the same time as browning.

Make sauce just before assembling. Heat oil and butter. Add flour and cook, stirring until nut-brown. Slowly stir in milk and when thickened, remove from stove and add seasoning and 200 ml of the cheese. Pour a little of the hot sauce onto yolks, mix and then stir into rest of sauce. Pour into bowl and fold in stiffly whisked whites.*

To assemble, cover base of a 30 cm x 20 cm baking dish with half the brinjals. Top with half the lentil mixture. Sprinkle with the remaining 175 ml cheese. Cover with the rest of the brinjals and spoon over the rest of the lentil mixture, spreading evenly. Spoon the fluffy white sauce over the top, sprinkle with Parmesan and bake at 180 °C for about 45 minutes until golden brown and puffy.
Serves 8.

* As with all moussakas, this dish takes a while to prepare. However, if you wish, it may all be done in advance. In this case, make the cheese sauce, but do not add the egg whites. Refrigerate the sauce, then fold in the whisked egg whites just before using.

SPICES

When frying spices, for a curry, for example, keep the heat low to prevent scorching, but do allow enough time for the flavours to be released or the finished dish won't taste as it should. With experience, your nose will tell you when you can start adding the rest of the ingredients.

The best curry powders are those that are home-made and fresh and are made up of ground spices in varying quantities. I don't like chillies (you will doubtless notice their omission), but if you like hot dishes, add ground chillies or chilli powder to taste, or a masala which contains chillies and/or black peppercorns.

PARSLEY

'Parsley is gharsley,' wrote Ogden Nash. Nevertheless, I use it liberally; it adds colour, flavour and vitamin C to a dish. However, it does have quite a strong flavour and so, unless used in a cooked dish, remember that less is better than more. For convenience, wash a whole bunch, dry thoroughly in a salad spinner, and store, unchopped, in the fridge.

LENTIL AND BRINJAL CURRY

A simple, spicy stove-top dish which is extremely economical, but for the almonds. Pass chutney, coconut and a green salad.

50 ml sunflower oil
1 large onion, chopped
2 cloves garlic, crushed
10–15 ml curry powder
2 ml each ground cumin, turmeric and cinnamon
5 ml each ground fennel and coriander
375 ml brown lentils, picked over and rinsed
350 g brinjals, cubed and dégorged
750 ml vegetable stock or water
125 ml chopped parsley
5 ml sea salt
7 ml brown sugar
1 x 410 g can Tomato-And-Onion Mix*
toasted almond strips

Heat oil in large saucepan, add onion and fry lightly. Add garlic and all the spices and stir over low heat for a minute or two. Add rest of ingredients, except almonds. Stir to mix, then cover and simmer gently for 50 minutes to 1 hour, stirring occasionally. Add extra liquid now and then to ensure a good sauce — the mixture should not become too thick or dry. When done, remove from heat and allow to cool in suitable container, if time allows, for flavours to blend. Reheat gently until piping hot, and serve on brown rice or pasta. Top each serving with toasted almonds, for a delicious flavour and crunch.
Serves 6.

* Look for the brand without artificial flavouring or colouring.

BREYANI

This version is layered with hard-boiled eggs instead of vegetables. (See page 48 for a breyani recipe with vegetables.) Once again, the spicy flavour is very subtle because this is my preference, but if you like stronger flavours, increase the quantities of spices. It may be assembled in advance and baked when wanted and is a most delicious and economical meal. Serve with bowls of chutney, coconut, sliced bananas, thick yoghurt and a tomato and onion salad. This dish is even good served cold as a spicy salad.

250 ml brown rice
5 ml turmeric
250 ml brown or green lentils, picked over and rinsed
vegetable stock or water
50 ml sunflower oil
2 large onions, sliced into thin rings
2 cloves garlic, crushed
2 fat sticks cinnamon
4 whole cloves
5 ml each ground fennel, cumin and coriander
6 eggs, hard-boiled and sliced into rings
30–50 ml butter, slivered

GARNISH
15 ml sunflower oil
2 ml masala for breyani (more if you like it hot)
100 ml slivered almonds
100 ml seedless raisins

Parboil the rice in 550 ml salted water with turmeric for 30 minutes. Parboil the lentils in 500 ml salted water. In both cases, cook over lowest heat. (The cooking process will be completed in the oven.) Drain both in a colander over a bowl and make up liquid to 500 ml with vegetable stock or water.

Heat the sunflower oil in a large pan and lightly fry the onions and garlic over medium heat until glossy and golden. Add all the spices and toss together for a few minutes until smelling delicious.

Mix together the rice, lentils and onion mixture, and spoon one third onto base of oiled baking dish — a deep pie dish, diameter 23 cm, is just right. Arrange half the eggs on top. Cover with another third of rice mixture, the remaining eggs and, finally, the last of the rice mixture, making sure that no cloves or cinnamon sticks lie on the top. Pour reserved liquid round the sides and dot the top with slivers of butter. If necessary, cover and set aside now. Bake, tightly covered, at 160 °C on middle shelf of oven for 50 minutes.

Meanwhile, prepare garnish by heating oil in a small pan. Keeping heat very low, add masala, almonds and raisins and toss until almonds are lightly browned and raisins plumped. Sprinkle over breyani before serving.
Serves 6.

LENTIL AND TOMATO STEW

Believe me, this easy and low-cost dish is much tastier than it sounds. It may be served on rice and sprinkled with grated cheese, or spooned into a large pie dish, covered with mashed potato and cheese and heated under the grill. Serve with a green vegetable or salad.

375 ml brown lentils, picked over and rinsed
5 ml sea salt
50 ml sunflower oil
1 large onion, chopped
2 cloves garlic, crushed
3 medium carrots, diced
1 green pepper, seeded and diced
100 ml chopped parsley
2 ml dried origanum
400 g juicy tomatoes, skinned and chopped
25 ml tomato paste
10 ml light brown sugar
5 ml sea salt and milled black pepper to taste
125 ml Marmite stock (see box on page 60)

Put lentils into a saucepan with 750 ml water and 5 ml salt, bring to the boil, cover and simmer for about 50 minutes until soft and liquid is absorbed.

Meanwhile, heat the sunflower oil in a large saucepan and sauté the onion, garlic, carrots and green pepper. When softening, add all the remaining ingredients, except the cooked lentils, stir to mix, then cover and simmer gently for 20–30 minutes, stirring occasionally to mash the tomatoes.

Stir in the cooked lentils and leave on low heat for 5–10 minutes, stirring once or twice. The mixture should be moist and juicy, so a low heat throughout is important. If a little thickening is necessary, you could stir in some toasted wheatgerm for extra nourishment, or do it the conventional way with a beurre manié. (See box on page 53.)

Serve as suggested
Serves 5–6.

SOYA BEAN CURRY

This is one of the nicest bean dishes and an excellent introduction to soya beans for those not familiar with them. Served on brown rice, it also makes an incredibly low-cost meal. On the side, apart from the usual sambals such as chutney and sliced bananas, I like to serve a cabbage slaw tossed with plenty of coconut — it complements the curried beans perfectly. Also good is slivered avocado pear sprinkled with toasted sesame seeds. Allow sufficient time when making for the sauce to be cooled down and reheated for the full flavour to develop.

60 ml sunflower oil
2 onions, chopped
10–15 ml curry powder
2 ml turmeric
5 ml each ground cinnamon, cumin and fennel
1 knob root ginger, peeled and grated
2 cloves garlic, crushed
2 eating apples, such as Star King, peeled and finely diced
2 large tomatoes, skinned and chopped
2 carrots, diced
2 sticks table celery, sliced, plus some leaves
100 ml chopped parsley
5 ml sea salt
20 ml fresh lemon juice
10 ml honey
2 bay leaves
750 ml cooked soya beans
100 ml seedless raisins
± 650 ml vegetable stock or water

Heat the sunflower oil in a large saucepan and fry the onions lightly. Add curry powder, all the spices, root ginger and garlic and stir briefly over low heat. Add all the remaining ingredients, mix well, bring to the boil, then cover and simmer very gently for about 25 minutes, stirring occasionally and adding a little extra water if necessary to keep mixture nice and moist. If working ahead, turn the curry into a fridge container, cool and chill.

Reheat gently before serving. Check the seasoning and remove the bay leaves.

Serve as suggested.
Serves 6.

Spicy Two-Bean Stew (p. 68) and Ratatouille with Haricots (p. 68).

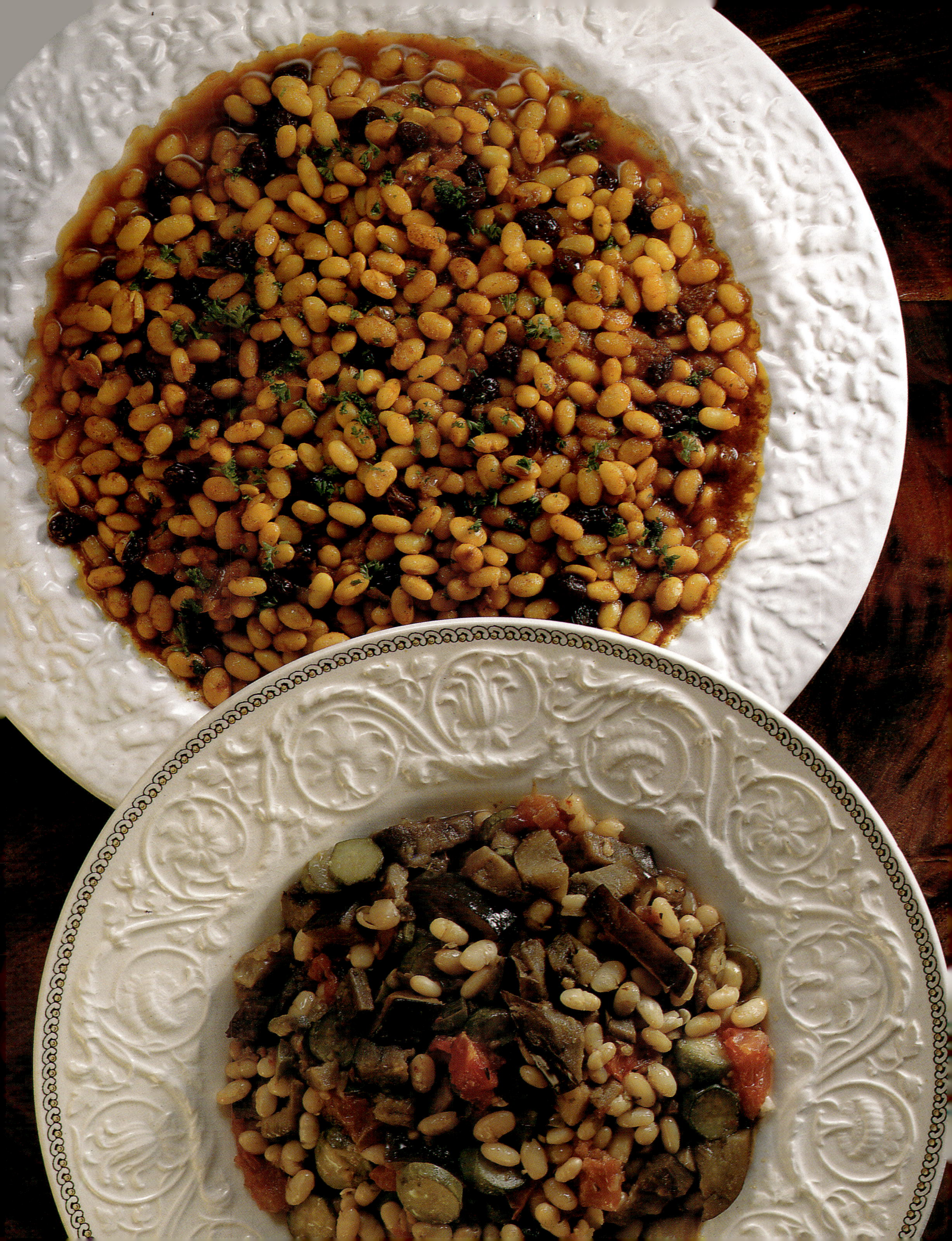

SPICY LENTIL CURRY

A surprisingly delicious curry. Serve on rice with sambals and a tomato and onion salad.

25 ml each sunflower oil and butter
2 large onions, sliced
1 green pepper, seeded and diced
2 cloves garlic, crushed
2 sticks table celery, thinly sliced
3 carrots, coarsely grated
10 ml curry powder
5 ml each ground cumin, turmeric and ground fennel (barishap*)
375 brown lentils, picked over and rinsed
1 bay leaf
100 ml chopped parsley
5 ml sea salt
10 ml brown sugar
175 ml tomato purée
a few spoons of sour cream
snipped chives and/or chopped cashew nuts for topping

Heat oil and butter and sauté onions, green pepper, garlic, celery and carrots. When softened, add spices and stir over low heat for a few minutes.

Add lentils, 750 ml water, bay leaf, parsley, salt, sugar and tomato purée. Mix well and spoon into a large baking dish. Bake, covered, at 180 °C for about 1 hour, or until lentils are soft, stirring once or twice. Remove from oven and streak in a few spoons of sour cream, sprinkle with chives and/or cashews and warm through for another 5 minutes before serving.
Serves 6.

* Available at speciality stores.

SAUCEPANS

Dishes like curries and other spicy mixtures are often best made in advance and left to stand for the flavours to develop before re-heating. As these dishes usually contain an acidic ingredient, like tomatoes, wine or chutney, they should not be left in the saucepan to cool, especially an aluminium or other metallic saucepan, which will react with acid. In any case, if you are still using aluminium cookware, perhaps it is time to invest in good quality, heavy stainless steel saucepans or baked enamelware.

HARICOT BEANS

Soak overnight in plenty of cold water. Drain, rinse and place in saucepan. Cover with water and simmer until soft, adding salt after 30 minutes. An alternative method is to bring the beans to the boil in a generous quantity of water, and then leave to soak for 2 hours. Drain and rinse, cover with fresh water, and boil until soft.

500 g uncooked haricot beans makes 7–8 cups when cooked.

HARICOT BEAN AND PUMPKIN CASSEROLE

This is a good choice for a simple but nourishing family meal. Serve with brown rice and creamed spinach spiced with nutmeg.

250 g haricot beans
50 ml sunflower oil
1 large onion, chopped
2 cloves garlic, crushed
500 g peeled, firm orange pumpkin
2 bay leaves
2 ml ground cinnamon
5 ml each ground coriander and ginger
15 ml honey
7–10 ml sea salt
125 ml chopped parsley
1 x 400 g can tomatoes, drained and chopped, juice reserved

TOPPING
125 ml fine, fresh wholewheat breadcrumbs
125 ml finely grated, strong Cheddar cheese
25 ml toasted sesame seeds

Soak beans overnight. Drain and rinse.

Heat oil in a large saucepan and fry onion and garlic. Add beans and 500 ml water. Bring to the boil, reduce heat, cover and simmer for 20 minutes. Cut pumpkin into dice-sized cubes and add, together with bay leaves, spices, honey, salt, parsley and tomatoes. Cover and simmer for about 50 minutes or until beans are tender, stirring occasionally.

If vegetables have not cooked to a pulp at end of cooking time, mash gently with a wooden spoon to make a thick sauce, taking care not to break up the beans.

Check seasoning and, if necessary, add the reserved tomato juice to ensure a moist mixture. Remove the bay leaves and spoon the mixture into a 30 cm x 20 cm baking dish. If working ahead, set the casserole aside at this stage.

Just before baking, mix all the ingredients for the topping and sprinkle over the casserole. Bake, uncovered, at 180 °C for about 30 minutes, until hot and bubbling. Serve as suggested.
Serves 6.

LENTILS AND BRINJALS IN BARBECUE SAUCE

A thick, savoury stew, which is delicious served on pasta or brown rice, topped with crumbled feta or grated Cheddar or Parmesan cheese. A lettuce and avocado salad tossed with French dressing is a good accompaniment, with crusty rolls an optional extra.

250 ml brown lentils, picked over and rinsed
50 ml sunflower oil
300 g young brinjals, cubed or 1 medium brinjal, cubed and dégorged
1 large onion, chopped
2 cloves garlic, crushed
1 small green or red pepper, seeded and diced
4 baby marrows (200 g), scrubbed and sliced
250 ml tomato purée
15 ml honey
25 ml soy sauce
100 ml chopped parsley
250 ml water
5 ml dried basil

Boil lentils gently in 500 ml salted water for about 50 minutes until soft.

Meanwhile, heat the sunflower oil in a large pan and add the brinjals, onion, garlic, pepper and baby marrows. Toss over low heat for 5 minutes.

Add the remaining ingredients, except the cooked lentils, cover and simmer gently for 30 minutes.

Add cooked lentils and, if necessary, another 125 ml water, or enough to make a good sauce. Simmer very gently for another 15 minutes.

Adjust seasoning — it may need a pinch of sea salt or a little sugar — and serve as suggested above.
Serves 4.

LENTIL AND POTATO PIE

Brown lentils are a good source of plant protein and if you like their distinctive, rather earthy flavour, you'll enjoy this pie, in which they're baked between layers of sliced potatoes and onions and topped with cheese. This simple dish is one of our favourite vegetarian meals, especially when accompanied with buttered cabbage and baked pumpkin.

375 ml brown lentils, picked over and rinsed
800 g potatoes, thinly sliced
2 large onions, thinly sliced
salt and milled black pepper to taste
750 ml hot stock or 10 ml Marmite in 750 ml hot water
grated Cheddar cheese for topping
butter for topping
paprika for topping

Cover lentils with water and leave to soak for about 2 hours. Grease a deep 23-cm pie dish and cover the base with half the potatoes and onions. Season lightly. Top with drained lentils, spreading evenly. Cover with remaining onions and potatoes, and season lightly again. Pour hot stock over the mixture, cover with greased foil, shiny side up (or with a lid) and bake at 180 °C for 1 hour.

Remove cover and sprinkle thickly with cheese, dot with butter and dust with paprika. Bake, uncovered, for a further 20 minutes, by which time potatoes and lentils should be soft, liquid absorbed and cheese melted and bubbling.
Serves 6–8.

SPLIT PEAS

They are usually reserved for soups, which is a pity. Green split peas are tasty, nutritious, and — presto! — do not need pre-soaking. They will, in fact, cook to a mush in about 30 minutes. (Use 250 ml rinsed peas to 750 ml water.) I even do them in the oven, if it is already on. Use the same quantities as when you are boiling them, and cover the baking dish. When soft, they can be puréed and served instead of mashed potatoes or creamed with mint and butter. This is an economical and neglected pulse.

NUTS AND SUNFLOWER SEEDS

Nuts are expensive but indispensable in any kitchen. I buy them in bulk and keep them in the freezer. Chopping in a food processor makes them go further. Use the grinding blade and be careful not to reduce them to powder. Toasting brings out the flavour. Spread the chopped nuts on baking trays and place them in a moderate oven until they are golden brown.

Sunflower seeds are much cheaper, rich in protein, vitamins and minerals, and can often be substituted for nuts. As they are often somewhat dusty, rinse them well in a colander first and then dry them out in a low oven, spread on baking trays. This is a nuisance as they take a while to dry, but dry they must or you cannot store them. For convenience, do a jumbo batch at a time and remember that their flavour is even better if they are slightly toasted.

CASSEROLE OF LENTILS AND RICE WITH PIZZA TOPPING

Serve with creamy mashed potatoes, cinnamon-baked pumpkin and a salad.

250 ml brown lentils, picked over and rinsed
125 ml brown rice
25 ml sunflower oil
10 ml butter
2 medium onions, finely chopped
2 green or red peppers, seeded and diced
100 ml chopped parsley
125 ml fresh wholewheat breadcrumbs
2 eggs
125 ml buttermilk
sea salt and milled black pepper to taste
3–4 firm tomatoes, thinly sliced
grated mozzarella or Cheddar cheese
grated Parmesan cheese
2 ml dried origanum
1 ml dried basil
35 ml olive oil

Simmer lentils in 500 ml salted water for about 50 minutes or until soft. Cook rice in 300 ml salted water for about 45 minutes.

Heat oil and butter and sauté onions and peppers. Spoon lentils and rice into a large bowl and add cooked onions and peppers, parsley and breadcrumbs. Beat eggs with buttermilk and add to lentil and rice mixture together with seasoning. Mix well, without mashing, and spoon into a deep, buttered 23-cm pie dish.

Level top and cover with layers of tomatoes, plenty of grated mozzarella or Cheddar, and a sprinkling of Parmesan. Sprinkle herbs over cheese and drizzle with oil. Bake at 180 °C for about 25 minutes, until bubbling and cheese has melted.
Serves 6.

POT BEANS

This is a hot and savoury version of the popular fasoulia. Economical, easy to prepare and remarkably good served on brown rice with a green salad.

500 g haricot beans
100 ml sunflower oil
2 large onions, chopped
5 ml each dried thyme and origanum
1 x 115 g can tomato paste
4 cloves garlic, crushed
2 bay leaves
15 ml honey
salt and milled black pepper to taste
vegetable stock or water
1 bunch spinach, shredded (optional)
125 ml chopped parsley
soy sauce to taste
grated Cheddar cheese for topping (optional)

Soak beans overnight, then drain and rinse.

Heat oil in a large saucepan and add onions. When softened, add beans and toss over medium heat for 5 minutes. Add herbs, tomato paste, garlic, bay leaves, honey and seasoning. Add enough stock or water to cover, then cover saucepan and simmer gently for 1 hour 30 minutes, or until beans are soft and liquid is thick and reduced. Add spinach, if using, and parsley. Cover and simmer for another 30 minutes. To serve, add soy sauce to taste, then spoon over servings of rice and top with grated cheese.
Serves 6–8.

Overleaf: Chickpea and Tomato Curry (p. 68) and Soya Bean Curry (p. 62), served with chutney, chopped tomato and onion, sliced bananas in yoghurt, atjar and rotis.

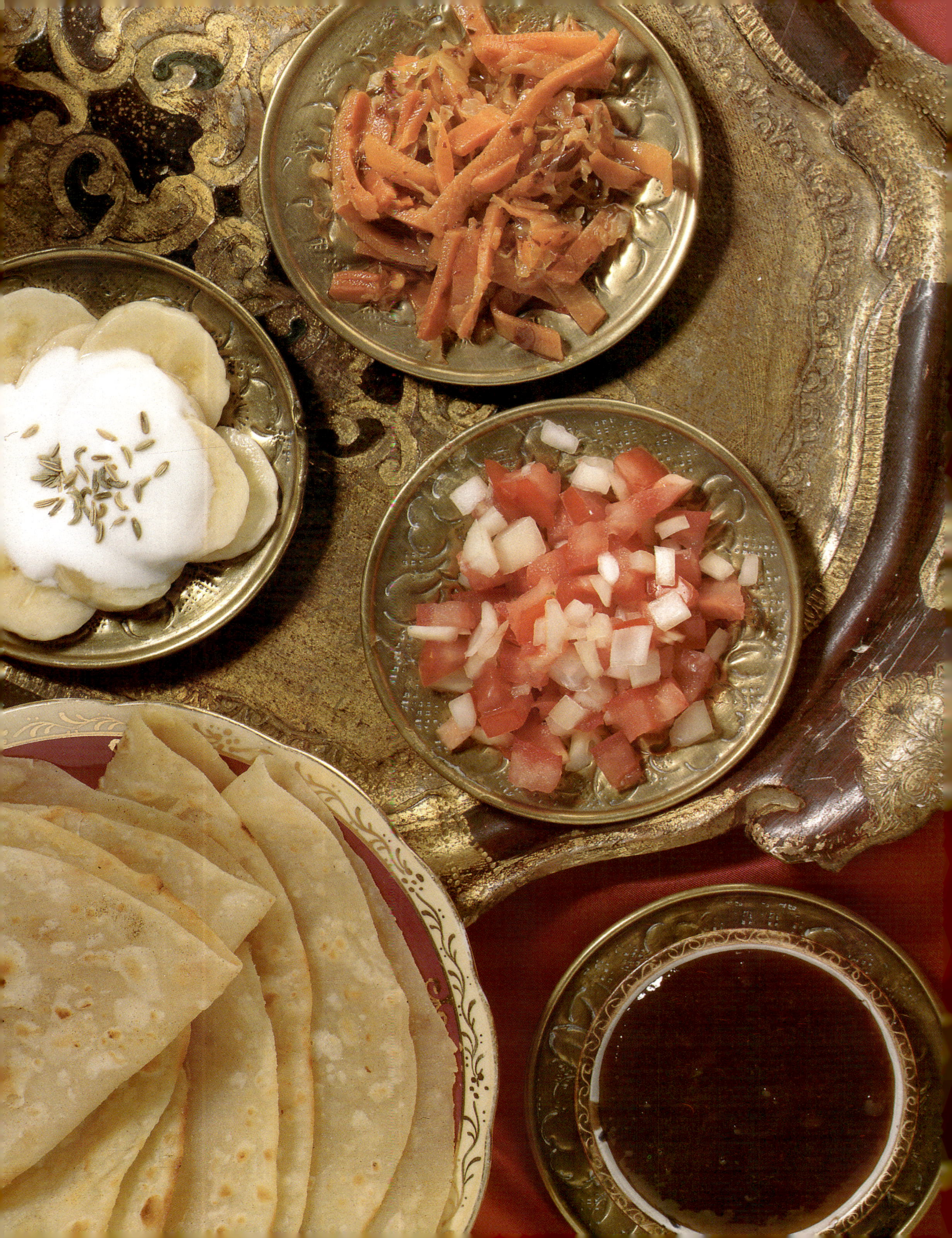

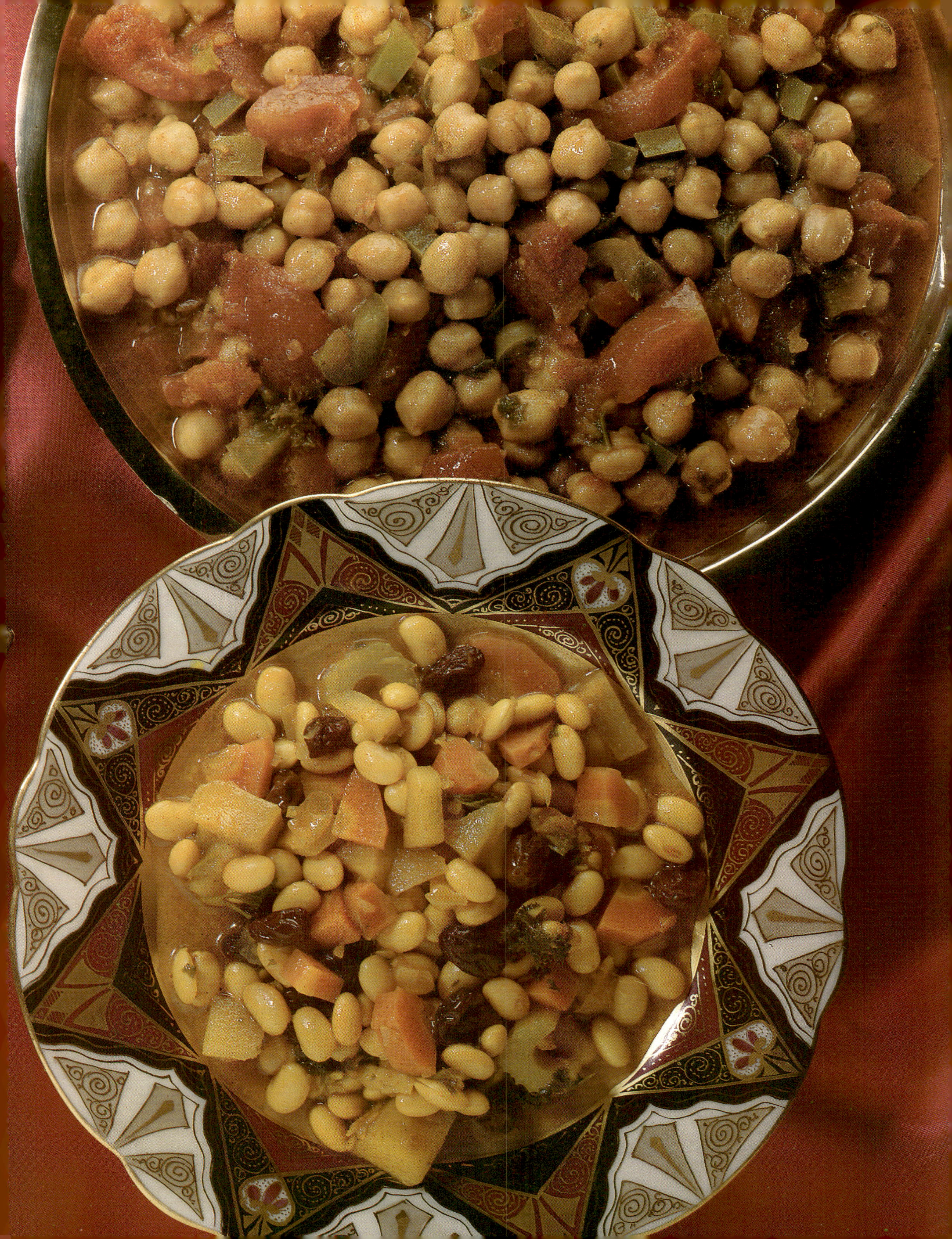

RATATOUILLE WITH HARICOTS

Here, traditional ratatouille — the delicious vegetable concoction from France — becomes an equally good vegetarian meal-in-a-dish with the addition of beans. The result is an aromatic, attractive and very economical dish. Serve on brown rice, sprinkled with grated cheese; a creamy cabbage and carrot slaw makes a good accompaniment. The dish reheats well.

**25 ml each sunflower and olive oil
2 large onions, chopped
2 cloves garlic, crushed
1 green pepper, seeded and diced
500 g brinjals, cubed and dégorged
500 g baby marrows, pared and sliced
5 ml sea salt and milled black pepper to taste
2 bay leaves
5 ml dried origanum
5 ml light brown sugar
500 g juicy tomatoes, skinned and chopped
750 ml cooked haricot or soya beans
chopped parsley for garnish**

Heat oils in a large saucepan and add onions, garlic and green pepper. Cook very gently, without browning, for 10 minutes, shaking pan occasionally. When softened, add brinjals and marrows, seasoning, bay leaves, origanum and sugar. Mix well, then cover and leave to simmer slowly for about 20 minutes until not quite tender. Add tomatoes and beans. Mix well, then cover and simmer for another 20 minutes, or until everything is soft and juicy, adding just a little water if necessary. Never boil ratatouille to a mush — the vegetables should be identifiable. Remove bay leaves, check seasoning and sprinkle with parsley.
Serves 6.

SPICY TWO-BEAN STEW

This dish was created one evening when I unexpectedly had to feed some hungry vegetarians with little on hand but a few cups of left-over cooked beans. It has become a great favourite. It's easy, economical, delicious and very nourishing — and if you cook beans in bulk and freeze them, you can make it at almost a moment's notice. Serve on brown rice and pass bowls of coconut and chutney. A green salad should also accompany the meal, while thick yoghurt and sliced bananas are optional extras.

**100 ml sunflower oil
3 large onions, chopped
3 cloves garlic, crushed
10 ml each turmeric, ground cinnamon and curry powder
5 ml ground cumin
750 ml cooked soya beans
750 ml haricot beans
750 ml vegetable stock or water
50 ml tomato paste
2 bay leaves
10 ml each sea salt and light brown sugar
250 ml seedless raisins
50 ml chutney
parsley or chopped coriander leaves for garnish (optional)**

Heat oil in a large pan and soften onions and garlic. Add all the spices and allow to sizzle for a few minutes. Add remaining ingredients, except parsley or coriander, bring to the boil, then cover and simmer on lowest heat for about 45 minutes, stirring occasionally. By end of cooking period the sauce should be reduced, thick and flavoursome. Check seasoning and remove bay leaves. Sprinkle with parsley or coriander, if liked.
Serves 6–8.

CHICKPEA AND TOMATO CURRY

A mild, creamy curry, using basic ingredients; easy to prepare, and sure to become a favourite way of serving this protein-rich pulse. Serve on brown rice with chutney and a green salad.

**30 ml sunflower oil
1 large onion, finely chopped
2 cloves garlic, crushed
1 green pepper, seeded and diced
10 ml curry powder
5 ml each ground cinnamon and coriander
2 ml each turmeric and ground cumin
500 g juicy tomatoes, skinned and chopped
375 ml vegetable stock or water
15 ml tomato paste
5 ml sea salt
2 bay leaves
10 ml light brown sugar
750 ml cooked chickpeas
100 ml chopped parsley
50–60 ml desiccated coconut
50–60 ml cultured sour cream**

Heat oil, add onion, garlic and green pepper and allow to soften. Add all the spices and stir for a minute or two to release the flavours. Add remaining ingredients, except coconut and sour cream. Bring to the boil, then cover and simmer gently for about 25 minutes, stirring occasionally.

If time allows, transfer to suitable container and cool for flavour to develop, before reheating. The dish may also be refrigerated overnight.

Reheat over low heat, adding extra liquid as necessary for the sauce. Check seasoning, stir in coconut and when thoroughly heated, swirl in cream.
Serves 4–6.

SOYA BEANS

Like 'em or not, the fact remains that soya beans — possibly the world's oldest food crop — are a highly concentrated source of vegetable protein. Rich in oil, yet low in carbohydrates, they also contain lecithin and plenty of fibre, as well as calcium and iron. Soya protein contains all eight amino acids essential for human needs. Apart from oil and flour, the beans are also used to make textured vegetable protein (TVP).

Soak overnight in plenty of cold water. Drain and tip into a large bowl. Add plenty of fresh water and then rub beans between palms of hands to remove skins (unlike chickpeas, from which skins are removed after cooking). As skins float to the top, pour off water. Repeat this process several times. If only half the skins come off, don't worry as they will rise to the top when the cooking water starts to boil rapidly, so simply skim them off with the froth a few times. Rubbing off the skins is a step which is seldom specified, but I always do, as they don't look nice floating on top of a dish, and must surely be indigestible.

To cook, simmer soya beans in water for about 2½ hours, adding salt towards the end of cooking period. An amount of 500 g uncooked soya beans make 6 x 250 ml when cooked.

VEGETARIAN BOBOTIE

The following dish, based on my favourite recipe for traditional bobotie, is a good place to start experimenting with TVP, an economical and healthy source of protien. Serve with buttered rice, cinnamon-baked pumpkin, a green vegetable and extra chutney.

500 ml soya mince
10 ml Marmite, mixed with
750 ml boiling water
1 fairly thick slice crustless wholewheat bread
375 ml milk
50 ml sunflower oil
2 large onions, chopped
2 cloves garlic, crushed
25 ml curry powder
7 ml sea salt
25 ml chutney
15 ml smooth apricot jam
15 ml Worcestershire sauce
5 ml turmeric
15 ml brown vinegar
100 ml seedless raisins
100 ml chopped, toasted almonds
3 eggs
a big pinch each of salt and turmeric
100 ml desiccated coconut
bay leaves

Place soya mince in a bowl, pour Marmite stock over it and leave to hydrate for 15 minutes.

Soak the wholewheat bread in the milk, full-cream or half-and-half.

Heat the sunflower oil and lightly fry the onions and garlic. Add the curry powder and sizzle for a minute or two. Add the sea salt, chutney, jam, Worcestershire sauce, turmeric and vinegar and mix well.

Squeeze the soaked bread (reserve the milk) and add it to the pan together with the soya mince, which will be swollen, with almost all the liquid absorbed.

Add the raisins, almonds and 1 beaten egg and mix all the ingredients together.

Spoon the curry mixture into an oiled baking dish, no larger than 30 cm x 20 cm, spreading it evenly.

Beat the remaining 2 eggs with the reserved milk — you should not have less than 300 ml. Add a big pinch each of salt and turmeric, and the coconut. Pour evenly over the curry mixture, and top with a few bay leaves.

Stand the dish of bobotie in a large pan of water — like a roasting tin — and bake at 180 °C for 1 hour. Serve as suggested.
Makes 6 large servings.

TVP

Some people may query the sense in using this meat substitute (which does not taste anything like the real thing) in a vegetarian diet. But TVP (textured vegetable protein) or TSP (textured soya protein) is such a powerful, protein-rich food, and so economical, that it is worth experimenting with this soya bean product in home-made dishes. You're probably eating TVP anyway, without knowing it, tucked into all sorts of manufactured foods, such as an extender in meat products, to ensure freshness in biscuits, and so on. It is available as granules and chunks, which need to be re-hydrated before use, or in ready-made, frozen, vegetarian sausages or burgers.

VEGETARIAN BOLOGNAISE

Vegetarians who use soya mince to add protein to their diets should find this recipe useful. Although it looks just like the traditional meaty sauce so often served with pasta, the flavour and texture are totally different, and although TVP might not be everybody's cup of tea, it does make a singularly nourishing and economical meal. Apart from a crisp salad, a bowl of fried mushrooms seasoned with soy sauce makes a good but optional accompaniment.

500 ml soya mince
10 ml Marmite, mixed with
750 ml hot water
25 ml each sunflower oil and butter
2 large onions, chopped
2 cloves garlic, crushed
1 green pepper, seeded and diced
5 ml dried origanum
2 ml dried thyme
1 x 400 g can tomatoes, chopped, plus the juice
125 ml tomato purée
5 ml sea salt
10 ml light brown sugar
100 ml red wine
100 ml chopped parsley
50 ml grated Parmesan cheese

Place soya mince in a bowl, pour over Marmite stock and stand for 15 minutes. Heat oil and butter in a large frying pan and lightly fry onions, garlic and green pepper. Add herbs and toss until hot and aromatic. Add mince and remaining ingredients, except cheese. Bring to the boil, then cover and simmer very gently for 45 minutes, stirring occasionally. When done, the sauce should be thick and juicy.

Stir in the Parmesan, heat through and serve on pasta, brown rice or with mashed potatoes. If serving on pasta, serve extra Parmesan separately.
Makes 6 large servings.

TOFU WITH MUSHROOMS, ONIONS AND CHEESE

Tofu is a soya bean curd, widely used in Japanese cooking. It is bland in flavour, high in protein and low in fat and may be found in the fridges of wholefood shops. Once purchased, you should take it home, cover it with water and chill, as it goes off very quickly. It may be served in salads, soups and sauces, or in a casserole as in this recipe. As it is served here in the dish in which it was cooked, use a presentable frying pan or a serving dish which can be placed on top of the stove. Serve on brown rice, or rice mixed with cooked brown lentils in equal quantities and tossed with a little finely chopped parsley and a nut of butter, with an accompaniment of a fresh green salad or vegetables.

25 ml sunflower oil
10 ml butter
2 large onions, thinly sliced
25–40 ml soy sauce
250 g brown mushrooms, wiped and sliced
1 green pepper, seeded and diced
250 g tofu
50 ml toasted sesame seeds
25 ml sherry
grated Cheddar cheese

Place oil, butter, onions, 25 ml soy sauce, mushrooms and green pepper in saucepan. Cover and cook over low heat for about 10 minutes until softened.

Meanwhile, pat tofu dry (using paper towels), cut into cubes and roll the cubes in sesame seeds.

Add the sherry and extra soy sauce to taste to the mixture in the pan. Top with the tofu cubes, cover and simmer gently for 10 minutes. Sprinkle generously with the grated Cheddar cheese, turn off heat and leave for 5 minutes before serving.

Serve as suggested.
Makes 4 large servings.

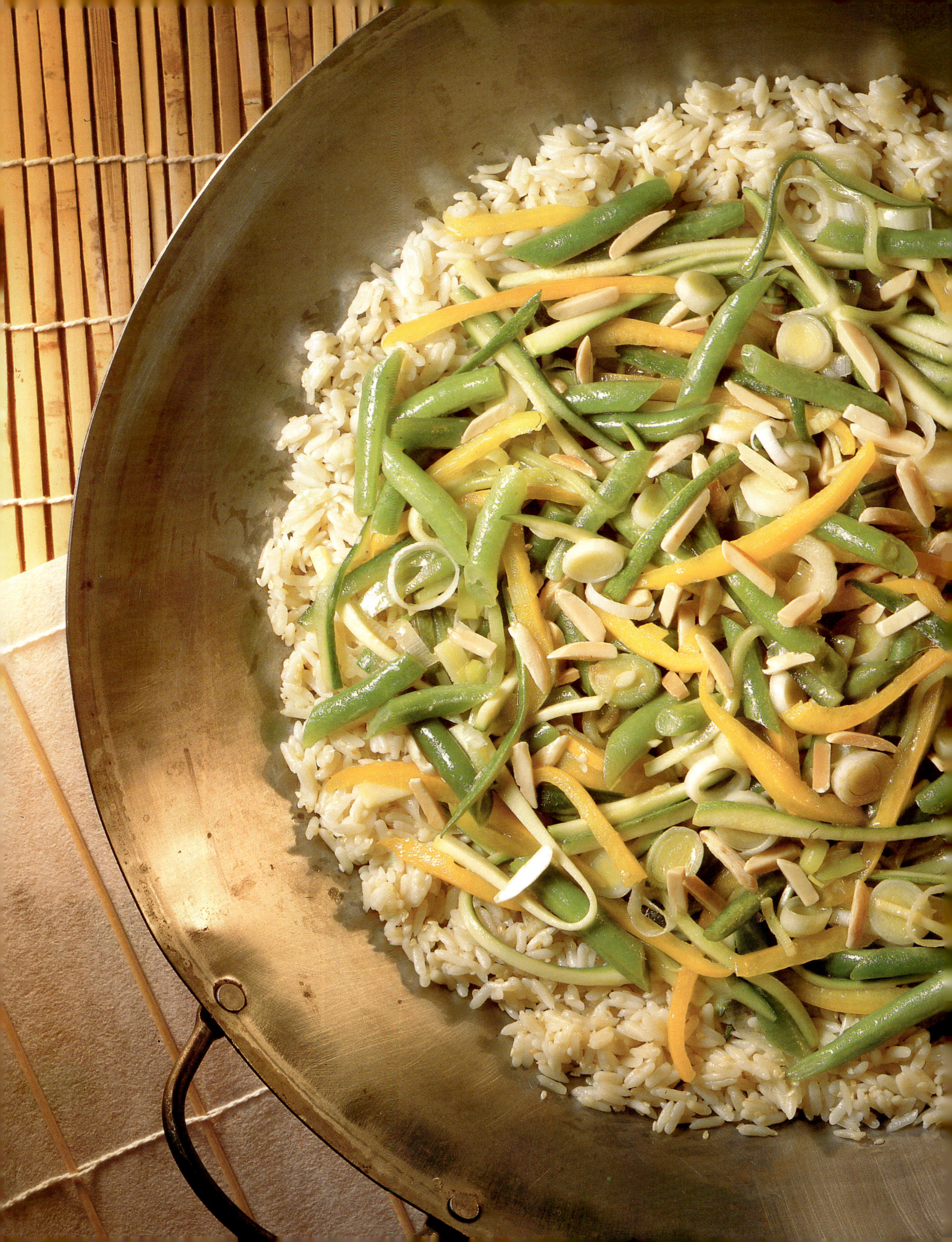

Vegetables

VEGETABLE PAELLA

50 ml each sunflower and olive oil
2 large leeks, sliced
1 onion, chopped
3 cloves garlic, crushed
1 green pepper, seeded and diced
375 ml brown rice
250 g mushrooms, wiped and sliced
1–2 brinjals (250 g), dégorged and diced
5 ml each turmeric, dried origanum
and dried basil
400 g tomatoes, skinned and chopped
500 ml chopped green beans or
500 ml peas
100 ml chopped parsley
sea salt and milled black pepper to taste
a pinch of sugar
500 ml vegetable or Marmite stock
125 ml white wine
250 g feta cheese, diced

Using a large saucepan, heat oils and add leeks, onion, garlic and green pepper. When softened, add rice and toss until coated with oil. Reduce heat and add mushrooms, brinjals, turmeric and herbs. Toss for a minute or two, then add tomatoes (or can of tomatoes, plus the juice), beans or peas, parsley, seasoning, sugar, stock and wine. Mix well, then turn into a large 30 cm x 26 cm baking dish. Cover and bake at 180 °C for 35 minutes. Stir lightly with a fork, then continue baking for another 20–25 minutes until vegetables are cooked and the liquid absorbed. The mixture should be moist but not at all watery. Turn off oven heat and cover top with diced feta and return to oven for 5–10 minutes to heat through.
Serves 6.

Vegetable Stir-Fry with Noodles and Chinese Sauce (p. 80).

SPICY FRUIT AND VEGETABLE CURRY

One can make a tasty vegetable curry using almost any combination of ingredients; the following is a good, basic version. Although the list of ingredients is long, they are mostly well-known items. Serve on brown or Basmati rice with extra chutney and coconut on the side and a tomato and onion salad.

100 ml sunflower oil
2 large onions, finely chopped
3 cloves garlic, crushed
1 knob root ginger, peeled and grated
15–20 ml curry powder
5 ml each ground cinnamon, turmeric, coriander and green cardamom or fennel
2 ml ground cumin
4 carrots, finely diced
2 sweet apples, peeled and diced
2 large sticks table celery, chopped, plus a few leaves
4 x 250 ml shredded cabbage
½ small head cauliflower florets
600 ml vegetable stock or water
10 ml sea salt
125 ml desiccated coconut
50 ml chutney
125 ml seedless raisins
25 ml fresh lemon juice
3 bay leaves
10 ml honey
2 bananas, thinly sliced
125 ml toasted almond strips
cultured sour cream

Heat the sunflower oil in a very large, deep saucepan and gently fry the onion, garlic and ginger. Add all the spices and toss until sizzling. Add the carrots, apples, table celery, shredded cabbage and cauliflower florets. Toss over low heat until vegetables are coated with spices, then add the stock or water, sea salt, coconut, chutney, raisins, lemon juice, bay leaves and honey. Bring to the boil, mix well, then cover and simmer over low heat for about 20 minutes, stirring occasionally without breaking up the cauliflower and adding a little more stock or water if necessary.

If time allows, cool the curry, transfer to a suitable non-metallic container, and refrigerate overnight for flavours to blend.

To serve, remove the bay leaves and reheat the curry gently. Mix in the bananas, almond strips and enough cultured sour cream to make a good sauce and bring to full heat, without boiling.

Serve as suggested.
Serves 8.

PHYLLO PARCELS WITH SPROUTS, FETA AND ALMONDS

This vegetable mixture makes a delicious filling. Serve with Tzatziki (page 76) and a creamy cabbage salad. Tissue-thin, feathery phyllo pastry requires special treatment (see box).

500 g frozen phyllo pastry, thawed in fridge for 24 hours
oil or melted butter

FILLING
500 ml mung bean sprouts
200 g feta cheese, rinsed and diced
100 ml chopped toasted almonds
2 egg yolks
25 ml soy sauce
2 sticks table celery, finely chopped
6 spring onions, chopped
4 small baby marrows, pared and coarsely grated
a pinch of sugar

Combine ingredients for filling. Remove three sheets of phyllo — they should measure about 37 cm x 42 cm. Brush each sheet with oil, garlic oil or melted butter (or, if cutting down on fat, brush only the top sheet; the results will be just as good), and place the sheets one on top of the other. Place a mound of filling in the centre and then draw up the corners to form a parcel, twisting the top to seal. Brush outside of parcel with oil or butter and sprinkle lightly with water. Make five more parcels in the same way, place on two large, oiled baking sheets and bake at 200 °C for 20 minutes until golden brown.
Makes 6 parcels.

USING PHYLLO PASTRY

The day before using, transfer phyllo to fridge to thaw. Unwrap and lay out on a dry kitchen towel. Cover with another dry towel and then with a damp towel, and leave to stand for 10 minutes, always keeping the sheets you are not working with covered in this way. They quickly become brittle and dry when exposed to air.

Brush each sheet (or only the top sheet) lightly with melted butter (for sweet or savoury dishes) or oil (for savoury dishes) before using.

MUSHROOM CROSTINI

This is not a main-course recipe, but it makes a marvellous, one-mouthful snack to serve with drinks when entertaining on a vegetarian theme. I think it's worth buying this book for this recipe alone! Not only are the crisp bread rounds (piled with an aromatic topping) perfect finger food as they do not drip, but the topping can be made and chilled the day before, the bread cut and crisped hours in advance, and the whole lot can be assembled, refrigerated until needed and baked just before serving.

12–16 slices slightly stale white or plain brown bread
20 ml butter and 40 ml oil, melted together
50 ml butter
250 g white or brown mushrooms, wiped and very finely chopped
50 ml white flour
250 ml milk
6 spring onions, finely chopped
1 ml dried origanum, crushed
sea salt and milled black pepper to taste
8 olives, pitted and slivered (optional)
grated Parmesan cheese

Slice crusts off bread and stamp out rounds using a 5-cm scone cutter. Place rounds on a baking tray and brush both sides with the melted butter and oil. Bake at 180 °C for 10–12 minutes, until golden brown and crisp, turning once. Leave to cool.

Melt the 50 ml butter in a small saucepan, add mushrooms and toss over low heat until soft and all liquid has evaporated. Sprinkle in flour, slowly add milk, bring to the boil, and stir until very thick. Remove from stove and add onions, origanum and seasoning to taste. If working ahead, cool, cover and refrigerate until needed.

To bake, spread the mushroom mixture thickly on each bread round, top with the slivered olives, if using, and sprinkle with the grated Parmesan. Bake at 200 °C for 12–15 minutes until piping hot. Serve immediately.
Makes about 36, depending on size.

VEGETABLE COTTAGE PIE (1)

This is a large simple pie, but nourishing and inexpensive. Apart from topping, it may be assembled in advance. Serve with cinnamon-baked pumpkin and green peas or a salad.

200 ml brown rice
250 ml brown lentils, picked over and rinsed
25 ml sunflower oil
1 large onion, chopped
2 cloves garlic, crushed
3 carrots, finely diced (250 ml)
5 ml mixed dried herbs
3 juicy tomatoes, skinned and chopped (300 g)
500 ml shredded cabbage
125 ml chopped parsley
3 eggs, beaten
250 ml buttermilk
250 ml grated Cheddar cheese
25 ml soy sauce
4 large potatoes, scrubbed
a little hot milk
a few nuts of butter

Cook the rice in 450 ml salted water until done. Cook the lentils in 500 ml salted water until soft and water is absorbed. Meanwhile, heat oil in small frying pan. Sauté onions and garlic and when softened add the carrots, herbs and tomatoes. Cover and simmer until the tomatoes are pulpy — for about 10 minutes.

Tip cooked rice and lentils into a large bowl. Add cabbage, parsley, eggs, buttermilk, 125 ml cheese and the soy sauce. Do not add salt, as the soy sauce should salt it sufficiently. Add tomato mixture and mix gently but thoroughly. Spoon into a lightly oiled 30 cm x 20 cm baking dish, spreading evenly. If working ahead, cover and set aside. Heat oven to 160 °C and bake, covered, on middle shelf for 35 minutes.

Meanwhile, boil potatoes until soft. Mash with milk and butter, then swirl over pie. Sprinkle with rest of cheese, and return to oven, uncovered, for about 20 minutes until hot and cheese has melted.
Makes 6 large servings.

VEGETABLE COTTAGE PIE (2)

As vegetables and rice do not constitute a complete meal, it is a good idea to add lentils as a complementary protein. Also, when mixed with rice, their somewhat dominant flavour is mellowed. The following dish is a good way of combining the two. Served with baked pumpkin and peas or a green salad, it makes a satisfying, simple meal. You can use left-over rice or lentils, if you have them, or put them on to cook before doing the vegetables.

25 ml each butter and sunflower oil
1 large onion, chopped
2 cloves garlic, crushed
4 medium carrots, julienned
2 sticks table celery, plus some leaves, chopped
1 green or red pepper, seeded and diced
250 g brown or white mushrooms, wiped and sliced
1 x 410 g can tomatoes, chopped, plus the juice
100 ml chopped parsley
4 x 250 ml coarsely shredded spinach (about half a bunch)
2 ml sea salt and a big pinch sugar
500 ml cooked brown rice
250 ml cooked brown or green lentils
25 ml soy sauce
30 ml chopped fresh mixed herbs (e.g. thyme, marjoram and sage)
potatoes mashed with a little milk and butter
250 ml grated Cheddar cheese

Use a large, deep saucepan in which to heat butter and oil. Sauté onion and garlic. Add carrots, celery, pepper and mushrooms and toss until softening. Add tomatoes, parsley, spinach, salt and sugar, mix well, then cover and simmer until just cooked — for about 6 minutes. The mixture should be moist. Lightly fork in rice, lentils, soy sauce and herbs and when combined, spoon into an oiled 30 cm x 20 cm baking dish. Cover with mashed potatoes, sprinkle with cheese, and bake on middle shelf of oven at 160 °C for 40 minutes.
Serves 8.

CHEESE-TOPPED VEGETABLE BAKE

The sort of wholesome dish you'd expect to find at an unpretentious vegetarian restaurant. Rice and lentils add substance, and preparation time is minimal. Serve with a salad or vegetables of choice, like new potatoes, creamed spinach, stuffed brinjals or stir-fried baby marrows.

60 ml sunflower oil
2 large onions, chopped
2 cloves garlic, crushed
2 large stalks table celery, plus some leaves, chopped
250 g brown mushrooms, wiped and sliced
400 ml coarsely grated raw butternut squash
200 ml brown rice
200 ml brown lentils, picked over and rinsed
5 ml dried origanum
2 ml dried thyme
800 ml hot Marmite stock
5 ml sea salt
100 ml chopped parsley
50 ml soy sauce
250 ml lentil or mung bean sprouts

TOPPING
125 ml buttermilk
125 ml cultured sour cream
2 eggs, separated
2 ml sea salt and a pinch of sugar
5 ml prepared mustard
250 ml finely grated Cheddar cheese
paprika

Heat oil and sauté onion and garlic. Add celery, mushrooms and butternut. When softening and smelling good, but not shrunken, turn off heat and mix in remaining ingredients, except sprouts. Turn into an oiled baking dish — a deep, 25-cm pie dish is ideal — and spread evenly. Cover and bake at 160 °C for 1 hour. Remove and fork in the sprouts. For topping, whisk together buttermilk, cream, egg yolks, salt, pinch sugar, mustard and 125 ml cheese Stiffly whisk egg whites and fold in. Pour over baked mixture, sprinkle with remaining cheese and paprika, and bake uncovered for 20–25 minutes or until set.
Serves 8.

Overleaf: Greek Green Bean and Brinjal Casserole (p. 88), Baked Souffléd Potatoes (p. 76) and Vegetable Cottage Pie (1) (this page).

PESTICIDES AND VEGETABLES

To pare or not to pare vegetables like baby marrows and cucumbers is a matter of choice. It's a pity to do so, but I do, because of the pesticides used on our vegetables. Tomatoes should also be well washed if you are using them with their skins.

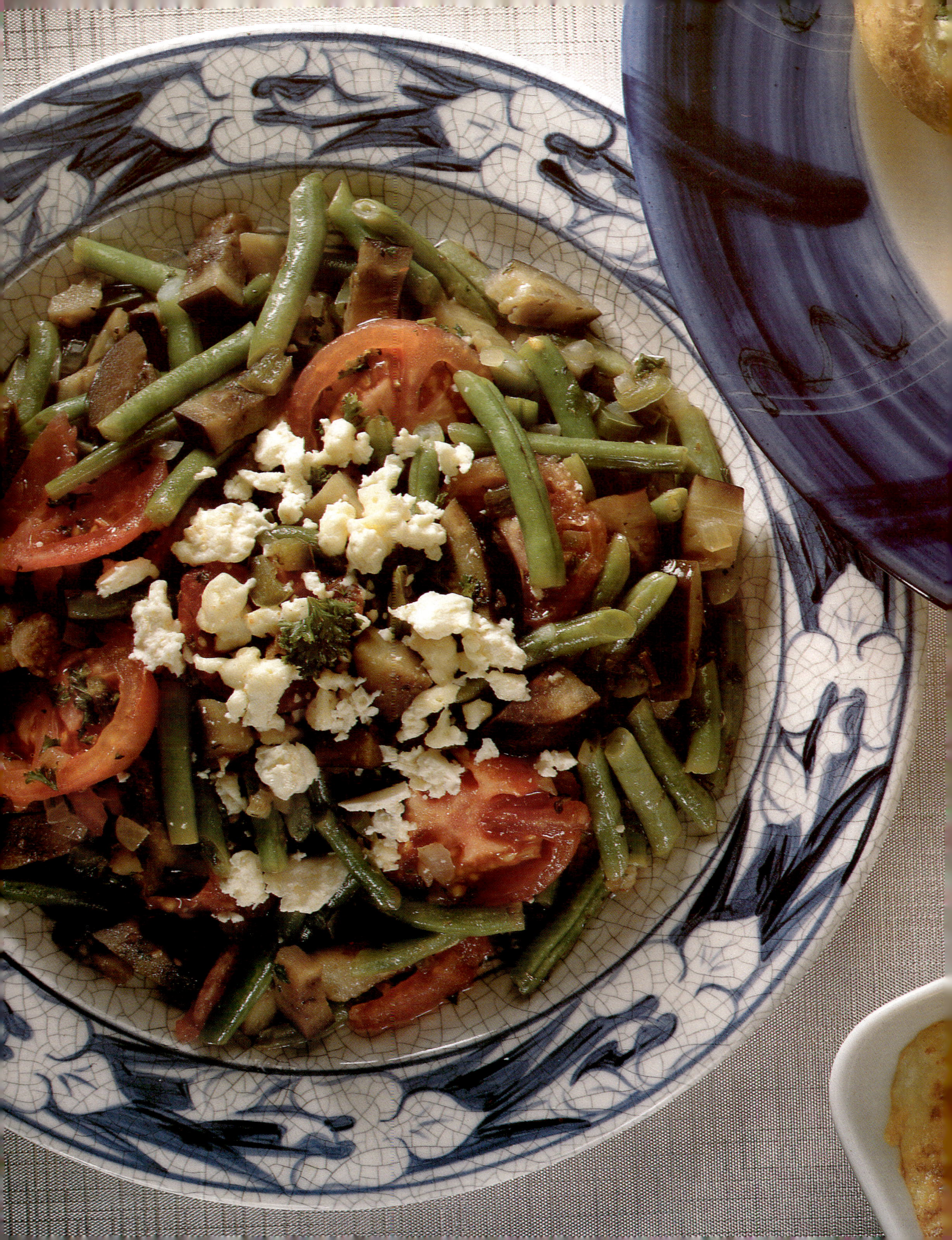

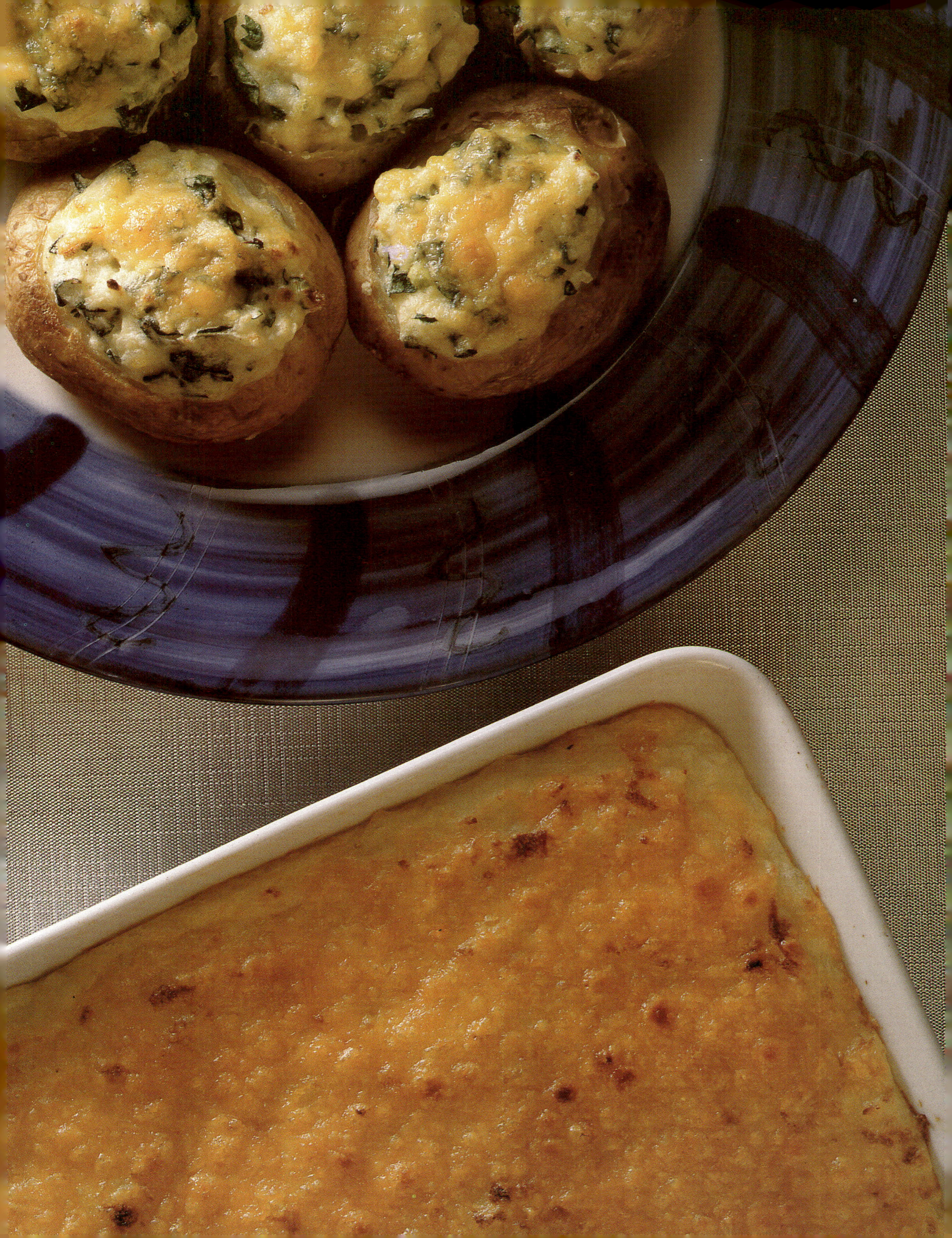

SPINACH AND FETA PIE WITH TZATZIKI

My version of the popular Greek pie with phyllo, using a roll of bought puff pastry to simplify preparation. It's a super recipe which may be prepared and chilled until about 40 minutes before dinner, then baked and served piping hot, golden brown and plump with filling. The one proviso is that you must use fresh spinach. You will also need a very large saucepan. The recipe for tzatziki is a short-cut method, side-stepping the need to drain the yoghurt overnight. Serve with baked potatoes and a brinjal salad, if liked.

TZATZIKI

½ small English cucumber
250 ml thick Bulgarian yoghurt
1 small clove garlic, crushed
a pinch of sea salt
10 ml finely chopped fresh mint
10 ml olive oil
a pinch of sugar

Pare and grate cucumber coarsely and leave, weighted, to drain in a colander for about 20 minutes. Squeeze dry between paper towels, then fold all ingredients together until well mixed. Cover and chill for several hours.
Makes about 250 ml.

PIE

2 large bunches fresh spinach
25 ml each sunflower and olive oil
2 large onions, finely chopped
2 cloves garlic, crushed
5 ml dried dill
2 ml dried origanum
3 eggs, beaten
250 g feta cheese, rinsed and crumbled
2 ml sea salt and milled black pepper to taste
25–50 ml grated Parmesan cheese
1 x 400-g roll frozen puff pastry, thawed in fridge
milk or lightly-beaten egg for glazing

Trim stalks from spinach (weight should then be 500 g). Wash and shake dry.
Heat oils in a very large saucepan and soften onions and garlic. Add herbs and spinach leaves, cover and cook until soft, tossing now and then to mix. If spinach draws moisture, cook over high heat for 1–2 minutes, then drain very well in a colander. When cool, chop finely, and tip into a large bowl. Mix in eggs, feta, seasoning and Parmesan.

Dampen a 25 cm x 20 cm baking tin. Line base of tin with half of pastry — should just cover the bottom. Spread spinach mixture evenly over top, then cover with rest of pastry. With dampened fingers, pinch all round edges to seal, and mark into six large squares.* If working ahead, chill at this stage.
Brush with milk or egg-wash and bake at 220 °C for about 40 minutes or until pastry is golden brown and puffed. Slice through squares and lift onto hot plates.
Serves 6.

* Or make crescent-shaped pies, using two packets of puff pastry, cut into twelve circles of 16-cm diameter. Divide filling between them, spooning down one side, fold over, damp edges and seal with fork. Brush with milk or egg-wash and bake on dampened sheet for 30 minutes.

STUFFED BAKED POTATOES

This simple stuffing makes a change from plain baked potatoes. Serve with a salad for an inexpensive, light meal or team up with a bean or chickpea casserole or a stir-fry for heartier appetites.

4 large baking potatoes
30 ml melted butter
± 150 ml hot milk
250 ml grated Cheddar cheese
sea salt and milled black pepper to taste
2 ml prepared mustard
30 ml chopped parsley
paprika

Scrub potatoes, prick, rub skins with oil and bake at 200 °C for about 1 hour until soft. Slice off the tops. Scoop flesh into a bowl, leaving a firm shell. Mash with the melted butter and milk, then add remaining ingredients, except paprika. Pile into shells, brush lightly with milk and dust with paprika, or top with a little more cheese and a small knob of butter. Reheat at 180 °C.
Serves 4.

> To avoid having to stand and toss a stir-fry all the time, I add a dash of water, and, with the pan three-quarters covered, let the steam do the cooking. Just toss now and then.

BAKED SOUFFLÉD POTATOES

Big potatoes, first baked and then stuffed with a mixture of cheese, spinach and eggs, then baked again until puffy and golden brown — these make a marvellous change from the usual baked spud and sour cream. I always serve them with a rather special bean salad, which is quite the nicest accompaniment: sliced green beans, garlic onions, and diced red pepper, stir-fried in sesame oil with a dash of sherry, soy sauce and lemon juice added, and then left to marinate until cold. Just before serving, I add a handful of chopped walnuts.

8 large baking potatoes, scrubbed, pricked and brushed with oil
12 large leaves spinach or Swiss chard
50 ml soft butter
250 ml finely grated Cheddar cheese
10 ml prepared mild mustard
4 eggs, separated
6 spring onions, chopped
5 ml sea salt and milled black pepper to taste
a big pinch of grated nutmeg
± 100 ml milk

TOPPING
60 ml finely grated Cheddar cheese
slivers of butter (optional)

Bake the potatoes at 200 °C for an hour and 15 minutes or until done.
Meanwhile, blanch the spinach leaves in boiling water for a few minutes, then drain and chop finely. You should have 200 ml, firmly packed for measuring.
As soon as potatoes are cool enough to handle, cut a slice about 1 cm thick across the tops and scoop out the insides into a large bowl, leaving just enough of a 'lining' to keep the shells firm and standing upright. Arrange them close together in a lightly oiled baking dish.
Mash the scooped-out potato well with the butter, cheese, mustard, egg yolks, onions, seasoning, nutmeg, spinach and just enough milk to make a softish but NOT sloppy mixture. Stiffly whisk the egg whites and fold in.
Mound the filling into the shells. Top each potato with the extra cheese and place a sliver of butter, if using, on each. Return to oven for 20–25 minutes.
Serve, as suggested, with a bean salad (see notes above).
Serves 8, with the salad.

ONIONS

The most amazing claims are being made concerning the health-giving properties of the humble onion. But, apart from any medical benefits, they certainly are indispensable in cooking and I use them in huge quantities. Buying pockets of large onions is a good habit as you will be tempted to use a whole, big onion every time, and you can hardly ever have too much onion in a dish.

To chop an onion after peeling, slice it in half from top to bottom, place the flat side down on a chopping board, make vertical slices, then give the board a half turn and slice several times again. *Voilà*, you will have lots of little dice in no time.

Keep onions in the fridge to prevent your eyes from streaming when you chop them.

VEGETABLE CURRY WITH COCONUT MILK AND RAITA

A simple but delicious curry with a subtle mix of flavours which is particularly good served on top of spiced mixed rice and vegetables. The Raita should be made in advance and refrigerated, preferably overnight. Prepare the Coconut Milk before starting to make the Curry.

RAITA

250 ml Bulgarian yoghurt*
1 x 4-cm piece English cucumber, pared, seeded and diced
2 spring onions, chopped
25 ml finely chopped parsley
a pinch of sea salt
25 ml chopped fresh mint
1 ml ground cumin

Fold all the ingredients together and then chill, covered.

* For a slightly thicker consistency, the yoghurt may first be drained in a muslin-lined sieve, but this is not essential.

COCONUT MILK

250 ml desiccated coconut
500 ml boiling water

Pour water over coconut and stand until cold. Strain, pressing as much liquid through sieve as possible. Reserve coconut.

CURRY

50 ml sunflower oil
15 ml brown mustard seeds
2 large onions, chopped
2 cloves garlic, crushed
1 red pepper, seeded and diced
20–25 ml curry powder
5 ml each ground cumin and turmeric
6 white cardamom pods
2 star anise
400 g brinjals, cubed and dégorged
6 medium carrots, julienned
500 g cauliflower florets
400 g ripe tomatoes, skinned and chopped or 1 x 400 g can plus juice
2 sticks cinnamon
2 bay leaves
5 ml each sea salt and light brown sugar
250 ml vegetable stock or water

Heat oil in a large pan, add mustard seeds and fry over medium heat until sizzling. If heat is too high, they'll pop right out of the pan. Add onions, garlic and red pepper. When softening, add curry powder and spices and toss for 1–2 minutes. Mix in brinjals, carrots and cauliflower and when coated with spices, add rest of ingredients and Coconut Milk. Bring to boil, then cover and simmer on lowest heat, stirring occasionally, for about 30 minutes or until mixture has thickened and vegetables are cooked. Remove cinnamon, anise and bay leaves and, if possible, transfer to suitable container and cool for flavours to develop.

To reheat, add a little vegetable stock or water, if necessary, and check seasoning. It will probably need a little salt. Stir in reserved coconut. It will add flavour and thicken the juices. Serve on a mixture of cooked rice and lentils. Optional extras are sliced hard-boiled eggs or toasted cashew nuts sprinkled over the top. Serve the Raita separately and a bowl of chutney.
Serves 8.

BUTTERMILK

Cultured buttermilk makes a good substitute for cream or sour cream in many recipes. It is lower in kilojoules, yet adds a creamy texture. It is also less tart than natural yoghurt.

BAKED POTATOES WITH CHUNKY TOPPING

The humble baked spud rises to new heights when served with this tasty topping — a mixture of lightly fried vegetables, cottage cheese and sour cream. Chunky, rather than smooth cottage cheese is always nicest with baked potatoes, but those little lumps do nothing for the appearance of the dish. So, use a bit of camouflage: before serving, spoon the mixture into a pretty pottery bowl and cover entirely with the sesame seeds, parsley or chives. Voilà — it will look as good as it tastes. Serve with steamed vegetables or a crisp salad.

6 large baking potatoes, scrubbed, pricked and brushed with oil

TOPPING

50 ml sunflower oil
1 onion, finely chopped
1–2 cloves garlic, crushed
1 red pepper, seeded and finely diced
250 g brown mushrooms, wiped and finely chopped
2 sprigs fresh rosemary
40 ml sweet sherry
25 ml soy sauce
250 g chunky cottage cheese
a little sea salt and milled black pepper to taste
125 ml cultured sour cream
several pats of garlic or herbed butter
toasted sesame seeds or chopped chives or parsley to garnish

Bake potatoes at 200 °C until done.

Meanwhile, heat the sunflower oil in a large pan and lightly fry the onion, garlic and red pepper. Add the mushrooms and rosemary and stir-fry over medium heat until softened and browned. Add sherry and soy sauce and continue cooking until mixture is shiny and moist, but all moisture must have evaporated. Spoon mixture into a bowl, remove rosemary and cool. Mix in cheese and sour cream, check seasoning and set aside until potatoes are cooked.

Serve one potato per person; cut a cross in the potato, squeeze to open, top with a pat of the garlic or herbed butter, then spoon topping over. Sprinkle with garnish.
Serves 6.

Overleaf: Spicy Fruit and Vegetable Curry (p. 72), and Vegetable Paella (p. 71), served with chopped tomato and onion.

VEGETABLES 77

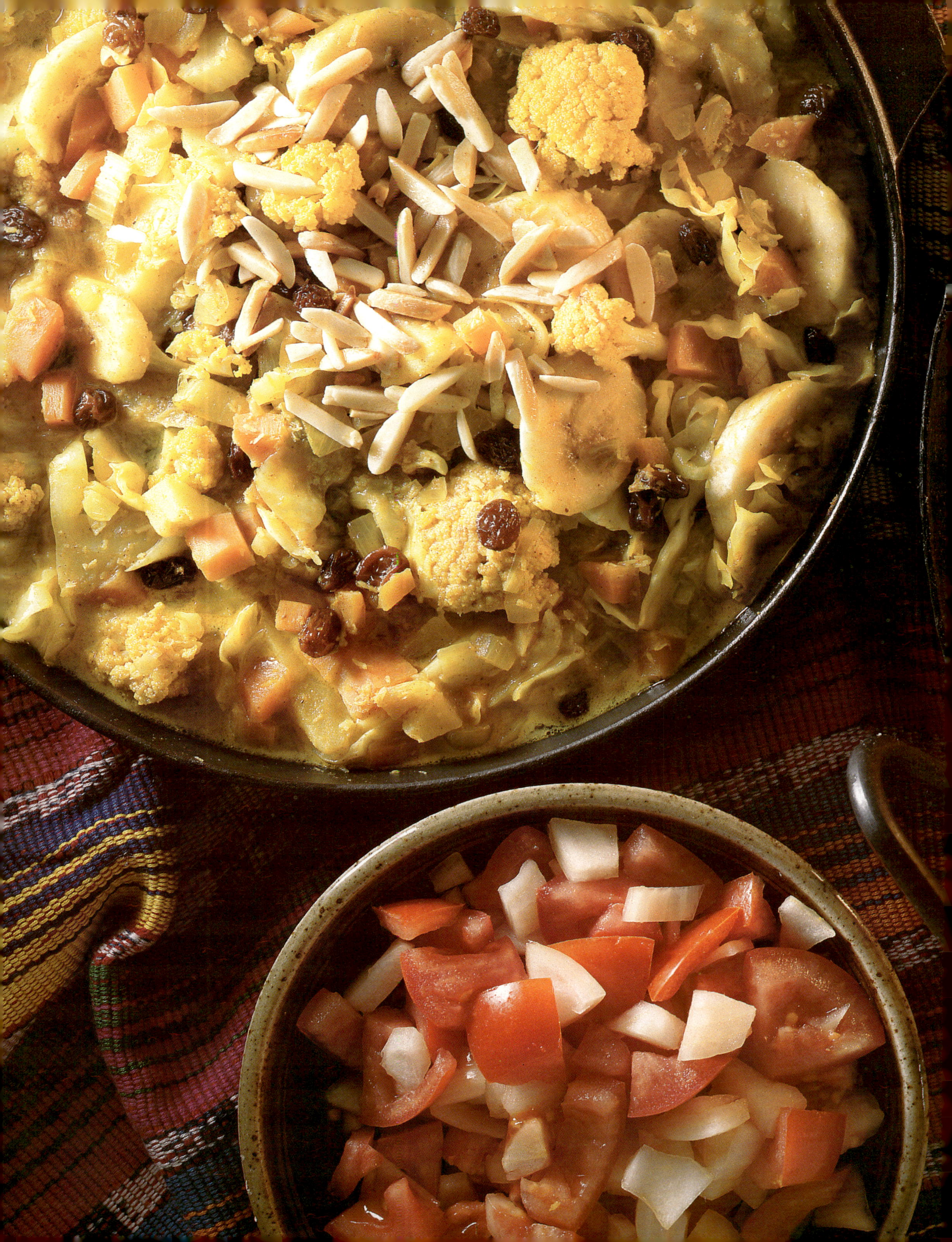

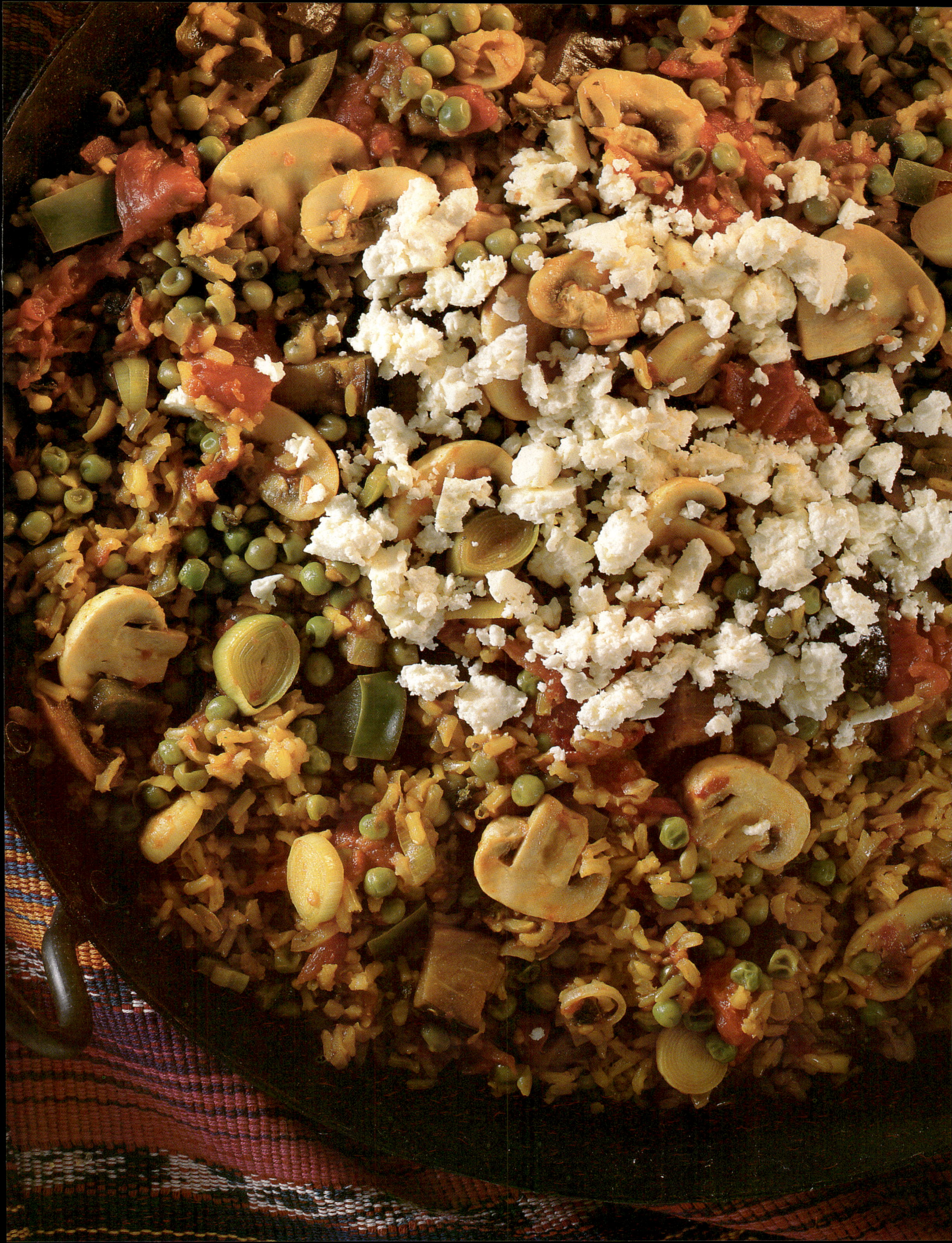

VEGETABLE STIR-FRY WITH NOODLES AND CHINESE SAUCE

An attractive and succulent stir-fry, combining green beans, baby marrows and cucumber in a tasty brown sauce, with the subtle flavours of ginger and sesame adding an Oriental touch.

30 ml sunflower oil
15 ml dark sesame oil
2 large leeks, sliced
1 small onion, chopped
1 red pepper, seeded and diced
2–3 cloves garlic, crushed
300 g young green beans, trimmed and sliced
300 g baby marrows, pared and julienned
½ English cucumber, pared and julienned
375 ml rice-shaped pasta noodles
30 ml toasted sesame seeds
toasted, slivered almonds for garnish

SAUCE
375 ml vegetable stock or water
1 small knob fresh root ginger, peeled and grated (about 2 ml)
15 ml sherry
25 ml cornflour
5 ml honey
20 ml soy sauce
15 ml fresh lemon juice

Heat sunflower and sesame oils in a large pan. Add leeks, onion, red pepper and garlic and allow to soften. Add beans, marrows, cucumber and 50 ml water and cook until tender-crisp. As raw beans are not nice, the water is added to encourage steaming, and if the pan is half-covered and the heat kept to medium, the vegetables should cook through while remaining succulent. Toss occasionally, using a wooden spoon. When ready for the sauce, the vegetable mixture will have reduced considerably.

Meanwhile, cook noodles quickly in plenty of rapidly boiling salted water, drain well, then toss with a dash of oil and the sesame seeds. Take care that the noodles don't become stodgy and stick together.

For the sauce, whisk together all the ingredients. Add it to the vegetable stir-fry mixture and bring to the boil, stirring. Check seasoning and serve at once, ladling the lovely thick vegetable mixture over each serving of noodles. Top generously with the slivered almonds.
Makes 4 large servings.

TABLE CELERY

Wash well, strip off the outer 'strings' from the thick ribs, and then slice thinly on the diagonal. Use very sparingly in salads, or more liberally in stir-fries.

STIR-FRY WITH CAULIFLOWER, GREEN BEANS AND WALNUTS

… and leeks, cucumber and carrots, with sesame oil adding a subtly delicious flavour. This is a chunky and generous mixture, so if you do not own a very large stove-top to table casserole, you may complete the cooking in a baking dish in the oven. Serve on brown rice, or combine rice and lentils in equal quantities for extra nourishment.

50 ml sunflower oil
3–4 leeks, sliced
2–4 cloves garlic, crushed
500 ml sliced green beans (about 200 g)
3 sticks table celery, sliced
sea salt and milled black pepper to taste
25 ml sesame oil
50 ml sherry
½ English cucumber, pared and julienned
florets from ½ cauliflower, coarse stems removed (about 400 g)
4 young carrots, julienned
250 ml vegetable or Marmite stock
25 ml soy sauce
5 ml ground ginger
20 ml cornflour
250 ml coarsely chopped walnuts
crumbled feta or grated Cheddar cheese for topping

Heat sunflower oil in large pan, add leeks, garlic, beans and celery and stir-fry for about 5 minutes. Remove to another pan or baking dish, season lightly and keep warm. Add sesame oil and sherry to pan, then add rest of vegetables. Lower heat and cook, half-covered, until tender-crisp, tossing occasionally. Mix all vegetables together in baking dish or saucepan.

Combine stock, soy sauce, ginger and cornflour. Stir into vegetables and add nuts. Cover and cook on medium heat, stirring occasionally and adding extra stock or water as necessary, until just done; or bake, covered, at 180 °C for 20–30 minutes. Top each serving with cheese of choice.
Serves 5.

BASIC VEGETABLE STIR-FRY SAUCE

It is useful to have a basic sauce mixture to add flavour and succulence to a vegetable stir-fry. The following recipe may be used for 1 kg of mixed vegetables of choice. Once prepared (that is, washed, scrubbed or peeled, and sliced, chopped or julienned) they should be steamed or lightly poached until tender but still crisp; stir-frying is not necessary as oil is used in making the sauce.

10 ml dark sesame oil
15 ml sunflower oil
1–2 cloves garlic, crushed
1 bunch spring onions, chopped
half a knob root ginger, peeled and grated
375 ml vegetable stock or water
20 ml cornflour
25 ml sweet sherry
25 ml soy sauce
1 kg vegetables of choice, steamed or poached

Heat both oils and sauté garlic, onions and ginger. Add stock or water. Slake cornflour with sherry and soy sauce, add to pan and stir until boiling and thickened. Pour into pan with the just-cooked and lightly seasoned vegetables and allow to boil up. Ladle over servings of brown rice and top with toasted, slivered almonds. Serve extra soy sauce separately, if desired.
Serves 4.

GOMASIO

An Oriental seasoning salt: a marvellous condiment with the sesame seeds being rich in calcium, lecithin and unsaturated fats. Gomasio is best freshly made, but will keep for a few days stored in a sealed glass jar in the fridge.

**125 ml husked sesame seeds
20 ml sea salt**

Spread seeds in a non-stick frying pan and place on medium heat until golden brown. Shake pan occasionally and watch for burning. Remove, add salt, then pound, in batches, using a pestle and mortar. Do not pound to a pulp; the mixture should retain some texture.

There are certain ingredients which may be favourites of yours, which simply don't feature anywhere. That's because, like everyone else, there are certain foods which do not appeal to me and, therefore, it is no pleasure for me to use them. In a cordon bleu cuisine this could create a problem, but the type of cooking explored in this book is wide open to additions and alterations. Frequently vegetables, pulses, herbs and spices can be happily interchanged; substitute seasonal alternatives for vegetables in recipes. The results will not, of course, be quite the same as in the original recipe, but invention through necessity is how some of the best dishes are born.

MUSHROOM AND SPROUT STIR-FRY

This is a fine example of how to 'bake' a stir-fry.

50 ml sunflower oil plus a little extra
4 leeks, thinly sliced
1 small onion, chopped
2 sticks table celery, sliced
2 medium carrots, julienned
2 cloves garlic, crushed
50 ml soy sauce
200 ml vegetable stock or water
20 ml cornflour
a pinch of sugar
250 g mushrooms, wiped and sliced
500 ml shredded cabbage
½ English cucumber, pared and cubed
250 ml lentil sprouts
toasted almonds

In a large frying pan heat 50 ml oil and stir-fry leeks, onion, celery, carrots and garlic. After about 5 minutes on medium heat, transfer to a large, warmed dish and place in an oven preheated to 160 °C.

Mix the soy sauce, stock, cornflour and pinch of sugar. Put aside.

To pan add a dash more oil and mushrooms, cabbage and cucumber. Sauté until softened, stirring, then add the sprouts and soy sauce mixture. Cover and simmer for a few minutes, then mix into the other vegetables in the oven dish. Return to oven for about 10 minutes, then serve on rice and top with plenty of toasted almonds. It should not be necessary to add salt.
Serves 4–6.

QUICK-MIX STIR-FRY

Although the bottom line in wholefood and vegetarian cookery always reads Fresh Ingredients, sometimes you don't have the time to prepare a mound of fresh vegetables. On these occasions, a packet of frozen vegetables is a boon. I have used several varieties with equal success; the stir-fry mixes are particularly good. Serve on a mixture of brown rice and lentils, cooked together for added convenience. For 250 ml of each, you'll need just over 1 litre of salted water. Bring to the boil, then cover and simmer slowly until cooked and liquid is absorbed. Fork in a nut of butter and some chopped parsley. Top each serving generously with toasted almonds. Serve with baby potatoes tossed in butter and chopped chives, and a green salad.

30 ml each dark sesame and
sunflower oil
1 onion, chopped
2 leeks, sliced
2 cloves garlic, crushed
250 g brown mushrooms, wiped
and sliced
1 sprig rosemary needles, chopped
1 kg frozen mixed vegetables
50 ml soy sauce
250 ml vegetable stock or water
50 ml sherry
25 ml cornflour

Heat both oils in a large pan and sauté onion, leeks, garlic, mushrooms and rosemary. When softening, add the frozen vegetables and toss over medium heat until half-cooked. Mix together soy sauce, stock or water, sherry and cornflour. Add to pan, stir to mix, then cover and simmer for about 10 minutes until thickened and the vegetables are tender.
Serves 6.

SOY SAUCE

Also called shoyu or tamari, this is a marvellous condiment which enhances the flavour and colour of foods, and is especially good in vegetable stir-fries and rice dishes. Some kinds are darker and saltier than others; some naturally fermented, some not. Check the labels, choose the purest, and store in the fridge once opened, as many of the good varieties do not contain preservatives. Always reduce or omit salt when using soy sauce.

SPECIAL STIR-FRY

I have called this a special stir-fry for two reasons: firstly, you use a frozen stir-fry mixture NOT ordinary frozen mixed vegetables (and this makes it especially convenient when time is short); secondly, it is one of the nicest ways in which to woo reluctant bean-eaters. Served on brown rice, Weet-rice or pasta, it really is very good and extremely nutritious as well.

25 ml each sunflower and
dark sesame oil
500 g frozen stir-fry mixture (preferably
the one with mushrooms, peas, leeks)
an extra 250 g brown mushrooms,
wiped and sliced
2 cloves garlic, crushed
½ fresh pineapple, sliced into
rings and diced
500 ml cooked soya beans
500 ml vegetable stock or Marmite stock
25 ml sherry
30 ml cornflour
25 ml soy sauce
10 ml light brown sugar
5 ml ground ginger
500 ml lentil or mung bean sprouts
sea salt to taste
toasted, slivered almonds for garnish

Heat both oils in a large pan. Add frozen stir-fry mixture,* mushrooms and garlic and toss over medium heat until softening. Add pineapple and beans. Stir together stock, sherry, cornflour, soy sauce, sugar and ginger and add to pan. Bring to the boil, stirring, then cover and simmer over low heat for about 10 minutes — the mixture should be fairly thick, but juicy. Fork in sprouts, check seasoning (it will probably need a little salt) and serve, as suggested, with a sprinkling of almonds.
Serves 6–8.

* If frozen mixture is icy and clumped together, place in a colander and hold under cold running water to separate. Pat dry and use immediately.

Overleaf: Phyllo Parcels with Sprouts, Feta and Almonds (p. 72) and Spinach Pancakes (p. 89).

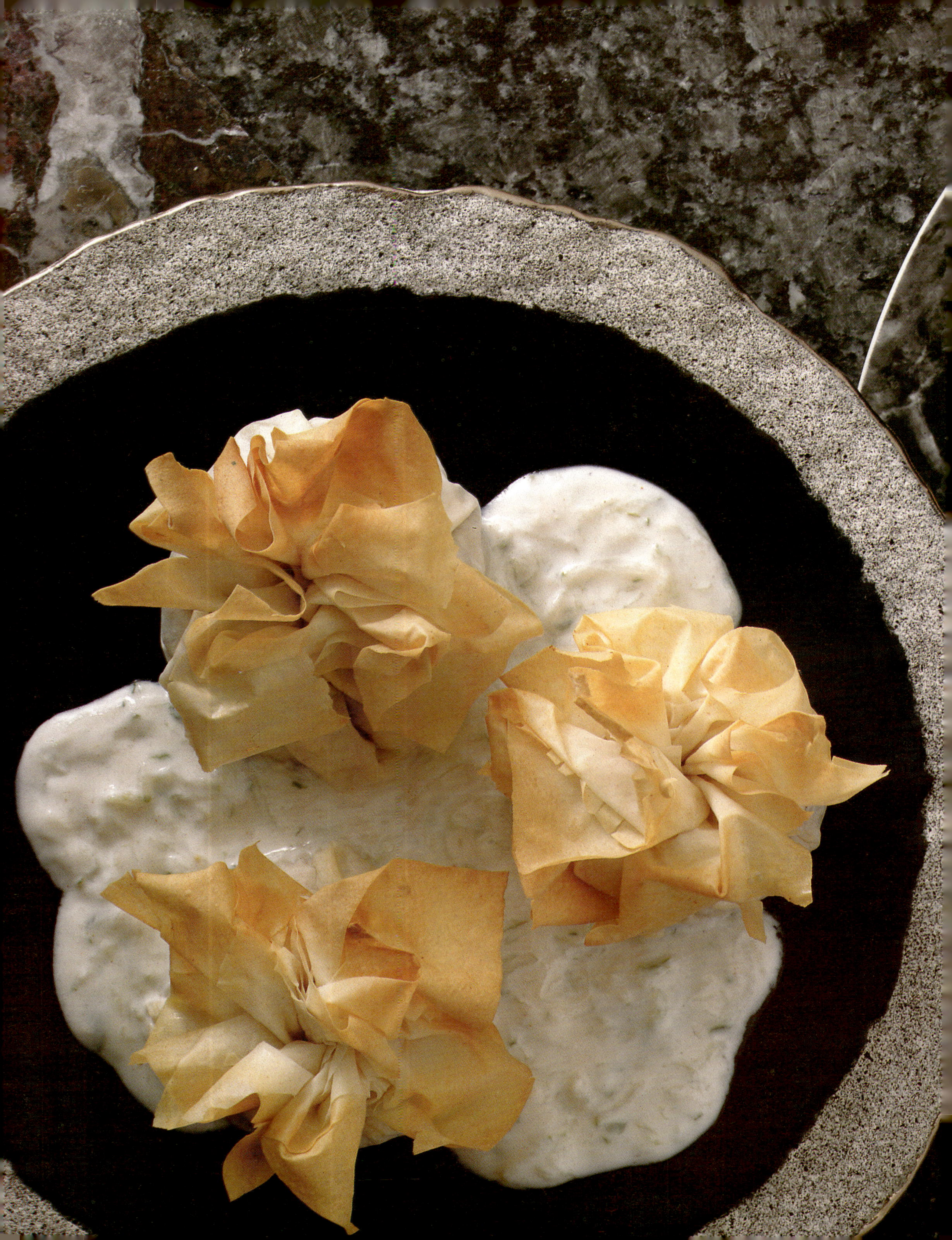

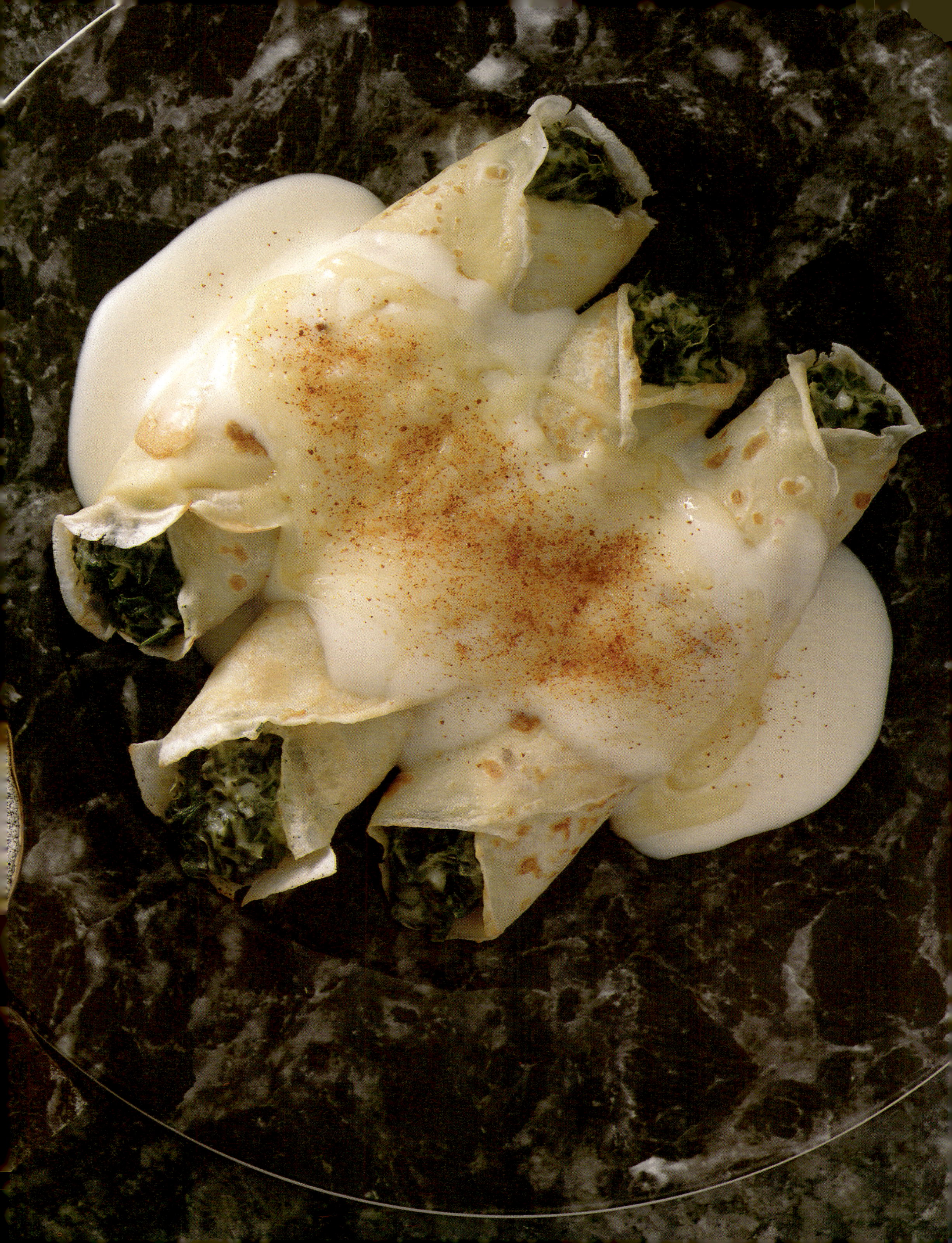

MIDDLE EASTERN BUFFET

Possibly the easiest and nicest way of feeding a crowd of vegetarians (or others with inquisitive palates) is to lay on a spread of salads, dips, pâtés and Pita Bread (page 93). The following recipes illustrate a few fine examples, to which you could add a hot dish, such as a Spinach and Feta Pie (page 76) and a bowl of Tzatziki (page 76). Although I have simplified the dips by using a processor, there is still a good deal of preparation involved in this type of meal as a wide variety of dishes is essential, but all the work can be done beforehand and the different colours and textures are a delight to the eye. Use your prettiest containers, the brightest of cloths, pots (rather than vases) of flowers and carafes of red wine.

HUMMUS

500 ml cooked chickpeas
100 ml liquid from cooking chickpeas or water
50 ml fresh lemon juice
3 cloves garlic
50 ml tahini
50 ml olive oil
sea salt to taste
finely chopped parsley

Drain chickpeas, reserving 100 ml of cooking liquid. Using the grinding blade of a food processor, purée chickpeas, lemon juice, garlic, tahini and olive oil. With motor running, pour in 100 ml reserved cooking liquid or water. The consistency should be that of thick mayonnaise. Add salt to taste, cover and chill. To serve, sprinkle with parsley and drizzle with a little olive oil.
Makes about 375 ml.

TAHINI

A rich and creamy paste (not unlike peanut butter) which is made from hulled, dried, roasted and ground sesame seeds, and is sold in cans or jars. Choose one made from pulped sesame seeds only, and which is free of preservatives and additives, and keep it refrigerated once opened. It really is worth experimenting with this delicious product, which is so popular in Middle Eastern cooking, but use it judiciously as it has a distinctive flavour. Try adding a little to sauces, mayonnaise or salad dressing.

Usually tahini separates and will be very thick at the bottom of the jar or can, so stir it very well, or spoon into a small bowl and whisk it until blended, then spoon out the required amount.

BEAN AND SESAME PÂTÉ *

500 ml cooked haricot beans, well drained
50 ml tahini
20 ml soy sauce
100 ml parsley sprigs
20 ml fresh lemon juice
6 slim spring onions, chopped
2 small cloves garlic
toasted sesame seeds for topping

Place all ingredients, except sesame seeds, in processor fitted with grinding blade. Process briefly. The mixture should not be absolutely smooth. Spoon into pottery container, cover and chill several hours, or overnight. Before serving, cover top generously with toasted sesame seeds.
Makes approximately 600 ml.

◆

SHERRIED BUTTER BEAN PÂTÉ *

20 ml each dark sesame and sunflower oil
2 cloves garlic
6–8 spring onions, chopped
2 x 410 g cans choice grade butter beans, drained
20 ml soy sauce
30 ml sweet sherry
30 ml melted butter

Heat both oils in small pan and sauté garlic and onions. Tip into processor fitted with grinding blade. Add remaining ingredients except butter and process until smooth. Spoon into pottery container, prick holes all over with skewer, pour melted butter over and swirl in until thoroughly mixed. Cover and chill several hours or overnight.
Makes approximately 600 ml.

* These recipes can easily be halved.

BRINJAL AND RED PEPPER SALAD

A version of the Yugoslavian ajivar, this is a simple salad using basic ingredients. If liked, 5 ml dried origanum may be added when sautéeing the vegetables.

800 g brinjals
60 ml olive oil
2 red peppers, seeded and sliced into thin strips
2 cloves garlic, crushed
2 leeks, thinly sliced
5 ml sea salt and milled black pepper to taste
20 ml fresh lemon juice
100 ml finely chopped parsley
natural yoghurt

Wash brinjals, remove bud ends, prick all over, place in baking dish and bake at 200 °C until soft. When cool enough to handle, slice lengthwise into four and ease out flesh. Discard skin, chop flesh into chunks, and place in salad bowl.

Heat oil and lightly sauté red peppers, garlic and leeks. Add to brinjals, plus any oil left in pan. Season mixture and add lemon juice and parsley. Use a fork to toss gently until combined, then cover and chill several hours. Before serving, drizzle yoghurt over the top.

◆

ISRAELI BRINJAL SPREAD

600 g brinjals
5 ml sea salt
4 spring onions, chopped
2 small cloves garlic
2 ml each ground cumin and coriander
25 ml fresh lemon juice
30 ml thick mayonnaise
a large pinch of sugar
2 hard-boiled eggs, chopped
finely chopped parsley or chives for garnish

Wash brinjals, remove bud ends, prick all over, place in baking dish and bake at 200 °C for 45–60 minutes until soft. When cool enough to handle, peel, cube and place in processor fitted with grinding blade. Add remaining ingredients, except eggs and garnish, and process until smooth. Spoon into a pottery bowl, fold in eggs, cover and chill several hours or overnight.

Garnish with parsley or chives.
Makes approximately 500 ml.

84 VEGETABLES

> **LEMON RIND**
>
> When finely grated lemon rind is called for, use smallest holes on grater (not a zester) so that rind will be reduced almost to a pulp, and very little will be needed to add flavour to a dressing. Also, you won't have to chew it.

STUFFED VINE LEAVES

For these little parcels, stuffed with a delicately flavoured rice mixture, I use a packet of vine leaves in brine, available at certain delicatessens. Because the leaves are as fragile as phyllo pastry, I sometimes overlap two or three to hold the stuffing and seal any tears. The rice mixture will fill 20–25 parcels.

1 x 200 g packet vine leaves in brine
25 ml olive oil
1 small onion, chopped
250 ml brown rice
75–100 ml sunflower seeds, preferably toasted
5 ml dried dill
finely grated rind of half a lemon
60 ml currants (chopped, seedless raisins may be substituted)
2 ml sea salt
750 ml vegetable stock or water
40–50 ml each sunflower and olive oil
25 ml fresh lemon juice

Drain and carefully separate vine leaves. Cut off any stems, place in a large bowl and cover with boiling water. Stand for 1 minute, then drain well.

Heat olive oil and sauté onion. Add rice and toss until coated with oil. Add sunflower seeds, dill, lemon rind, currants, salt and 500 ml of the stock or water. Stir with a fork to mix, then cover and cook on low heat for about 35 minutes until rice is almost done. Remove from stove and toss again, using a fork.

Lay leaves out flat and put about 30 ml rice mixture in the centre of each, using two or three leaves, as suggested. Flap over sides, then fold over into parcels. Place, seam side down, in baking dish to fit snugly, side by side.

Mix remaining 250 ml stock, oil and lemon juice. Pour over parcels, cover securely, and bake at 160 °C for 45 minutes or until plump and soft. Cool in liquid, then chill for several hours or overnight, but serve at room temperature.

FELAFEL

Traditionally, felafel are deep-fried in oil, but here they are simply baked. Being less rich and moist, serve with Tzatziki (page 76).

750 ml cooked chickpeas, drained
2 ml sea salt
50 ml finely chopped parsley
2 cloves garlic, crushed
5 ml each ground cumin and coriander
25 ml wholewheat flour
1 egg, beaten
oil for baking

Preheat oven to 180 °C. Grind chickpeas in food processor to a dry, mealy mixture. Put into bowl and add salt, parsley, garlic and spices. Sprinkle in flour and bind with egg, then roll into fifteen small balls. Cover base of swiss roll baking tray with a fairly generous layer of oil and heat in oven. Roll balls in hot oil, then bake for 20 minutes. Using a spatula, turn carefully. Raise heat to 220 °C and bake for another 15 minutes or until crisp and brown.
Makes 15.

♦

STUFFED GREEN PEPPERS

6 large green peppers
80 ml olive oil
1 onion, finely chopped
150 ml quick-cooking, long-grain white rice
2 large tomatoes, skinned, chopped and seeded
50 ml chopped parsley
2 ml sea salt and milled black pepper to taste
5 ml each dried dill and mint
20 ml lemon juice

Cut a slice from stem end of peppers and reserve. Remove cores and seeds and rinse out shells. Heat 30 ml of oil, add onion and fry lightly, then add rice, tomatoes, parsley, seasoning and herbs. Mix well, then cover and simmer very gently for 15 minutes. Spoon mixture loosely into peppers, about three-quarters full, and arrange upright in small pan with lid. Mix 250 ml hot water with remaining oil and lemon juice, pour over and around peppers, re-position tops, then cover pan and simmer slowly for about 45 minutes or until soft. If necessary, add a little water. When done, cool in pan, spooning juices over until cold. Chill well, preferably overnight, before serving.

BABA GHANOUJ

This is my version of this ethnic speciality. In the Middle East, it is usually served in one big bowl and diners scoop out servings with chunks of Pita Bread (page 93). The brinjals are sometimes charred, rather than baked, but personally I find the smoky flavour unpalatable. This recipe can easily be halved.

800 g brinjals
5 ml sea salt and milled black pepper to taste
2 cloves garlic
50 ml fresh lemon juice
50 ml tahini
20 ml olive oil
2 ml each ground cumin and paprika
finely chopped parsley or chives or toasted sesame seeds for garnish

Wash brinjals, remove bud ends, prick well, place in baking dish and bake at 200 °C for 45–60 minutes until soft. When cool enough to handle, peel and chop. Place pulp in processor fitted with grinding blade. Add remaining ingredients, except oil, spices and garnish, and process until smooth. Spoon into pottery bowl. Mix oil and spices, pour over top of mixture and, using a skewer, swirl in until thoroughly combined. Cover and chill for several hours, or overnight. Garnish with parsley, chives or sesame seeds.
Makes approximately 700 ml.

♦

HARICOT BEAN SALAD (2)

Simple bean salads (and stuffed peppers) are popular dishes in Greece and Turkey.

4 x 250 ml cooked haricot beans, well drained
40 ml fresh lemon juice
100 ml olive oil
2 ml sea salt and milled black pepper to taste
5 ml dried origanum
100 ml finely chopped parsley
2 tomatoes, diced
12 black olives, sliced
8 spring onions, chopped
feta cheese, rinsed and crumbled
3–4 hard-boiled eggs, sliced

Toss all ingredients, except cheese and eggs, until thoroughly mixed. Cover and chill several hours, or overnight. Before serving, top generously with feta cheese and garnish with hard-boiled eggs.

BUTTER

A mixture of oil and butter is best for sautéeing vegetables; butter adds extra flavour. However, in keeping with the mood of the book, I have used less, or omitted the butter altogether, in many of the recipes. Margarine is not an equivalent substitute.

STUFFED BRINJALS

2 medium brinjals
1 large tomato, skinned and chopped
½ small onion, finely chopped
75 ml wholewheat breadcrumbs
25 ml garlic blender mayonnaise
a little sea salt and milled black pepper to taste
2 ml dried basil
a pinch of sugar
rinsed, crumbled feta cheese
25 ml olive oil
black olives to garnish

Boil the brinjals in unsalted water for 8–10 minutes or until just softened. Cut in half and remove most of flesh, leaving the shells intact. Chop the pulp coarsely, and add the tomato, onion, breadcrumbs, mayonnaise, seasoning, basil and sugar. Fill shells and sprinkle with feta. Drizzle oil over the brinjals and bake, uncovered, at 160 °C for 45 minutes. Leave to cool. The liquid will slowly be absorbed. Serve at room temperature garnished with olives.

OILS

Avoid using mixed oils, which can be high in saturated fatty acids. Stick to sunflower oil or a good quality extra virgin olive oil.

Brinjal and Red Pepper Salad (p. 84), Stuffed Brinjals (above), Baba Ghanouj (p. 85), Stuffed Green Peppers (p. 85), Felafel (p. 85), Hummus (p. 84), Stuffed Vine Leaves (p. 85), and Pita Bread (p. 93).

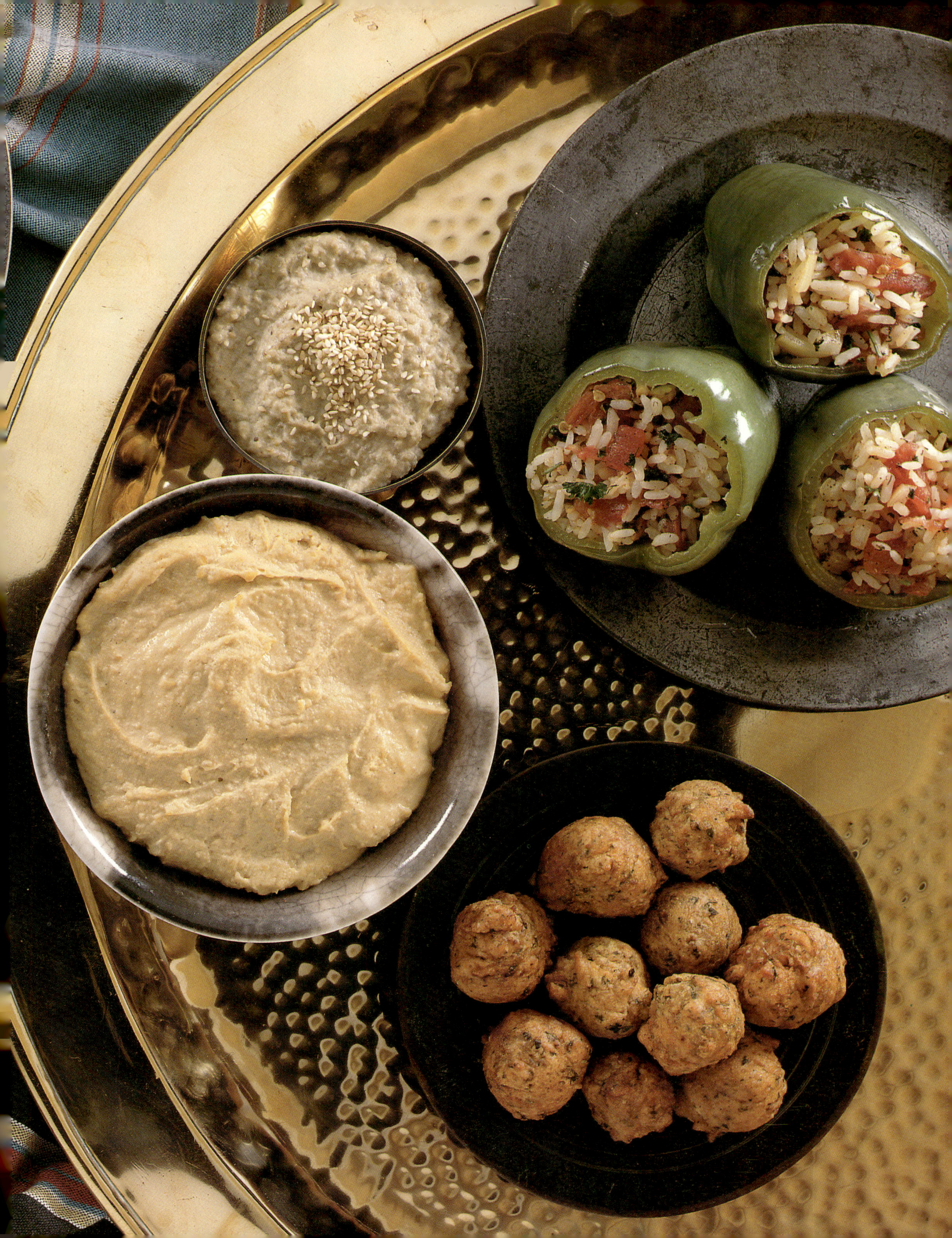

GREEK GREEN BEAN AND BRINJAL CASSEROLE

An aromatic vegetable stew with a Plaka-type flavour and wonderful visual appeal. Serve on pasta, with Pita Bread (page 93) and a green salad, tossed with olive oil dressing and a few black olives.

**25 ml each sunflower and olive oil
1 large onion, chopped
1 green pepper, seeded and diced
3–4 cloves garlic, crushed
300 g brinjals, cubed and dégorged
400 g young green beans, trimmed and sliced
400 g fresh, juicy tomatoes, skinned and chopped
2 ml each dried origanum and basil
1 ml dried thyme
2 bay leaves
100 ml chopped parsley
sea salt and milled black pepper to taste
5 ml brown sugar
50 ml white wine
250 g feta cheese, rinsed and diced for topping
toasted sesame seeds for topping**

Heat oils in a large saucepan and lightly fry onion, green pepper and garlic. Add brinjals and beans, and sweat on low heat for a few minutes, tossing until vegetables are glistening. Add tomatoes, herbs, seasoning, sugar, 125 ml water and wine. Bring to the boil, then reduce heat, cover and cook slowly, stirring the mixture occasionally, until the vegetables are tender. Remove the bay leaves and, if necessary, bind the sauce with beurre manié (page 53). Sprinkle with feta, top with sesame seeds, cover and heat through for 5 minutes; or spoon into a serving dish, add topping, and heat through in an oven.
Serves 4.

SOUR CREAM

The brand I use is as thick as Guernsey cream. Unopened cartons should be stored upside down in the fridge. Once opened, spoon what hasn't been used into a glass jar with a lid, and keep refrigerated. Sweet cream and Bulgarian yoghurt are also best stored in glass jars once opened.

STUFFED CHEESY BRINJALS

I hope, with this absolutely super recipe, to inspire restaurateurs to feature this dish on their menus. Although it is not difficult to prepare, the average cook, unused to exploring vegetarian meals, just might pass it over as being too fiddly, whereas diners, in search of an alternative to meat and fish, will surely love it: halved brinjals, stuffed with a mixture of vegetables, spiked with mustard, enriched with cream and blanketed with melting cheese, with chickpeas or beans tucked inside for a nutritional boost. Served with Pita Bread (page 93) and a spinach, sprout and hard-boiled egg salad, it makes a superb meal.

**2 brinjals, weighing 300 g each
50 ml olive oil
25 ml sunflower oil
1 small onion, finely chopped
1–2 cloves garlic, finely chopped
2 ml mixed dried herbs
250 g baby marrows, pared, sliced thinly lengthwise and diced
50 ml thick, cultured sour cream
250 ml cooked chickpeas or soya or haricot beans or a mixture of chickpeas and beans (depending on what you have on hand)
5 ml prepared mustard
2 ml sea salt
plenty of sliced Mozzarella or low-fat cheese**

Wash brinjals, remove bud ends and slice in half lengthwise. Score the flesh lightly in a diamond pattern, sprinkle with some sea salt and stand for 30 minutes. Rinse off the salt and pat the brinjals dry.
Heat olive oil and 25 ml water in a large frying pan with a lid. Add brinjals, cut side down, and cook gently, covered, until just tender but not wrinkled or collapsed — for about 25 minutes. A dash of extra water may be necessary if moisture evaporates too quickly. Place shells in baking dish to fit fairly closely, and when cool enough to handle, scoop out most of the pulp with a grapefruit spoon or knife, leaving a firm shell. Reserve the pulp.
Heat the sunflower oil in the same pan, add onion, garlic, herbs and marrows, then cover and cook gently until soft. Add cream, chickpeas/beans, mustard, salt and reserved brinjal pulp. Mix well and then spoon into brinjal shells, mounding high. Top each 'mountain' with plenty of cheese, then bake on middle shelf of oven at 180 °C for 30 minutes.
Serves 4.

GREEK VEGETABLE CASSEROLE WITH BEANS AND FETA

A bright, attractive and delicious medley of Mediterranean-type vegetables. Serve on brown rice with a lettuce and avocado salad tossed in garlicky French dressing.

**25 ml each sunflower and olive oil
1 large onion, chopped
2 leeks, sliced
1 green pepper, seeded and diced
2 cloves garlic, crushed
1 large brinjal (250 g), cubed and dégorged
6 baby marrows (250 g), pared and sliced
4 large, juicy tomatoes, skinned and chopped
750 ml cooked soya or haricot beans
5 ml sea salt and milled black pepper to taste
5 ml each dried origanum and basil
5 ml sugar
250 ml vegetable stock or 5 ml Marmite in 250 ml water
black olives, sliced
200–250 g feta cheese, rinsed and coarsely crumbled**

Heat oils in a large pan and sauté onion, leeks, green pepper and garlic. When softened, add brinjal, marrows and tomatoes. Cover and sweat for 5 minutes over low heat. Add drained beans, seasoning, herbs, sugar and stock. Stir to mix, then turn into large baking dish. Bake, covered, at 150 °C for 1 hour 15 minutes, stirring once or twice and adding more liquid if needed.
Before serving, add olives and sprinkle with feta. Return to oven to heat through.
Serves 4–6.

BRINJALS

It is much better to buy several small brinjals, which, if fresh and young enough, don't need dégorging. This is a process by means of which the bitter juices are extracted. Wash brinjals, slice or cube them, place in colander, salt quite heavily, and put weight on top. Leave for 30–45 minutes, then rinse and dry. Drying the brinjals is important, to avoid adding excess liquid to the dish. Use either a salad spinner or kitchen paper towels.

SPINACH PANCAKES

Also called Crêpes Florentine, this dish takes a while to assemble, but can be prepared in advance and baked when required. The pancake batter (which makes lacy, light crêpes) and the cheese sauce are both made in a blender, which cuts down on preparation time.

CRÊPES
250 ml white or sifted brown flour
1 ml sea salt
1 egg plus 1 yolk
250 ml milk
125 ml water
25 ml sunflower oil

FILLING
2 x 250 g packets frozen spinach, thawed
1 ml sea salt
1 ml freshly grated nutmeg

SAUCE
600 ml milk
50 ml white or 60 ml brown flour
125 g Gruyère cheese, grated
2 ml each dry mustard and sea salt
50 ml soft butter

grated Parmesan (or Cheddar or Gruyère) cheese and paprika

Put all the ingredients for the crêpes into blender, blend well and leave to stand for at least 30 minutes. The consistency should be creamy and medium-thick, and the batter will be enough to make 10 crêpes, 18–20 cm in diameter. Stack, after cooking, with sheets of greaseproof paper between the crêpes.

For the filling, cook spinach, drain very well in colander, and press out all moisture. Season with salt and nutmeg.

For sauce, put 500 ml of the milk, the white or brown flour, Gruyère cheese, mustard, salt and butter into blender, blend well and then pour into saucepan and cook over low heat, stirring, until thick and cheese has melted.

Stir 125 ml of the sauce into the spinach purée and mix well.

Fill each crêpe with a large spoonful of the purée and roll into cigar shapes. Place side by side, close together in a shallow, buttered baking dish.

Thin the remaining cheese sauce with the remaining 100 ml milk and pour over crêpes. Sprinkle generously with Parmesan cheese (or Cheddar or Gruyère if preferred) and dust with paprika. Bake at 180 °C for 30 minutes.
Serves 10 as a starter or 5 as a main course.

SESAME OIL

Some sesame oils are stronger and darker in colour than others, with a pronounced smoky flavour.

Dark sesame oil should be used very sparingly (a teaspoonful can flavour an entire dish), while the lighter type can be used far more liberally. I usually use the dark oil (a product of Hong Kong) as it adds terrific zest to stir-fries and salad dressing. Remember that a little goes a long way, so use it in conjunction with sunflower or olive oil, just for the flavour.

CRÊPES RATATOUILLE

In this dish, pancakes are wrapped round a savoury vegetable filling, covered with a white sauce, sprinkled with a topping of cheese, and then baked. This dish can be assembled successfully ahead of time, and baked when required.

BLENDER CRÊPES
250 ml white or sifted brown flour
1 ml sea salt
1 egg
250 ml milk
125 ml water
25 ml sunflower oil
2 ml dried origanum (optional)

FILLING
15 ml each sunflower and olive oil
1 medium brinjal, cubed
1 green pepper, seeded and diced
1 onion, chopped
5 small baby marrows (200 g), scrubbed and sliced
sea salt and milled black pepper to taste
2 large tomatoes, skinned and chopped
2 cloves garlic, crushed
5 ml dried basil
5 ml sugar

SAUCE
a knob of butter
25 ml sunflower oil
50 ml white flour or 60 ml brown flour
500 ml milk
sea salt and black pepper to taste
5 ml prepared mustard

TOPPING
grated Cheddar or Gruyère cheese
25 ml grated Parmesan

Put all ingredients for crêpes into a blender and blend well, stopping to scrape down sides once or twice. Stand for 1 hour, blend again, then make thin crêpes in an 18-cm frying pan. As they are done, stack on large plate with a circle of greaseproof paper between the crêpes.

For the filling, put oils, brinjal, green pepper, onion, baby marrows and seasoning into a large saucepan. Cover and stew slowly, stirring occasionally, for about 35 minutes or until soft. Add tomatoes, garlic, basil and sugar. Half-cover saucepan, and cook until tomatoes are pulpy. If necessary, remove lid and boil rapidly to reduce excess liquid. Cool, then divide between crêpes, roll into cigar shapes and place side by side in buttered baking dish. The filling is enough for 8–10 crêpes.

Make white sauce by melting butter with oil, stirring in flour, then adding milk slowly, stirring constantly. When thick, add seasonings and pour over crêpes. Sprinkle generously with Cheddar, top with Parmesan and heat through at 160 °C for about 40 minutes.
Serve 1–2 crêpes per person.

YOGHURT

In Greek cooking, especially, yoghurt is used in sauces in many baked dishes. Our natural yoghurt, however, cannot be heated without it curdling, unless it is first stabilised. It remains characteristically tart, but it is a useful addition to sauces* for those cutting down on cream or sour cream.

To make stabilised yoghurt, first rinse a small, heavy-based saucepan with water, as this low-fat sauce scorches easily. Pour in 500 ml natural yoghurt and then stir in 25 ml cornflour slaked with 25 ml milk. Bring to a slow boil, stirring all the time with a wooden spoon, in one direction only. For some reason this is very important. When mixture comes to the boil, reduce heat to very low and simmer, uncovered, for 10 minutes. Cool, cover and refrigerate. Expect it to thin somewhat on reheating, but it should not curdle.
Makes 500 ml.

* In all other cases (e.g. for tzatziki), always use the thick, set type of Bulgarian yoghurt rather than natural, pouring yoghurt.

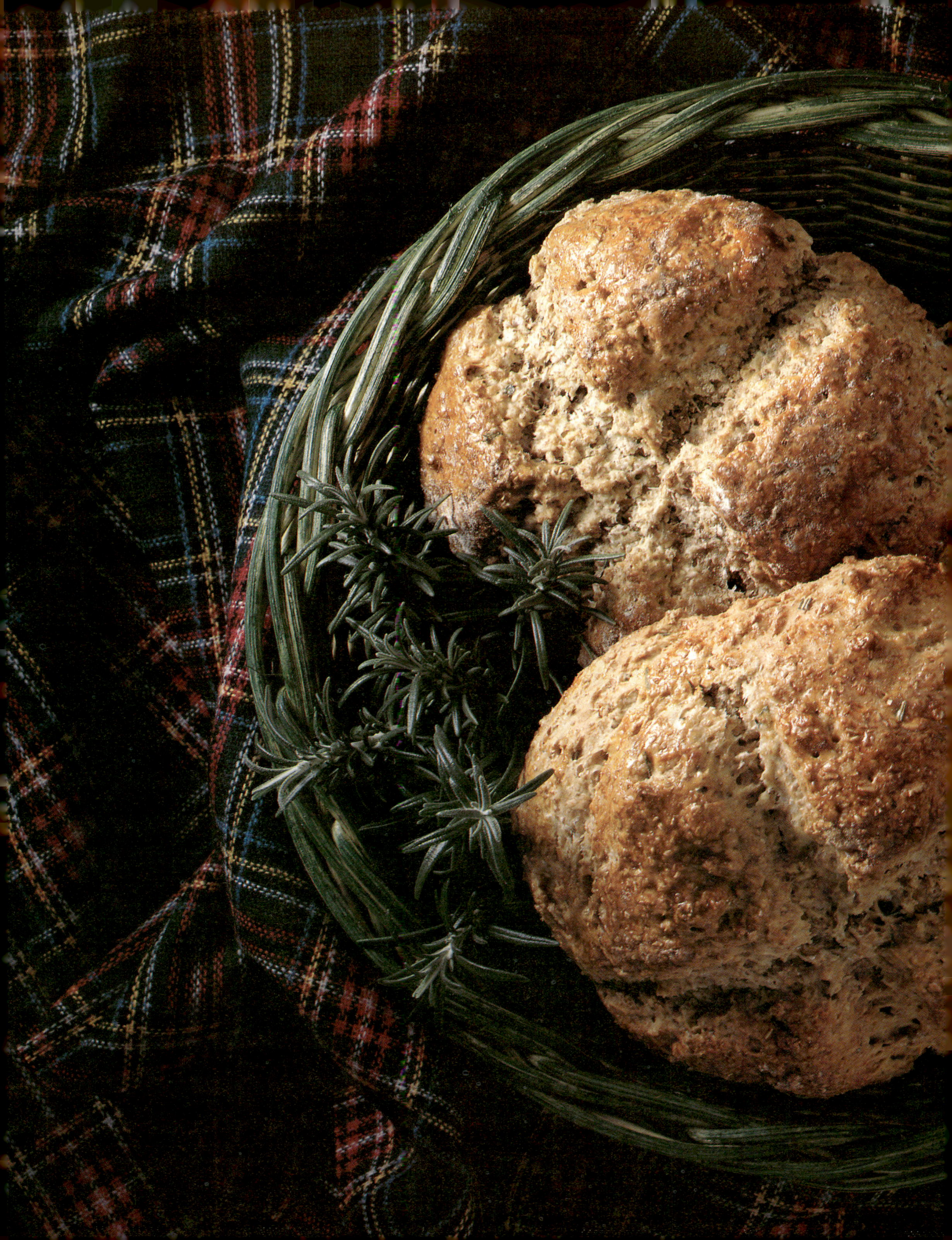

Breads & Rolls

WHOLEWHEAT BUTTERMILK BREAD

A reliable version of this favourite loaf. The quantity of bicarbonate of soda used is small, but it is enough for the batter to rise without imparting the sometimes overt bicarb flavour.

**4 x 250 ml wholewheat flour
5 ml sea salt
5 ml bicarbonate of soda
15 ml sunflower oil
15 ml honey or molasses or brown sugar
100 ml seedless raisins (optional)
500 ml buttermilk or natural drinking yoghurt
sesame seeds for topping**

Mix flour and salt. Sift in the bicarbonate of soda (this is important). Add oil, honey and raisins, if using. Stir to mix and then pour in buttermilk or yoghurt. Stir, using a wooden spoon, until ingredients are thoroughly combined — the batter will be soft and sticky. Turn into an oiled 23 cm x 8 cm x 7 cm loaf tin, sprinkle with sesame seeds and make a slight depression down the centre of the loaf.

Bake on middle shelf of oven at 180 °C for 1 hour. Stand for 5 minutes, then turn out and return to oven for 5 minutes to crisp the sides. Cool on wire rack.
Makes 1 loaf.

VARIATION

Use 3 x 250 ml wholewheat flour and 300 ml muesli. Avoid using muesli containing sunflower seeds as these will turn green in this bread.

Wholewheat Soda Bread with Rosemary (p. 94).

> **WHEATGERM**
>
> Wheatgerm is literally the germ (or centre) of the grain and is chock-full of nutrients, especially vitamins B and E, several amino acids, and a supply of unsaturated fatty acids. There's plenty of wheatgerm in wholewheat flour and none in refined white flour, which is yet another good reason to rather eat brown or wholewheat bread.
>
> Raw wheatgerm has a pronounced flavour and is usually tucked into cereals in small quantities, or used in baking, when the flavour dissipates. It also deteriorates very quickly, as the fatty acids become rancid, and it should therefore always be kept in the fridge. I usually toast wheatgerm as soon as I buy it. This does destroy some of the nutrients, but gives it a nice, nutty flavour.
>
> Add it to muesli, bread dough, and biscuit, muffin or scone mixes, or use it to thicken gravy. Used judiciously, no one will notice and everyone will benefit as it really is an excellent food.
>
> To toast wheatgerm, spread it out on a large biscuit tray and place it in a moderately hot oven until it is a light golden brown. It burns easily, so watch it carefully.
>
> Store some in a jar next to the stove and add it when cooking, or sprinkle on salads. Keep the rest in the fridge. It may sound like a hassle to use, but the inclusion of wheatgerm in your diet is a healthy habit that is worth cultivating.

INSTANT WHOLEWHEAT BATTER BREAD

This is the perfect bread for reluctant bakers — no kneading required

3 x 250 ml wholewheat flour
250 ml white bread flour
100 ml crushed wheat
7 ml instant dry yeast
5 ml sea salt
100 ml sunflower seeds
25 ml sunflower oil
25 ml honey
approximately 450 ml warm water
extra sunflower seeds for topping

Mix flours, crushed wheat, yeast, salt and sunflower seeds. Mix in oil and honey. Add 300 ml of the water, then stir in just enough of the remaining water to make a soft, sticky dough. Mix well, then turn into an oiled 23 cm x 9 cm x 8 cm loaf tin, sprinkle with sunflower seeds, pressing in lightly, and leave to rise in a warm place until 1–2 cm over top of tin. Cover, if liked, with a large plastic bag, allowing it to balloon over the top so that it does not stick to the rising dough.

Remove plastic bag and bake on middle shelf of oven at 200 °C for 30 minutes and then at 180 °C for 20–30 minutes. Turn out onto wire rack to cool.
Makes 1 medium loaf.

ENRICHED BATTER BREAD

A delicious loaf, packed with healthy ingredients. It rises well, has an even, flat top and slices neatly.

25 ml honey
475 ml warm water
10 ml dried yeast
3 x 250 ml wholewheat flour
125 ml crushed wheat
75 ml soya flour
75 ml fat-free milk powder
100 ml wheatgerm
250 ml brown bread flour
7 ml sea salt
25 ml sunflower oil
sunflower seeds for topping

Dissolve the honey in 125 ml of the warm water. Sprinkle in the yeast, cover and then leave to froth.

Mix the remaining ingredients (except the sunflower seeds). Give the frothy yeast a quick stir, and then pour it into a well in centre of dry ingredients. Mix, using a wooden spoon, and gradually add the remaining 350 ml water, or just enough to give you a thick, sticky batter.

Turn the batter into an oiled loaf tin measuring 26 cm x 9 cm x 7 cm, which should be nearly two-thirds full. Sprinkle the top thickly with sunflower seeds, pressing them in lightly. Leave to rise in a warm place for 45–60 minutes.

Bake on middle shelf of oven at 200 °C for 15 minutes, then at 180 °C for 45–60 minutes. Stand a few minutes, run a knife round the edges and turn out onto wire rack to cool.
Makes 1 loaf.

> **GARLIC BUTTER**
>
> Cream 50 ml butter with 1–2 cloves crushed garlic and a dash of fresh lemon juice.

NUTTY BROWN BLOOMER LOAF

A beautiful bread, incorporating two flours, wheatgerm and sunflower seeds, and as professional-looking as anything you can buy. It requires only one rising, which is quite lengthy due to the unrefined ingredients, but it is nevertheless easy to make and is tops on the taste test.

3 x 250 ml wholewheat flour
10 ml sea salt
15 ml instant dry yeast
350 ml warm water
25 ml honey
25 ml sunflower oil
2 x 250 ml white bread flour
125 ml wheatgerm
125 ml sunflower seeds
milk to brush batter with
melted butter to brush top of bread with

In a large mixing bowl combine 375 ml of the wholewheat flour, the sea salt and the yeast. Mix together the water, honey and oil. Stir into the flour mixture and mix to a sloppy dough. Cover and leave to rest for 10 minutes. Add the remaining 375 ml wholewheat flour, the white flour, wheatgerm and sunflower seeds. Mix with a wooden spoon and then with your hands to form a dough, adding up to 75 ml warm water if necessary. Knead in the bowl for 8–10 minutes — this is a firm dough which requires some hard kneading. When the mixture forms a smooth ball and leaves the sides of the bowl clean, shape the batter into a 25 cm x 12 cm bloomer (or slab) with blunt ends.

Place on an oiled baking tray and tuck two cloths tightly on either side so that the dough rises upward rather than sideways. Make six deep diagonal slashes across the top, then leave to rise for about 1 hour or until doubled. Brush with milk.

Bake the bread on the middle shelf of the oven at 200 °C for 30 minutes. Cool on wire rack, then brush the top with melted butter for a shiny finish.
Makes 1 loaf.

HERBED OAT BATTER BREAD

No kneading required for this wholesome, crunchy loaf perfumed with fresh rosemary.

**about 375 ml warm water
5 ml sugar
10 ml dried yeast
400 ml wholewheat flour
200 ml white bread flour
200 ml crushed wheat
250 ml rolled oats
5 ml sea salt
3–4 cloves garlic, crushed
25 ml finely chopped fresh rosemary needles
25 ml sunflower oil
25 ml honey**

Pour 250 ml of the water into a jug. Stir in sugar, sprinkle in yeast, then cover and stand until frothy — for about 15 minutes. Mix flours, crushed wheat, oats, salt, garlic and rosemary. Stir oil and honey into yeast mixture, then add to flour mixture. Mix, and then slowly stir in remaining 125 ml water or enough to make a sloppy dough. When well combined, turn into an oiled 20 cm x 9 cm x 7 cm loaf tin. Smooth the top, then leave to rise in a warm place until 1 cm over the top of the tin — for about 45 minutes.

Bake at 200 °C for 30 minutes, then at 180 °C for 20–25 minutes. Stand for 1 minute, run a knife round the edges and turn out onto a wire rack to cool. Brush top with melted butter.
Makes 1 loaf.

FOUR-SEED BATTER BREAD

A nutritious, crunchy, flat-topped loaf, excellent for sandwiches as it slices so well.

**25 ml honey
550 ml warm water
15 ml dried yeast
4 x 250 ml wholewheat flour
250 ml white bread flour
50 ml each sesame seeds and linseeds
100 ml sunflower seeds
5 ml sea salt
poppy seeds for topping**

Mix honey into 250 ml of the warm water and stir to dissolve. Sprinkle in the yeast, cover and leave to froth. Mix flours, sesame seeds, linseeds, sunflower seeds and salt. Stir the risen yeast, pour it into a well in the centre of the flour mixture, stir, then slowly add the remaining 300 ml water, or just enough to make a sticky but quite stiff dough. Pat firmly into an oiled 26 cm x 9 cm x 7 cm loaf tin, sprinkle the top with poppy seeds, and leave the dough to rise in a warm place for 1 hour or until it is just over the top of the tin.

Bake at 200 °C for 30 minutes, and then at 180 °C for 20–30 minutes. Run a knife round the sides and leave the bread in the tin for 1 minute before turning out onto a wire rack to cool.
Makes 1 loaf.

MUFFIN TIN WHOLEWHEAT ROLLS

A basic wholewheat batter is used for these quickly-made muffin-shaped 'rolls'.

**500–550 ml warm water
a pinch of sugar
10 ml dried yeast
3 x 250 ml wholewheat flour
250 ml white bread flour
125–250 ml seedless raisins (optional)
100 ml rolled oats
5 ml sea salt
25 ml sunflower oil
25 ml honey or half honey, half molasses
125 ml sunflower seeds
extra sunflower seeds or crushed wheat for topping**

Mix 250 ml of the water with a pinch of sugar. Sprinkle in yeast, cover and leave to froth. Mix remaining ingredients, except sunflower seeds and crushed wheat for topping, in a large bowl. Stir frothy yeast and pour into well in centre of dry ingredients. Mix, and then slowly stir in remaining 300 ml warm water or just enough to make a thick, moist dough. Spoon into large, oiled muffin tins — they should be just over halfway filled with batter. Top with extra sunflower seeds or crushed wheat pressed in lightly. Leave to rise in a warm place until batter rises (will be slightly humped) to just over the tops of the tins — for 50–60 minutes.

Bake just above centre of oven at 200 °C for about 25 minutes until browned and firm. Stand a few minutes and then run a knife round the edges to loosen. Cool on a wire rack, and eat freshly baked.
Makes 14–16 large rolls.

PITA BREAD

Much experimenting has resulted in what are, to my mind, quite the best of home-made pitas. Fun to make, the shaping is quite different from that of ordinary bread rolls. They rise in the oven like fat little cushions and form perfect pockets for stuffing. A high baking temperature is important and to ensure the formation of pockets, the dough should not be creased when rolling or pinched when turned over just prior to baking.

**10 ml sugar
300 ml warm water
10 ml dried yeast
4 x 250 ml cake flour
5 ml sea salt
30 ml sunflower oil**

Stir sugar into water. Sprinkle in yeast, cover and leave to froth.

Sift the flour and salt into a large bowl. Add the oil. Stir the bubbly yeast and pour it into a well in centre of the dry ingredients. Combine, using a wooden spoon, and then mix to a dough with your hands, adding about 40 ml extra water, or enough to make a kneadable dough. Turn the dough onto lightly floured board and knead well for 10 minutes until the mixture forms a pliable ball. Return to bowl, brush the top of the dough with oil, cover the bowl with a kitchen towel and leave the dough to rise for about 1 hour or until doubled.

Punch down the dough and pinch off ten equal pieces. Roll them into balls between the palms of your hands, rest for 5 minutes and then, using a rolling pin, roll the dough into thin ovals. Place the ovals on ungreased baking trays dusted with cake flour. Leave to prove, uncovered, for about 30 minutes until they are puffy and doubled in thickness. Turn over carefully and sift a little flour over them.

Bake, a tray at a time, just above the centre of the oven at 240 °C for 7 minutes. Remove from oven and wrap in a cloth to soften. Slice off the tops and press the sides gently to open out pockets.
Makes 10.

WHOLEWHEAT PITA BREAD

Use 500 ml white bread flour and 500 ml wholewheat flour. Sift the white flour with 5 ml salt, add the wholewheat flour, then proceed as for white pitas. A little extra water may be necessary, but the rising and proving times are about the same.

MOCK BUTTER

If you process butter and oil, you get a creamy mixture which spreads like margarine, but retains the natural flavour and goodness of butter. The addition of sunflower oil makes healthy good sense as it contains a high proportion of unsaturated fatty acids. Make a big batch, keep some on hand in the fridge, and freeze the rest.

500 g soft, unsalted butter, diced
5 ml sea salt
200–250 ml sunflower oil

Place butter and salt in processor fitted with the grinding blade, and process to a soft paste. Slowly dribble in the oil, keeping the motor running. If necessary, stop and run a spatula round the sides, then continue blending until well mixed. The mixture will be sloppy. Turn into fridge containers. Keep chilled.

For Herbed Mock Butter, follow the above recipe, but add the following to the butter and salt:

a few tufts of parsley
16 large, fresh basil leaves
4 sprigs each origanum and marjoram, leaves only
2 cloves garlic
4 sage leaves

Process the herbs and garlic to chop, with the butter and salt, before adding the oil.

WHOLEWHEAT HONEY BREAD

A lovely, malt-coloured health loaf using instant yeast. Apart from simplifying mixing, instant yeast also cuts down on rising time.

1 x 10-g packet instant dry yeast
100 ml wheatgerm
4 x 250 ml wholewheat flour
125 ml seedless raisins
5 ml sea salt
100 ml sunflower seeds
approximately 500 ml warm water
50 ml honey
15 ml sunflower oil

Mix yeast, wheatgerm, flour, raisins, salt and sunflower seeds in a large mixing bowl. Whisk 250 ml of water with honey and oil. Pour into dry ingredients and mix, then add remaining 250 ml water, or enough to make a batter with consistency of a fruit cake. Turn into an oiled 23 cm x 8 cm x 7 cm loaf tin. Leave in a warm place until batter rises to just over top of tin — for about 30 minutes. Bake at 200 °C for 30 minutes, then at 180 °C for 20 minutes. Turn out onto wire rack to cool.
Makes 1 large loaf.

WHOLEWHEAT SODA BREAD WITH ROSEMARY

Soda bread is a traditional Scottish bread served on Burns night with Finnan Haddie Soup and Haggis. Flavoured with fresh rosemary, this version makes a lovely, perfumed bread. Serve freshly baked, broken into quarters, with butter.

500 ml cake flour
5 ml each sea salt, bicarbonate of soda and sugar
500 ml wholewheat flour
15 ml finely chopped fresh rosemary needles
25 ml butter
about 400 ml buttermilk
beaten egg or milk for topping

Sift flour, salt and bicarbonate of soda. Add sugar, flour and rosemary. Rub in butter. Add buttermilk and mix to a soft dough. Shape into two 15-cm rounds and place on a floured baking tray. Using back of knife, score deeply into quarters. Brush tops with eggs (or milk, but egg gives a better colour). Bake at 200 °C for 30 minutes.
Makes 2 loaves.

OAT, RYE AND CARAWAY BATTER BREAD

about 400 ml warm water
5 ml sugar
10 ml dried yeast
500 ml wholewheat flour
300 ml rye flour
250 ml rolled oats
5 ml sea salt
5 ml caraway seeds
25 ml sunflower oil
25 ml honey

TOPPING
50 ml sunflower seeds
2 ml caraway seeds

Pour 250 ml of the water into a jug. Stir in sugar, sprinkle in the yeast, then cover and stand until frothy — for about 15 minutes.

Mix flours, oats, salt and caraway seeds. Stir oil and honey into yeast mixture, then add to flour mixture. Mix, then slowly stir in remaining 150 ml water, or enough to make a sloppy dough. When well combined, turn into oiled 20 cm x 9 cm x 7 cm loaf tin. Smooth top and sprinkle with topping. Leave to rise in warm place until 1 cm over top of tin — for about 45 minutes.

Bake at 200 °C for 30 minutes, then at 180 °C for 20–25 minutes. Stand for a minute, run a knife round the edges and turn out onto a wire rack to cool.
Makes 1 loaf.

GREEK GARLIC BREAD

Sliced bread, baked with a topping of herb butter mixed with Parmesan cheese and sesame seeds, makes a delicious accompaniment to many Mediterranean-style dishes, and affords a welcome change from the usual garlic French loaf. Use a fat, crusty white loaf — definitely not regular white bread — and cut into 2-cm slices.

250 g soft butter
3–4 cloves garlic, crushed
a few grinds of black pepper
50 ml grated Parmesan cheese
50 ml dehusked sesame seeds
5 ml dried marjoram
oil to brush pan with

Mash butter with rest of ingredients. Brush a large baking tray with oil, lay bread slices on it, spread with half butter mixture, then turn over and repeat. Bake at 160 °C for 20 minutes, turn slices, and bake until golden brown. (Alternatively, toast bread on one side, spread the other side generously with butter mixture, then grill until bubbling.) Serve hot.

Pita Bread (page 93), Four-Seed Batter Bread (page 93) and Muffin Tin Wholewheat Rolls (page 93).

INDEX

B
beurre manié *53*
bouquets garnis *8*
breads and rolls:
  Enriched Batter Bread *92*
  Four-Seed Batter Bread *93*
  Greek Garlic Bread *94*
  Herbed Oat Batter Bread *93*
  Instant Wholewheat Batter Bread *92*
  Muffin Tin Wholewheat Rolls *93*
  Nutty Brown Bloomer Loaf *92*
  Oat, Rye and Caraway Batter Bread *94*
  Pita Bread *93*
  Wholewheat Buttermilk Bread *91*; Variation *91*
  Wholewheat Honey Bread *94*
  Wholewheat Pita Bread *93*
  Wholewheat Soda Bread with Rosemary *94*
butter *86*
  Garlic Butter *92*
  Herbed Mock Butter *94*
  Mock Butter *94*
buttermilk *77*

C
cheese:
  Cheddar *34*
  feta *28*
  marinated feta *40*
Coconut Milk *77*

D
dressings and sauces (*see also* mayonnaise):
  Basic Blender Salad Dressing *17*
  Raita *77*
  Sherried Sesame Seed Dressing *25*
  soy sauce *81*
  Spinach, Onion and Rosemary Cream Sauce *32*
  Tahini and Yoghurt Dressing *25*
  Tzatziki *76*
  white sauce *36*

E
egg dishes:
  Baked Eggs Florentine *46*
  Coronation Egg Salad *24*
  Curried Eggs *24*
  Piperade *24*
  soufflés *33*

H
herbs and spices *21*
  bouquets garnis *8*
  coriander *24*
  garlic *16*
  parsley *61*
  rosemary *29*
  spices *61*

L
lemon rind *85*

M
Marinated Mushrooms with Sprouts *16*
mayonnaise *12*
  Blender Aïoli *8*
  pesto-flavoured mayonnaise *20*
  Quick Home-Made Mayonnaise *21*
Middle Eastern Buffet:
  Baba Ghanouj *85*
  Bean and Sesame Pâté *84*
  Brinjal and Red Pepper Salad *84*
  Felafel *85*
  Haricot Bean Salad (2) *85*
  Hummus *84*
  Israeli Brinjal Spread *84*
  Sherried Butter Bean Pâté *84*
  Stuffed Brinjals *86*
  Stuffed Green Peppers *85*
  Stuffed Vine Leaves *85*
Mushroom Crostini *72*
mustard *9*

N
nuts and sunflower seeds *65*

O
oils *86*
  sesame oil *89*

P
pasta *33* (*see also* salads; pasta, sauces for):
  Creamy Mushroom, Walnut and Pepper Pasta *36*
  Favourite Macaroni Cheese *40*
  Macaroni, Cheese and Spinach Bake *34*
  Noodle, Cheese and Vegetable Casserole *29*
  Pasta and Brinjal Casserole *36*
  Pasta Primavera *33*
  Pasta Ratatouille with Marinated Feta *40*
  Pasta with Herbs and Eggs *27*
  Pasta with Mushroom Sauce *33*
  Pasta with Vegetables and Herbs *37*
  Pasta, Mushroom and Ricotta Bake *36*
  Pasta, Vegetable and Lentil Bake *32*
  Quick Tomato Macaroni Cheese *33*
  Quick Vegetable and Bean Lasagne *34*
  Two-Sauce Noodle Casserole *37*
  Two-Sauce Pasta *29*
pasta, sauces for:
  Italian Tomato Sauce with Fresh Herbs *29*
  Mediterranean Vegetable Sauce *28*
  Parsley Pesto *28*
  Pesto *28*
  Spinach and Mushroom Sauce *34*
  Vegetable Sauce *32*
pesticides and vegetables *73*
phyllo pastry, using *72*
Pizza with Wholewheat Crust, Easy *37*
pulses *52*, *57* (*see also* salads):
  Boston Baked Butter Beans *56*
  Breyani *62*
  Butter Bean, Mushroom and Walnut Curry *52*
  butter beans *56*
  Casserole of Lentils and Rice with Pizza Topping *65*
  Chickpea and Tomato Curry *68*
  Chickpea Stew *53*
  Chickpea Stew with Tahini Sauce *52*
  chickpeas *52*
  Chickpeas and Broccoli in Mustard Sauce *53*
  Haricot Bean and Pumpkin Casserole *64*
  haricot beans *64*
  Lentil and Brinjal Curry *61*
  Lentil and Potato Pie *65*
  Lentil and Tomato Stew *62*
  Lentil and Vegetable Moussaka *61*
  Lentil Dahl with Eggs and Masala Sauce *60*
  lentils *57*
  Lentils and Brinjals in Barbecue Sauce *64*
  Mediterranean Chickpea Casserole *53*
  Mushroom and Lentil Moussaka *57*
  Pot Beans *65*
  Quick Butter Bean and Mushroom Goulash *65*
  Ratatouille with Haricots *68*
  Soya Bean Curry *62*
  soya beans *68* (*see also* TVP)
  Spiced Chickpeas *51*
  Spiced Lentils and Mushrooms with Coriander *60*
  Spiced Mixed Rice and Lentils *53*
  Spicy Lentil and Mushroom Stew *57*
  Spicy Lentil Curry *64*
  Spicy Stove-Top Beans *60*
  Spicy Two-Bean Stew *68*
  split peas *65*
  Tofu with Mushrooms, Onions and Cheese *69*
  TVP *69*
  Vegetable and Butter Bean Hurry Curry *56*
  Vegetarian Bobotie *69*
  Vegetarian Bolognaise *69*

Q
quiches:
  Asparagus and Spring Onion Quiche *41*
  Italian Quiche *41*
  Spinach and Brown Mushroom Quiche *41*

R
rice and grains (*see also* salads):
  barley *49*
  brown rice *44*
  bulgur *24*
  Bulgur, Lentil and Tahini Pilaff *46*
  couscous *49*
  Couscous with Chickpea and Vegetable Stew *49*
  Kitcheree with Fried Eggs *45*
  millet *46*
  Millet Pilaff with Eggs Florentine *46*
  Mushroom Rice with Sprouts and Tahini *49*
  Nutty Barley and Vegetable Bake *43*
  Nutty Millet Pilaff *46*
  Nutty Rice and Mushroom Casserole *44*
  Nutty Vegetable Rice with Stuffed Mushrooms *48*
  One-Pot Rice, Mushroom and Sprout Risotto *44*
  Oriental Rice *45*
  Rice with Lentils, Mushrooms and Almonds *44*
  Spiced Mixed Rice and Lentils *53*
  Spiced Rice, Lentils and Vegetables with Yoghurt *45*
  Vegetable Breyani *48*
  Weet-rice *46*
  Wild Rice with Water Chestnuts *48*

S
salads:
  Aïgroissade with Aïoli-Yoghurt Dressing *8*
  Bean Slaw *7*
  Brinjal and Red Pepper Salad *84*
  Bulgur Salad with Rice and Mushrooms *12*
  Bulgur Salad with Tomatoes and Black Olives *17*
  Bulgur, Chickpea and Spinach Salad *25*
  Chickpea Salad with Cabbage and Walnuts *12*
  Chickpea, Rice and Sprout Salad *9*
  Chilled Mushroom and Cheese Tart *20*
  Coronation Egg Salad *24*
  Cottage Cheese, Cucumber and Pasta Mould *20*
  Creamy Curried Soya Bean Salad *9*
  Creamy Pasta, Cheese and Pineapple Salad *18*
  Curried Weet-Rice Salad *12*
  Green Pasta Salad with Herbed Dressing *17*
  Haricot Bean Salad (1) *8*
  Haricot Bean Salad (2) *85*
  Lentil Salad *13*
  Mediterranean Pasta and Vegetable Salad *18*
  Moulded Cream Cheese and Vegetable Salad *20*
  Pasta and Butter Bean Salad *18*
  Rice and Pecan Nut Salad *21*
  Rice and Sprout Salad with Sesame Dressing *16*
  Rice, Chickpea and Feta Salad *9*
  Rice, Lentil and Mushroom Salad with Fresh Herbs *13*
  Rice, Lentil and Pineapple Salad *13*
  Sesame Noodle Salad with Tahini *25*
  Sesame Rice Salad *17*
  Spicy Indian-Style Salad *21*
  Two-Bean Fruit and Nut Salad in Lemon Mayonnaise *21*
  Two-Grain Salad with Mushrooms and Baby Marrows *16*
salt *40*
  Gomasio *80*
saucepans *64*
sauces *see* dressings and sauces; pasta, sauces for
sauté and sweat *41*
sherry *60*
sour cream *88*
spices *see under* herbs and spices
sprouts *9*
stir-fries *76*
  Basic Vegetable Stir-Fry Sauce *80*
  Mushroom and Sprout Stir-Fry *81*
  Quick-Mix Stir-Fry *81*
  Special Stir-Fry *81*
  Stir-Fry with Cauliflower, Green Beans and Walnuts *80*
  Vegetable Stir-Fry with Noodles and Chinese Sauce *80*
stock, vegetable or Marmite *60*
sugar *13*

T
tahini *84*
TVP *69*

V
vegetables (*see also* salads; stir-fries; Middle Eastern Buffet; pesticides and vegetables)
  Baked Potatoes with Chunky Topping *77*
  Baked Souffléd Potatoes *76*
  brinjals *88*
  broccoli and cauliflower *52*
  butternut squash and beetroot *13*
  Cheese-Topped Vegetable Bake *73*
  Crêpes Ratatouille *89*
  Greek Green Bean and Brinjal Casserole *88*
  Greek Vegetable Casserole with Beans and Feta *88*
  onions *77*
  peppers *8*
  Phyllo Parcels with Sprouts, Feta and Almonds *72*
  Spicy Fruit and Vegetable Curry *72*
  Spinach and Feta Pie with Tzatziki *76*
  Spinach Pancakes *89*
  Stuffed Baked Potatoes *76*
  Stuffed Cheesy Brinjals *88*
  substitutes *86*
  table celery *80*
  tomatoes *24*
  Vegetable Cottage Pie (1) *73*
  Vegetable Cottage Pie (2) *73*
  Vegetable Curry with Coconut Milk and Raita *77*
  Vegetable Paella *71*

W
wheatgerm *92*

Y
yoghurt *89*